D0923356

To Al Skonski
as a token of friendship
with a prayerful wish that
he may derive great profit
and inspiration from its reading.
Darlington, New Jersey
Christmas, 1949
J. M. K.

You Can Change the World!

YOU *Can* CHANGE *the* WORLD!

The Christopher Approach

JAMES KELLER, M.M.

Longmans, Green and Company

NEW YORK · TORONTO

CUM PERMISSU SUPERIORUM

Nihil Obstat:
JOHN M. A. FEARNS, S.T.D.
Censor Librorum

Imprimatur:
✠ FRANCIS CARDINAL SPELLMAN, D.D.
Archbishop of New York
September 14, 1948

First Printing—November, 1948—55,000 copies
Second Printing—December, 1948—20,000 copies
Third Printing—January, 1949—25,000 copies
Fourth Printing—February, 1949—25,000 copies

Copyright 1948
by The Christophers, Inc.

Printed in the United States of America
by H. Wolff, New York

EXPLAINING THE CHRISTOPHERS*

By Way of Introduction

Did you ever stop to think that the United States is being effectively undermined by less than *one percent* of the people of our country, of whom only a portion are Communists?

Nearly everyone in this one percent has a militant hatred for the basic truths upon which this nation is founded (and without which it cannot endure): that each and every human being is a child of God, created in His image and likeness; that he gets his fundamental rights from God, not from the State; and that the chief purpose of the state—as the Founding Fathers repeatedly affirmed in the Declaration of Independence—is to *protect* these God-given rights.

These few are not content to keep their hatred of God and

---

* The word *Christopher* is derived from the Greek word, *Christophoros,* meaning *Christ-bearer.*

country to themselves. As everyone driven by such a perverse hatred is automatically a "missioner," those in this group therefore want to poison the minds of many, not merely a few. Invariably they make it their business to get into one of the four influential spheres of activity which touch and sway the majority of the people: (1) education, (2) government, (3) labor-management, (4) writing (newspapers, magazines, books, radio, motion pictures, television).

It is our conviction that one percent of the normal, decent citizens of America can be found who are willing to get into the mainstream of American life as Christophers and work as hard to restore to it the divine truth and human integrity as the other one percent are striving furiously to eliminate these values. One of the best ways to get rid of weeds is to plant something in their stead. The big need, therefore, is to encourage people with good ideas to go into the market-place rather than to concentrate too much on driving out those with evil designs.

THE RÔLE OF THE CHRISTOPHER

The Christopher goes into the market-place, into a job of his or her own choosing, without fanfare, or flag waving, without doing anything sensational. His or her simple task is to insist on truth where others are intent on furthering falsehood, to establish order where others are spreading confusion. Where there is hate, he tries to bring in love; where there is darkness, he carries light. Always striving to implant more firmly the fundamentals which others are trying to uproot, the Christopher emphasizes the normal rather than the abnormal. Nothing remarkable may ever be required beyond a generous spirit of courage and daring. He or she expects to do the usual, not the unusual, the ordinary, not the extraordinary, knowing that while the steady fulfillment of duty often requires plodding devotion and day-by-day hard work, even monotonous drudgery, yet this continuing sacrifice is constantly lightened by a driving purpose. The most trivial and tiresome task achieves significance and dignity when done for Christ, Who said, ". . . *My yoke is sweet and My burden light.*" (*Matt.* 11:30)

The Christopher will often work quietly, even silently, as leaven works in dough, yet never stealthily nor underhandedly. The Christopher should ask no favors, seek no privileges, look for no special attention, be ready for neglect, misunderstanding, and suffering. He or she is ever aware that the important thing is to be *there,* as Christ commanded. Even if nothing more is achieved than filling one spot which otherwise might be occupied by one bent on subversion or perversion, this is no small accomplishment in itself. But far more than this results: the very presence of a bearer of Christ in any sphere means that Christ is also present there through a personal representative who acts as an instrument of His grace.

OVERCOMING EVIL BY GOOD

The over-all problem facing our country as well as the world is materialistic atheism. Communism is only one expression of this godlessness. Even if Communism disappeared overnight, the problem is still a tremendous one. An enormous missionary task still remains to be done. The de-spiritualizing process which has taken place during the last seventy-five years is approaching its logical conclusion in our own day and age—world-wide reduction of men to the level of the beast, with resultant misery, hatred, destruction, and wholesale murder.

In every country that the godless have undermined and eventually destroyed, they first swarmed into the main fields of public influence. They taught millions over the earth to have a false outlook on life, to ignore their eternal destiny. Too many of those who believe in God, instead of getting into the thick of things and overcoming evil with good, have withdrawn into a world apart from the frightening realities around them. For them the words of the Apostle Paul have an added significance: *"Be not overcome by evil, but overcome evil by good."* (*Rom.* 12:21)

The awful challenge of our times demands more than understanding and sympathy, more than token performance. We are bidden by the Prince of Peace not to cease our efforts until we have brought His sublime message to *"all men of all nations."*

The object of the Christopher movement, therefore, is to develop a sense of personal responsibility and initiative in bringing back into the market-place the major truths which alone guarantee peace for all mankind.

The achievements of tens of thousands who have already gone as Christophers into the four fields of influence are inspiring hope for the *peaceful* transformation that will take place when their number reaches a million.

Each Christopher carries Christ with him, individually and personally, into the dust and heat of the market-place, into the highways as well as the byways, thereby helping to change for the better the trends abroad in the world today. Each Christopher knows he is called by Christ Himself to be a "*fisher of men.*" But he knows, also, that the best fisherman in the world cannot catch a single fish if he is two miles away from the water, just talking about fish.

THE DISTINGUISHING MARK

Love of *all* people should be the distinguishing mark of every Christopher. He must guard against the dangerous tendency which is developing among many people of otherwise sound judgment who are beginning to return hatred for hatred, instead of meeting hatred with love. As never before, we need to remember that Christ died for *all* men, even for those who crucified Him. Upon this basic principle rests the whole spirit of the Christopher movement: *"By this shall all men know that you are my disciples, if you have love for one another."* (*John* 13:35). The more one brings Christ into his own personal living, the better will he be able to bring Christ into the lives of others. He will:

(1) PRAY FOR ALL. This means of showing love for all is at the disposal of everybody.

(2) GO TO ALL. One of the greatest tributes ever paid Christ was that *"He went about doing good."* We likewise must mingle with all men, even those who know Him not, so far as it is in our power to do so. We should not expect them to come to us.

(3) TEACH ALL. People are won or lost by ideas, *not by things.* Subversives, seldom putting one stone upon another in building anything, stick tenaciously to the realm of ideas. Through ideas, fallacious as they are, they have swayed the outlook of millions over the earth. They knew that whoever controls the thought of man controls all else. *But* the only way to overcome *bad* ideas is to replace them with *good* ideas, the immutable principles of Christ. Christ tells us to *"preach the gospel* to *every creature."* He bids us *"go into the whole world . . . to all men."* To be daring for love of others He urges us to *"launch out into the deep,"* with the assurance that *"I am with you all days."*

A positive, personal love of *all*, even of those who hate, is absolutely essential. Complaining and criticizing accomplish little or nothing. A Christopher spends his time improving, not disapproving, because he knows that *"it is better to light one candle than to curse the darkness."*

If a million persons go as Christ-bearers into every sphere of life, they will bring love where there is hate, the light of Christian principles where there has been only darkness and error.

SCOPE OF THE CHRISTOPHERS

Rather than institute a new organization, the Christopher movement limits itself to one phase of a big problem: emphasis on *individual responsibility* and *individual initiative* for the common good of all, regardless of whether one is working on an individual basis or in any one of many excellent and essential organizations.

Because Christophers realize they are not merely individuals, but also social beings, they do not stand aside. Realizing their kinship with all others because they are brothers and sisters in Christ, they feel a sense of personal responsibility to work for the corporate good of all, no matter what sacrifice may be entailed. They do not necessarily seek to go *up* to material success in life. They seek to go *deep* into life, into anything that concerns the welfare of mankind. They may be in positions which are in themselves unimportant, but which they make of the greatest importance because, as Christ-bearers, they can be effective instruments of His truth and love.

PURPOSE OF THIS BOOK

This book is submitted as a guidebook or textbook for the individual use of Christophers, either in the work they do alone, or in their work in any organizations to which they see fit to belong.

It is not intended as a book for experts. Neither is it a literary work. Rather it is an "A-B-C" for the average person who, becoming more and more disturbed by the rapid trend toward paganism, feels helpless and frustrated only because he is not aware of the vital role he can play, personally and individually, in reversing that trend. It was not prepared to be read at one sitting. Rather, it is a reference book or manual, and its various sections are addressed to persons with various objectives in life. Hence throughout this book there is an intentional repetition of the basic theme, because many will wish to read only those sections of particular interest to themselves.

This book, prepared with the advice of those who are experts in the specific fields covered in this volume, contains simple, fundamental ideas, repeated through varied applications which have been found practicable and worth while. Well-trained people—in far greater numbers than are now available—are needed, to be sure. But they must be supplemented by a million or more average men and women, who, as bearers of Christ into the market place, are thereby so many small channels of His grace. They depend much more on God, much less on the human techniques which ultimately fence in those who are against God. Millions are needed. Christ meant it that way. He wanted large numbers of lay apostles to work at the business of saving the world for *"The harvest is great, but the laborers are few."* (*Luke* 10:2)

CHRISTOPHER SCHOOLS

Introducing this book or any portion of it into a family circle, a classroom, a gathering, or an organization of any kind would constitute what we regard as the formation of a *Christopher school.* It is, for example, as though a women's club should introduce a cooking school, at which the members come together for a short time to study the principles of cooking, using an accepted cookbook as their text, and then go out and put those principles into practice in whatever sphere they find themselves.

The Christopher school, like the Christopher movement, is not a formal institution or organization, but the carrying or spreading of an idea to those who do not possess it by individual Christ-bearers acting as messengers. In short, the Christopher school, like the cooking school, may be introduced anywhere, with this guidebook serving as the basic textbook.

Since we limit our efforts to the developing of personal initiative and responsibility, *we do not authorize Christopher groups or clubs of any kind.* All we can authorize are the contents of this approved volume. Each individual chooses—as he or she thinks will best serve the cause—whether he or she will function individually or, under proper authority, will help spark some already-existing organization. We lay down no tailor-made techniques. We confine ourselves to the broad pursuit of major principles and rely on the refreshing resourcefulness God has placed in every individual to do the rest. This simple freedom allows greater originality, more imagination, enterprise, and daring, and more enduring dynamism.

THE CHRISTOPHER POSITION

The Christopher movement is under Catholic auspices. By the very fact that it is Catholic, it is deeply concerned, for time and for eternity, with the welfare of *all* men—of Protestants, Jews, those professing no faith, and those whose background makes them hostile to religion. In loving solicitude we are bound to include *all* and exclude *none.* Each is a child of God, at least through creation. Each, doing even one thing for Him, can start to be a Christopher, a Christ-bearer.

The movement has *no* chapters, *no* committees, *no* meetings. There are *no* memberships, *no* dues. Rather than have a large membership "paying dues and doing nothing," we have, from the beginning, set out to encourage tens of thousands to "do something and pay nothing."

Literature on the Christopher movement, including bimonthly News Notes, is sent *free of charge* to more than 120,000 people in this country and overseas. It may be obtained *without cost* by writing to the central headquarters of The Christophers in New York City.*

For the material means to carry on the Christopher program, our motto is the simple one inscribed on every American coin, "In God We Trust." For routine expenses of $150,000 a year, or approximately $12,000 a month, the Christopher movement depends entirely on the voluntary offerings of those who see fit to assist it. We are incorporated under the legal title of *The Christophers, Inc.*

God willing, this tiny spark may one day burst into a flame. Fortunately, we have to manufacture nothing; our product is made in heaven. All we have to do is become *distributors* of a changeless Truth in our changing times, ever conscious that there can be neither peace nor freedom without that Truth which "will make you free."

Above all, we are fortified with the reassuring conviction that none of us works alone. Christ works with and through each and every one who would be a Christ-bearer—a Christopher. By our living presence in the mainstream of life we can, with God's grace, help to renew the face of the earth!

James Keller

*THE CHRISTOPHERS
121 East 39th Street, N.Y., 16, N.Y.
Father James Keller, M.M., Director.

PROLOGUE

The First to "Go"

One hot, dust-laden day in Samaria long ago, a woman came to the Well of Jacob, just off the high road from Jerusalem to Galilee, to draw water . . . unaware that she was that day to become one of the outstanding instruments in a new program which was to revolutionize the world.

It was about noon, and the place was deserted but for the solitary figure of a Man. He was obviously a traveler and, to a Samaritan woman, just as obviously a Jew, and He sat with His back resting wearily against the stone parapet of the well. The chattering women of the village and their noisy offspring had long since returned to their homes, but the woman, head high and face proud, made no move to speak to the stranger. She was an outcast even among her own people, because she had taken to herself five husbands. Yet in her eyes, which had seen much and had not liked what they saw, was a hunger for something even she would have been at a loss to explain.

Leaning forward, she hooked the waterpot to the rope coiled about the top of the well and turned the windlass, unmindful of the Man watching her. As the vessel, brimming over, was pulled to the surface, the Man spoke: "Give Me to drink," He said, and in her surprise that a stranger, and a Jew, at that, should speak to her, she offered Him a measure of water. When He had drunk and the woman's puzzled "How dost thou being a Jew ask of me to drink who am a Samaritan?" (*John* 4:9) had been answered with a reply that gave a clue to His identity, the Man bade her *"Go call thy husband and come hither."*

Taken off guard by this strange and sudden command, the woman yet sensed quite well in His quiet dignity the superiority and authority of the Speaker. Tears squeezing through the corners of her eyes, with an instinct for self-preservation that counselled against revealing all the sordidness of her life, she answered, *"I have no husband."*

There was a pause before the Man made reply. He looked at her with an eye of complete and kindly understanding. He knew she had intended to deceive Him but, without rebuke, He finished her admission for her by saying, *"Thou hast said well I have no husband, for thou hast had five husbands, and he whom thou now hast is not thy husband."*

A sudden fear widened the woman's eyes, but in a moment was gone. Left only was the strange hunger to which she gave voice in a question that was also meant to distract Him. His answer was to tell her more, but this time of Himself and of His work. In later years when He was gone, she was to recall the day she had met Him and humbly thank God that in those early years she had heard from His own lips the declaration of His identity.

Now, however, joy in her new knowledge could not be

contained. She felt she had actually been commissioned—individually and personally—to go and share that knowledge with as many others as she could. She did not waste a moment. Leaving her waterpot in her haste, she hurried to the village. Behind her she left the Man Who, by this time, had been rejoined by His followers. The surprise on their faces at finding their Master talking with her she ignored, just as she failed to be mindful of the same old sneers and loathing which greeted her in the village. With beating heart, to all whom she saw she proclaimed triumphantly, *"Come and see a Man Who has told me all things whatsoever I have done. Is not He the Christ?"*

"Thus," as Archbishop Alban Goodier puts it so well, "was that poor woman, that poor, sinful, heretical, Samaritan woman, chosen to be the *first apostle of Christ Jesus in this world."*

Drawn out of herself, her words carried the ring of conviction to her listeners and, as the Gospel narrative continues: *"They went therefore out of the city and came unto Him . . . they desired that He would tarry there."* And Jesus, accepting their invitation, *"abode there two days."*

After He had departed, the villagers discussed among themselves all that He had said to them. Finally, coming to the woman, they told her somewhat ungraciously, *"We now believe, not for thy saying; for we ourselves have heard Him, and know that this is indeed the Saviour of the world."*

But the woman knew, and we know through the utter simplicity of the Gospel account how an outcast, a violator of the laws of human decency, was chosen as the connecting link, the "silken cord," between Christ and those who might never have known Him, but for her. To all appearances, she was the most unlikely messenger of Christ imaginable. She was also the first to go through the bitter experience for which every Christopher must be prepared—discovering that those she had brought to Christ, far from being grateful, were inclined to resent the part played by her and determined to minimize it. Yet, in the newness of her life, it probably mattered little to her that she had once more decreased in the estimation of her neighbors. The important thing to her was that Christ had increased.

In truth, did she "go," even hurry, into the market-place as a Christ-bearer. And, in going, she is an example for all to imitate who would bear Christ to others.

In these disturbing times there is a thrilling challenge in the realization that the world itself can be better because we are in it. No matter what our circumstances or failings, we can yet do *more* than say, *"Thy will be done on earth."* We can, with Christ's help, actually help *make* this tired old world of ours *the prelude to heaven*! And since that is what God wants it to be, truly it is a great time to be alive. Now—and for all eternity—we can look with deep consolation on the part we have played, no matter how small or insignificant, in shaping for the better the destiny of all mankind!

CONTENTS

You Can Change the World!

I

"EVERYTHING'S ALL RIGHT IN KOKOMO!"

A FEW MONTHS AGO while traveling through Indiana, giving talks in the smaller towns and cities of the state, one thing more than any other impressed itself on me. It was the *quality* of the people who made up the various audiences—farmers and factory workers, small businessmen and housewives—in short, the sound, solid folk who are the backbone of America.

No wild-eyed, irrational, heads-in-the-clouds visionaries were they. On the contrary, on their faces were the calm, down-to-earth expressions of people possessed of an honest sense of values. In their eyes was the quiet confidence born of such knowledge.

If ever a description fitted a group of individuals, it was the phrase, "salt of the earth." And in one talk frankly I told them so.

"If we had people with your plain common sense teaching

in our colleges, running our government, our trade unions, writing our newspapers, magazines, books, radio programs and movie scenarios," I said, "everything would be pretty much all right with our country . . . and the world."

After the talk one middle-aged gentleman came up to me. He seemed neither angry nor pleased with what I had just observed but, taking my hand, said simply, "I come from Kokomo . . . and everything's all right in Kokomo!"

If he had launched into a tirade of criticism or disagreement, his words would not have startled me half as much as that quiet statement of fact: "I come from Kokomo . . . and everything's all right in Kokomo."

Though he failed to realize it, that one little remark sums up only too well what probably is the chief obstacle to peace in the world. Most *good* people are taking care only of themselves while most *evil* people are taking care of everyone else. Most people with good ideas are thinking in small circles, in terms of a thousand separate "Kokomos" while the people who are out to wreck our civilization are planning and acting on a long-term, daring scale—in terms of centuries and over the span of the world!

THE HOPE THAT IS "KOKOMO"

To know that everything is all right in Kokomo, however, is encouraging . . . thank God for it. But for us, the refreshing hope in that knowledge is to release into the bloodstream of the whole country and the arteries of the world the confined goodness which makes Kokomo and communities like it what they are.

And tens upon tens of thousands of people of every age and in all walks of life are doing just that right now! They are getting out of themselves and into the thick of things. They are exerting their tremendous influence for good and hastening the day when peace will once more come to all mankind.

And that word "tremendous" is not misused.

For instance, still fresh in people's memories is the recent gigantic letter-writing campaign directed by the American people to the people of Italy, telling them what freedom and democracy mean in the United States and what they would mean to Italians if they only appreciated these rights enough to work for them.

Not just hundreds, or even thousands, but literally millions of letters went out from people of Italian descent in every section of this nation to their relatives in the "old country." Yet that campaign didn't just start by itself—somebody started it. And that somebody was *one man,* a barber in Southampton, Long Island, N. Y.

He had left Italy himself in 1913 and had come to the United States, determined to become a living part of our democracy for the rest of his days. He'd married, raised a family, and found life good. As the years went by, however, two things began to bother him. One was the constant stream of criticism from many quarters about what was wrong with our government and with the world in general. The second thing —and which irritated him even more than the first—was that those who did the complaining never seemed to do anything about making conditions any better.

Following World War II when news of millions of Italians flirting with Communism reached the American press, his patience reached the breaking point. *He decided to do something about it personally.*

First he wrote to his own relatives in St. Catherine, Sicily. Next he wrote to his wife's relatives who lived near the same town, telling all of them what the free way of life meant in America. Then he got his oldest boy, a doctor, and his oldest girl, a dietician, to write. He sent letters to the President and to all the newspapers in the New York area, asking for their support. The reaction to the idea was invariably good—but invariably it was accompanied with regrets that the project was too big to handle. Various organizations which he approached personally received him with smiles and wished him well . . . and that was all.

Faced with having the whole idea collapse on the spot, this barber still wouldn't quit. He kept writing and contacting his friends who had relatives in the old country, asking them to lend a hand. Gradually—providentially—the idea began to catch fire. Businessmen, young GI brides, housewives, veterans groups, civic societies, and religious leaders took up the fight. Soon a steady trickle (that in no time at all became a torrent) of heartfelt letters of thanks started coming back from Italy, promising to push the democratic concept of life. The result: hundreds of thousands of people in America began to do something no other agency or official group could possibly have done—reach the hearts of the Italian people.

And remember, one man started it all. One man, personally, was responsible for all of this because he got out of his own little world with its little ideas and into the big world with all its breathtaking potentialities.

OTHER SITUATIONS—OTHER WORKERS

Other men and other women in less spectacular ways, perhaps, but with equally far-reaching results, are carrying their individual Kokomos into the battle for a better world.

In the University of Wisconsin at this moment one particular teacher* is there at a great personal sacrifice simply because he finally realized how much more good he could do

* Personal names are used in relating incidents whenever the information has already been made public. In all other instances, names have been withheld, usually at the request of the individuals concerned.

in the classroom than by pursuing a successful business career. Once he had been a teacher but had given it up, as he put it, to "make more money on the outside." The money had come all right, but with it no real peace of mind.

The situation annoyed him. More than that, it puzzled him. Here he was with almost everything anyone could want and he wasn't happy. It was fantastic, unbelievable, yet until he happened across a Christopher pamphlet he was at a loss to know the reason. Reading it, he found out. In getting ahead in the world, in thinking only of himself, he was neglecting the good of others, particularly the youngsters he had been trained to teach. So—back to the classroom he went . . . and back to the satisfaction of knowing he was doing the most for his fellowmen in the best way he knew how.

In a sense this teacher-turned-businessman-turned-teacher had unconsciously been conducting an experiment with himself. He had been testing his own reactions to a problem which involved engrossing himself in selfish rather than selfless interests. And he had found the formula unsatisfactory. Only when the proper equation or relationship between himself and his neighbor was realized, did he count the experiment a success.

And speaking of experiments, just recently a scientist in the research laboratory of the Eastman Kodak Company, who had learned about the Christophers and what they were doing, sent us this letter:

"You're on the right track," he wrote. "I've been in the scientific field most of my life and have seen the wonderful things it's done. Lately, however, I've noticed a pagan trend becoming more apparent. Much of our scientific development in this country proceeds from the old German school which threw out the idea of God and the supernatural, and paved the way for Hitler. The only way to correct this condition, as you say, is to bring back Christian values into the teaching end of science. Maybe I can help in this. Anyway, I'm giving up my present job and becoming a science teacher at $1,000 less a year."

At a convention on the West Coast recently, the world's need for democracy was being discussed by the delegates at considerable length and with varying shades of opinion. In a corner of the huge meeting hall a housewife sat listening intently as the talk flowed on for the better part of two hours. Though she kept her silence, inside her was an undercurrent of excitement that was in sharp contrast to her earlier decision to pass up the convention and let her alternate go in her place. She'd felt, well . . . so inadequate. Conventions were something new to her. She knew nothing about their methods of procedure nor even what each delegate was supposed to do, and she almost made up her mind that it was useless for her to attend. Then the thought occurred to her that if everyone passed up the opportunity to do something constructive for the country—even if that something was very small—the nation could be lost by default.

Quietly, she listened to what the other delegates had to say, the feeling of excitement inside her now mingled with a mounting impatience at their ideas on democracy which sounded so confused and superficial. Finally, she stood up and quietly suggested to the convention chairman that it might be well to *define* democracy. "What does the word mean?" she asked, and listened to the murmur of surprise that swept the hall.

Several delegates offered halting, uncertain replies. When they'd finished, the housewife stood up again. "It's interesting to note," she observed, "that many definitions have been submitted, yet not one has included the basic idea which our Founding Fathers considered so important that they put it right at the beginning of the Declaration of Independence, namely: each individual man, woman and child receives his rights from God, not from the State, and one of the chief purposes of the State is to protect and respect those God-given rights."

When she sat down, no one was more surprised than she at the volley of applause that greeted her words. In one simple statement she had distinguished between Christian democracy and pagan totalitarianism.

What this woman did personally and individually, typifies the whole spirit of the Christopher approach. As one man (himself interested in the field of labor relations) put it in a recent letter from San Francisco:

"The magic of the Christopher idea—the shift from selfish defensive to unselfish offensive—has made me happier than I have been in a long time and in such a fundamental way . . . Now I shall plunge into the study of labor legislation with added fire . . ."

Of equal interest, and in a field so much in the public eye of late, is the case of a young lady of the Jewish faith who made her voice heard very effectively at the Communist-dominated meetings which she was accustomed to attend. Deeply concerned with the basic, sacred worth of each individual, she found her chance to express herself when a measure which violated the principles for which she stood came up for discussion on the floor one day.

Though she was the only *non-Communist* sufficiently interested to attend this particular meeting, she got up and told the rest of the gathering in a courteous friendly manner what she thought about the bill and the policy of the union in general.

Her words were received in stony silence. The expressions on most of the unionists' faces were openly scornful. The few others? It was impossible to tell what they were thinking.

When the vote was taken after the discussion had ended,

60 out of 75 union members present voted in favor of the measure; only one—this Jewish girl—voted against it. BUT, 14 Communist sympathizers present *abstained* from voting, so impressed were they by the courage and conviction of this one girl. Afterwards they came up to her, singly, and in groups of twos and threes and told her so. They didn't cease being party-liners right then and there, naturally. But the fact is, a start had been made in the right direction. For once they did not vote the Party line!

HERE, THERE AND EVERYWHERE

Literally and figuratively, this girl got "into the thick of things." She was alone. There was no friendly voice to shout encouragement, not even a perfunctory handclap when she sat down. Yet she made others respect her for what she believed, even though that fact will never be bragged about in Communist Party headquarters. Hers was a daring type of courage, but it isn't the only kind. Others, no less courageous, work quietly doing good. And sometimes the good they do means a sacrifice to others besides themselves.

In New York a few months ago a stock broker whose business gave him ample opportunity to feel the "pulse" of the nation, became alarmed when he realized the amazing inroads the Communists had made in this country, especially in the field of government. His business associates, apparently, didn't recognize the danger; but since he did, it was up to him to do something about it. His position in Wall Street involved high-level administrative skill, so he decided to try for a job in the State Department in Washington . . . until he remembered there were his wife and children to be considered. They had always been used to the best of everything, the finest clothes, the most modern luxuries of the home, and his wife in particular prized such possessions quite highly. If he went to Washington, he'd get far less money than he was making in New York.

Weeks of talking things over followed until, at last, they made their decision. Sacrifice or not, they'd make the change.

They've never regretted it. The ex-broker isn't "big time" any more—just a man in a government office doing a job. But what a job! His wife doesn't dress so well now. Her clothes are not as new and smart as they used to be. In fact, they're beginning to show signs of too much wear. Yet she doesn't care. The old phrase, "clothes make the woman" in her case is reversed. There is a radiance on her face that was never there when she was considered very much the fashionplate of style-conscious Manhattan. *Doing things for love of one's fellowman does that to people.*

A Baptist lawyer down in Texas is another who is finding that out, too. A man of about forty-five, he had been a captain in Army Intelligence during the recent war. And what he saw of the attempts to undermine our country made him fighting mad—not at anyone in particular—just fighting mad to do something about it.

Somehow he heard about the Christophers and, not long ago when I passed through Texas, he made it his business to see me. He asked my advice; but, before I gave it, I put just two questions to him:

"Do you believe in the basic idea that our Founding Fathers put in the Declaration of Independence—that man is a child of God and gets his rights from God?—that the problem of the State is to protect those rights?"

"I sure do," he answered.

"Are you willing to do something really constructive about it?"

"I sure am," came back the emphatic reply. "I'll even give up half my law practice to do it. That's how important I think it is!"

My suggestion to him was simply to go around and give as many talks as he could—at business functions, civic meetings, social gatherings, wherever the opportunity presented itself, and to encourage people with good ideas to get into the four great fields of education, labor-management, government, and the writing end of newspapers, radio, motion pictures, television and so on.

I told him, also, to try and have each person who heard him to get at least one other person to do the same thing, to get them working *as hard* putting basic American ideals *into* these fields as the doers of evil work trying to pull them *out.*

"BETTER TO LIGHT ONE CANDLE THAN TO CURSE THE DARKNESS"

If he succeeds in doing just that, and if the people who hear him follow suit, then the darkness of confusion, of evil, and of error in that part of the world, at least, will be illuminated by a light that cannot—and will not—be put out. Instead, of complaining about *evil,* they will be doing *good.*

An old Chinese proverb points up that fact so simply, yet so dramatically. "Better to light one candle," it goes, "than to curse the darkness." For a girl in a small California town, doing that meant the difference between a life of sickness and pain and grumbling frustration, and a life that has been—and still is—an inspiration to everyone around her.

Weakened by a series of recurring epileptic fits, her condition was aggravated to the point that hospitalization was the only course left open to her. Lying in bed, hour upon weary hour, gave her plenty of time to think about the future. She felt sorry for herself, but after a time even self-pity became a trifle tiresome.

Looking around for something different to occupy her time, she got an idea. Perhaps if she tried to forget about her own troubles and tried to help others . . . no, that wasn't quite it. Perhaps if she tried to help others *first,* then her own troubles might seem less important, less hopeless.

Though "no literary genius," as she put it, she did have some flair for writing. So she asked the hospital authorities to contact the editor of the town newspaper. "I want to write a column," she told him. "A column that will try to make people concentrate on . . . well, the good in life around them instead of always doing just the opposite." And she almost added, "like I've been doing."

Fortunately, the paper wasn't bound by the space limitations of a big city daily, and the editor agreed to give her a chance. Within three or four weeks after the column first appeared, letters began pouring in, thanking her, giving her a mental "pat on the back" for what she was trying to do.

And from that very first day on this same girl has rarely suffered another attack of epilepsy!

Doctors familiar with the case have not tried to minimize the change in her. Instead, they point out that the "getting out of herself," and out of her own narrow world, has given her a purpose in life, has done away with the mental and emotional frustration which, in their opinion, was apparently responsible for a serious physical disorder. And, while not attempting to generalize, they add that they know of similar cases where the cure was within the person himself as much as in any medical treatment.

FOR EACH LIFE—PURPOSE

To some of us, realization of this fact comes easily. But to others, it comes only after some tremendous experience has shaken them out of their complacency and self-satisfaction.

A young ex-naval officer had spent five and one-half years on active service during the recent war, both with the Board of Economic Warfare and with the Photographic Division of the Armed Forces. In the first post his job was to investigate and help allocate vital supplies to the countries assisting us and our allies in the war effort. In the second post, a lot of his work consisted in helping photograph much of the European mainland, the coast of Norway and the rough terrain of Czechoslovakia, in particular.

Both jobs called for technical skill and an extraordinary capacity to evaluate material and, because of the complexities of modern warfare, evaluate men as well.

However, when he was returned to inactive duty and began the task of getting back into the "feel" of civilian life, he found something had happened to him in the time he'd been away. While in uniform, he'd had a *purpose*—to help win for himself and his countrymen a victorious peace. All the inconvenience, the suffering, the ever-present threat of death had been made bearable because of that.

Now that he was back in "civvies" he wanted his life to have a purpose, also, a worthwhile goal to work toward, some field where he could do some good for others as well as for himself. It didn't call for simply making money, either, as the offer of an $8,000 a year job with a big New York banking house, while it tempted him, didn't persuade him to the point of acceptance.

The job meant security. But it also meant the plowing of an economic and social furrow that might become a *rut* as the years went by. So he decided, not without regret, "That's not for me!"

Well, how about the movies? In Europe he'd worked with several prominent Hollywood technicians and directors. Perhaps there was a place for him out there. But again, a blank wall. Oh, he was offered jobs all right—good ones, too. Yet, with one exception, they paralleled too closely the Wall Street offer—money—nothing more. The one exception possessed possibilities more to his liking, but only for the immediate future.

"The turn-over in this job is terrific, no matter how good you are," a friend on the inside told him. "In a year or two you'll be on the outside looking in. And once you're out, all your ideas, everything you've worked for, will wind up in some convenient wastebasket. If you want a job with a future, this isn't for you."

Discouraging? Most assuredly, yes! Yet, somehow the movies, their creative values, and their wonderful potential for the communication of good to millions of people, still stuck in his mind. Driving along in his car one night with a friend who happened to be a Christopher, he asked for and got a solution to his dilemma.

The answer, briefly, was this: as an exhibitor of motion pictures—that is, as an independent exhibitor—he would be in a position to encourage movies that were both entertaining and decent. And he could weed out and refuse to show any film that didn't meet these standards.

This ex-naval officer knew next to nothing about this phase of the film industry. But he decided to learn.

At a salary of $35 a week, he got a job in order to learn the field from the ground up. By the end of eighteen months —remember, he had a purpose—he had learned his work so well that with the help of a bank loan he was able to buy his own theater in an upstate New York college town. And, incidentally, he is making more money than he would have earned if he'd taken the job first offered him in Wall Street. A motion picture executive, noting his progress, commented recently that such a theater might well be the start of a string of theaters across the country similarly dedicated to showing only *good* screen plays.

More important at the present, however, is the fact that this man has already influenced the lives of thousands of people by giving them the best in screen entertainment. "If a picture doesn't deserve to be shown, I'll not show it, even if there's nothing else to put on the screen in its place," he announced not long ago. "If that happens, I'll close down the theater for a couple of days and put out a sign explaining why."

In his spare time this Christopher has completed a law course begun before he entered service and has also concerned himself in many activities offering opportunities to serve the general good.

For example, you may remember the uproar in the American press when Czechoslovakia succumbed to Communist pressure from Moscow and had to hoist the Red flag of surrender. Editorials proclaimed the catastrophe which had befallen a great people. The terse obituaries by radio commentators went out to every corner of the country, telling the soda jerker in Des Moines, the secretary in New York, the salesgirl in San Francisco of the latest manifestation of tyranny which had been flung in their faces from across the sea.

As in the case of the Long Island barber, one man—this theater owner—did something about it. And did it with equally far reaching results.

The morning after the papers first screamed the news, he took it upon himself to go down to the Slovak section of New York's midtown East Side, where he rounded up a few men who felt as indignant as he did, about what had happened in Central Europe.

"But what can we do about it?" they asked him.

"Why not picket the Soviet U.N. headquarters on Park Avenue?" came back the prompt reply. "Tomorrow!"

"But . . . but that's impossible. It's never been done before and on such short notice. I mean, where will we get the men?" one of the group asked.

"That's your job. This thing won't wait. You'll have to get the pickets somewhere. Leave the rest to me."

With that the Christopher turned on his heel and was off. An hour went by, an hour spent calling one sign contractor after another, trying to get a rush job done on some placards for the following afternoon. On the sixteenth call, his perseverance paid off. The signs would be ready when he wanted them.

Next he called the newspapers and motion picture newsreel companies, identified himself as a lawyer interested in Czechoslovak freedom, and told them of plans to picket the Communist headquarters the following afternoon.

And at three-thirty the following afternoon the pickets, all Slovak-Americans, were there, complete with signs protesting the Red seizure of their former homeland. And on the scene with them were newspaper reporters and photographers from practically every major newsreel company in the city, recording for posterity the *free expression* of what the man in the street thought about Communist imperialism.

Late that afternoon and all that evening word of the event went out to every part of the country and to different parts of the world. A few days later newsreels followed suit.

Shortly afterwards letters and telegrams to the United States began arriving from Europe. One letter from a man in Paris to the head of a Slovak paper in New York tells better than any long discourse how the news and pictures were being received on the continent.

"I wonder if you realize," the letter read, "what seeing things like these means to us who are fighting for a free way of life over here. It gives us courage and inspiration—and most of all, hope! Thank God for those who were responsible for them!"

One other event for which, in part at least, this same young

Christopher can claim credit, occurred at the U.N. Assembly at Lake Success. Mr. Gromyko had just made a vicious speech denouncing the United States as being responsible for much of the world's disorder and implying that we, not they, were guilty of aggression. He finished by stating that every cowboy in the country was aware of this . . . every taxi driver . . . every doorman.

Not long after, this Christopher helped arrange for a dozen cowboys and taxi drivers in uniform to parade outside the U.N. Assembly Hall carrying signs whose general theme was: "We don't know it, Mr. Gromyko! How come?"

THE IMPORTANCE OF ONE LITTLE LIGHT

What this one Christopher did should be an inspiration to everyone who would truly bear Christ. Once a million men and women like him carry their light into the darkness of confusion, misinformation and error, then this groping old earth of ours will truly come to reflect the brightness of Him Who is the Light of the world.

Those who witnessed a post-war ceremonial at Los Angeles Coliseum just after V-J Day can appreciate the physical accuracy of that statement. More than 100,000 spectators had jammed the huge stadium to witness a mighty pageant in honor of the city's war heroes. Thanks to the magic of Hollywood, the arena had been transformed into a terrifyingly realistic battle scene. Exploding land mines shook the earth, batteries of army tanks roared across the stadium, a mass formation of B-29's swooped down over the watching throng. The noise was deafening and the effect, thundering and overpowering, as if to emphasize the helplessness and insignificance of the human individual in the face of so much mechanical might.

Then something strange happened. Suddenly all the outburst stopped and stepping to the microphone the master of ceremonies began to speak to the listening thousands.

"Perhaps you sometimes say to yourself," he began, "'My job isn't important because it's such a little job.' But you are wrong. The most obscure person can be very important. Anyone here who wants to exert a far-reaching power may do so. Let me show you what I mean."

Abruptly, the giant searchlights that bathed every corner of the Coliseum were turned off. From day-like brightness the great arena was unexpectedly plunged into total darkness. Then the speaker struck a match, and in the blackness the tiny flame could be seen by everyone.

"Now you can see the importance of one little light," he said. "But suppose we ALL strike a light!"

From all over the stadium came the sound of matches being struck until, faster than it takes to tell, nearly 100,000 pinpoints of light lit up the summer night.

Everyone gasped with surprise. Quickly and effectively, there had been demonstrated to them the power of each single individual.

Coming out of the Coliseum and making our way through the crowds toward the waiting streetcars, we found ourselves thinking about how comparatively easy it would be to bring peace to a heartsick world if only enough of the wonderful people in it would make a constant effort to spread the light of truth, and combat the darkness of error.

People all over the earth are beginning to realize more and more that there is a very intimate connection between truth and freedom. Sobered by the scourge of war, even those opposed to religion are more disposed to admit the inescapable conclusion of what Christ meant when He said: "The Truth shall make you free." Once a sufficient number of people realize that falsehood is nothing more than the absence of truth, just as darkness is the absence of light, hate the absence of love, and disease the absence of health, then there is high hope that this old world of ours will one day come to know the blessing of a real, lasting peace.

Anyone can help in this task. You can. I can. And, naturally, the closer we are to Christ the better Christophers we will be. Yes, no one is so far away from Christ that he or she cannot share in some measure in this tremendous undertaking.

And startling as it may seem, even a pagan in darkest Africa or a Communist in the heart of America who learns even *one* of Christ's Truths—and tries to spread that truth in the lifestream of his land—is beginning to be a Christopher, whether or not he realizes it. The more he does for Christ, the closer he draws to Christ. With each truth-bearer he will have the consolation of knowing that he can be a bearer of that true light "which enlighteneth every man that cometh into this world." They can be partners with Him Who said: "I am the Way, and the Truth, and the Life." (*John* 14:16)

Every one of us can be a bearer of Christ—a Christopher.

II

THE PROBLEM HAS A CURE

"Those people who are not governed by God will be ruled by tyrants."

—WILLIAM PENN

OVER TWO HUNDRED AND FIFTY YEARS ago when the charter of the Commonwealth of Pennsylvania was being written, the Quaker, William Penn, sounded that very warning. Today, those words have for us a far greater, even a life-and-death, significance.

Make no mistake about it. We are at the crossroads of civilization. We stand on the brink of the greatest peace the world has ever enjoyed—or the most terrible nightmare of misery and chaos that mankind has ever known.

The issue is clear and narrows down to what is truth with regard to the human being. If he is not a creature of God and the noblest act of God, with rights from Him, then he is just a clod of earth or the merest tool of the almighty State. He must be one or the other. He cannot be both.

Karl Marx, the archprophet of Communism, in his *Das Kapital* expressed this fundamental point most clearly. *"The democratic concept of man is false because it is Christian,"* he wrote. *"The democratic concept holds that . . . each man is a sovereign being. This is the illusion, dream, and postulate of Christianity."* (First ed., ME, 1, 1. p. 590)

In this Marx was one with Adolf Hitler. In fact, Hitler took much of the Marxian philosophy and integrated it into his Nazi doctrine, voicing the same complete disregard for the sacred worth of the individual. As quoted in *The Voice of Destruction,* by Hermann Rauschning, here are Hitler's own words:

"To the Christian doctrine of the infinite significance of the human soul . . . I oppose with icy clarity the saving doctrine of the nothingness and insignificance of the human being."

Thus both Marx and Hitler testified that democracy depends on Christianity. They realized that to destroy all forms of democratic government the godless must discredit and eventually exterminate Christianity.

Before proceeding with suggestions on "where to go" and "what to do" to avert this threatened disaster, and to put into practice the *cure* we have at our disposal, those who would be Christophers might do well to review briefly the *particular* problems that face our country and the world.

Commenting editorially on the situation not long ago, *Fortune* magazine went on record with:

> "We Americans are unhappy. We are not happy about ourselves in relation to America. As we look out at the rest of the world we are confused; we don't know what to do. . . . As we look toward the future—our own future and the future of other nations—we are filled with foreboding.
>
> "We know how lucky we are compared to all the rest of mankind. At least two thirds of us are just plain rich compared to all the rest of the human family—rich in food,

rich in clothes, rich in entertainment and amusement, rich in leisure . . . *rich*!

"Yet we also know that the sickness of the world is also our sickness. We, too, have miserably failed to solve the problems of our epoch. And nowhere in the world have man's failures been so little excusable as in the United States of America. Nowhere has the contrast been so great between reasonable hope of our age and the actual facts of failures and frustration. . . . Naturally, we have no peace."

And the editorial continued:

"But, even beyond this necessity for living with our own misdeeds, there is another reason why there is no peace in our hearts. It is that we have not been honest with ourselves. In this whole matter of War and Peace especially, we have been at various times and in various ways false to ourselves, false to each other, false to the facts of history and false to the future. . . .

"If our leaders have deceived us it is mainly because we ourselves have insisted on being deceived. Their deceitfulness has resulted from our own moral and intellectual confusion. The trouble is not with facts. The trouble is that clear and honest inferences have not been drawn from the facts. The day-to-day present is clear. The issues of tomorrow are being befogged. If we dodge the issue, we shall flounder for 10 or 20 or 30 bitter years in a chartless and meaningless series of disasters."

THE GREATEST OBSTACLE

As this editorial makes evident, we have seemed unable to cope with the thousand-and-one problems all over the globe which the cessation of World War II has brought. And these problems have become magnified as the earth has "shrunk" in proportion to the advances of modern science with its jet-propelled planes faster than the speed of sound, and its atom bomb which can level all humanity to the common denominator of a lifeless, fetid pulp.

But great as these problems are, perhaps the most formidable problem of all which we have failed so far to solve is represented by the force of a group of men banded together to eliminate God from the face of the earth.

The greatest obstacle to our finding a solution to this problem as well as to most of the others is the *apathy* which comes from our lack of understanding that we followers of Christ have the salvation of the world in our hands. Far too many people are deluded into believing that we are living in a brave, new world where everything is different and values—human values—not what they used to be.

But let's not fool ourselves. *It is still the same old world.* Conditions have changed drastically, still we are fundamentally the same. The world will never be more than we are. If the world is in bad shape, it is because too many of *us* are in bad condition.

Many people are inclined to think once Communism is on the wane all over the globe, mankind will settle back automatically to an era of peace. Most emphatically, that cannot be true. Even if Communism were to disappear overnight—which it most certainly will not—the situation which makes *all* forms of totalitarianism possible still remains. And not only does it remain, it grows steadily worse. It is the "deficiency disease" in our society which, like the deficiency disease in a starving person, paves the way for an attack of scurvy or beriberi, poisons our national and international bloodstreams.

Those who fall for the attractive deceptions of the materialists are not merely those who are economically insecure, oddly enough. In far greater numbers they are those who have no spiritual moorings, no fixed beliefs in the Fatherhood of God and the dignity of man. In the United States alone, according to one prominent government official, the Communists, while numbering less than 100,000 card-carrying Party members, have in tow about *five million* fellow travelers and sympathizers. And, significantly, many of these are middle class, well-to-do. Confused and with little idea of true values, they are like immature children who fall for the glib half-truths of the kidnapper.

It is the hope and dream of the Communists to build this five million into twelve or fifteen million and then to "revolutionize" this country out of its present democratic form of government. That can easily be done because these millions will come, with but few exceptions, from among the 100,000,000 in our land who are living off the benefits of Christianity but who are becoming less and less conscious of the great Christian fundamentals which make all their freedoms possible. Of this one hundred million, seventy million belong to *no* church. Another thirty million, while "on the books" of various denominations, have drifted so far away that, for all practical purposes, they should properly be classed as "not belonging."

As time goes on, to them even the most elementary truths will fade into the hidden background as *more* and *more* people come to stand for *less* and *less.* Most are *against* Communism now, just as they were against Nazism and Fascism. But they don't know what they are *for.* They talk vaguely about the "free way of life" and the need for democracy, yet most of them have only a faint idea of the Cause which makes these *effects* possible. They are unaware that every time this Cause is removed, out the window go the effects as well.

If this steady trend toward paganism continues, it is only a matter of time before our nation will collapse—more from deterioration from *within* than from any force *without.*

IT IS NOT TOO LATE FOR AMERICA

This is what took place in Germany. But, thank God, *in the United States it is not too late to reverse this trend. It is not too late to do something about it!*

It seems safe to say that less than *one percent* of the American people are set on the destruction of our country. Furthermore, there is little danger of exaggeration in saying that every one of this tiny minority has a militant hatred of the immutable truth on which our nation is founded—that man is a child of God and is "endowed by his Creator with certain unalienable rights." Also, you will invariably find, once you investigate, that practically all of this minority are in key spots where they pass on their hatred, not to a few, but to the mass of the people. This is so because those who have an active hatred of God are *missionaries* at heart and are never content to keep that hatred to themselves. They strive incessantly to pass it into the bloodstream of our national life, defiling the minds and hearts of everyone they can reach with their foul ideas.

Ever on the job, they use every possible medium—education, government, labor, press, radio, movies, comic strips, magazines, books, and countless other channels to further their purpose. They are in a race for man's soul. Their program is well organized, unusually efficient, remarkably aggressive. They mingle with the people, they speak their language, they outsmart all others with their well-thought-out techniques and formulas of approach. Admittedly, it is difficult for many to resist their beguiling invitations and the honeyed promises they offer but seldom, if ever, fulfill.

Acknowledging all this, it is still very simple to correct

such a condition. One of the best ways to cure a starving patient is to build him up with good, nourishing food. The *best* way to cure this disease in our society is to build up society itself with good ideas and ideals and to eliminate those which are evil.

Our responsibility to our fellowmen in this respect is tremendous. Christ has put in our hands the Divine medicinal power, the restorative power of *love.* Ours is the mission to bring that love to all mankind, to "go to all men" and "to all nations." There is no substitute, no short cut.

"The great truth of the times," wrote Dave Boone not long ago in the *New York Sun,* "is . . . that in the terrible light of the atomic bomb it is clear now that nothing can save world civilization except acceptance and practice of the brotherhood of man. And the emphasis goes on 'practice.' Few things are accepted more and practiced less."

Those who have a burning love of God and of man, not merely of self, will go to the greatest lengths to put that brotherhood into practice. They will suffer everything to share that love with all mankind.

It is the Christopher thesis, therefore, that for the one percent bent on destruction, it should not be too difficult to find another one percent who will strive with even greater imagination and enterprise to show a devoted and continuing solicitude for our brothers of the one hundred million who are reached by no faith. As Christophers, as Christ-bearers, they will go into their very midst, into all the spheres that influence the destinies of mankind.

Most of these one hundred million are blessed with an abundance of common sense. They are extremely fair when they *know* the facts and are seriously interested in getting fair play for all men of all nations. They most certainly are *not* atheistic. A Gallup poll revealed that ninety-four percent of Americans believe in God, three percent list themselves as "not knowing," and only another three percent put themselves down as atheists. Their present drift from religion is probably much less their fault than it is that of the followers of Christ who fail to "go" and "keep going" to them with the same determination and thoroughness displayed by Christ's enemies in their relentless drive to enslave the earth.

This is a far from normal state of affairs. The strength of American life is rooted in Christian truth, as an editorial in *Fortune* magazine recently pointed out:

"The basic teachings of Christianity are in its bloodstream," it said. *"The central doctrine of its political system—the inviolability of the individual—is a doctrine inherited from nineteen hundred years of Christian insistence upon the immortality of the soul."*

The first Americans acknowledged this. They believed in the supernatural, as every important document of colonial history shows. From Georgia to the Massachusetts Bay Colony they had respect and reverence for fundamental Christian principles which modern totalitarians and materialists seek to destroy. Among these truths are the following:

(1) the existence of a personal God, Who has spoken to the world;
(2) Jesus Christ, true God and true man;
(3) the Ten Commandments;
(4) the sacred character of the individual;
(5) the sanctity of the lifelong marriage bond;
(6) the sanctity of the home as the basic unit of the whole human family;
(7) the human rights of every person as coming from God, not from the State;
(8) the right, based on human nature, to possess private property, with its consequent obligation to society;

(9) due respect for domestic, civil, and religious authority;
(10) judgment after death.

These basic truths are only a portion of "all things" which Christ commissioned His Church to teach "all nations" (*Matt.* 28:19-20). Upon them, the early Americans wisely built our nation. Proof that recognition of them was much more than lip-service to eternal truths, that they were actually a part of the lives of the men and women who first settled our country, is found in one account after another of the early days of this country's history. For example, in the field of education alone, 140 years before the signing of the Declaration of Independence the motto of Harvard University was given as *In Christi Gloriam* (For the Glory of Christ). The university's founder, John Harvard, was referred to as a *"godly gentleman and a man of learning"* in the legislative act in 1638 that authorized the founding of this world-famed institution. And, during the administration of the school's first president, Master Dunster, one of the student directives was even more explicit in emphasizing the spiritual values that characterized all phases of early American life. *"Let every student be plainly instructed,"* the directive reads, *"and earnestly pressed to consider well, the maine end of his life and studies is to know God and Jesus Christ which is eternal life. . . . Christ* [*is*] *the only foundation of all sound knowledge and learning."*

"WE HOLD THESE TRUTHS TO BE SELF-EVIDENT"

Thus these early Americans set the pace in acknowledging the Fatherhood of God and the brotherhood of man, and what was good enough for them should at least represent the minimum good for us. At any rate, their beliefs were good enough for our Founding Fathers who, right in the beginning, wrote these words into the Declaration of Independence: *"We hold these truths to be self-evident, that all men are created equal, that they are endowed by their Creator with certain unalienable Rights, that among these are Life, Liberty, and the pursuit of Happiness."*

And again quoting from the same document:

"To secure these rights governments are instituted among men, deriving their just powers from the consent of the governed."

The Founding Fathers, you see, were most explicit. They were God-fearing men. For them the idea of God had to be integrated with everything if men were not to forget that their rights, liberties, and life itself come from their Creator. They must have feared that, in the years ahead, those who would destroy America might subtly deny this *Truth.* So, leaving nothing to chance, they were most positive.

They took pains to emphasize the fact that the natural law itself depends on God, when they wrote: "When in the course of human events, it becomes necessary for one people to dissolve the political bands, which have connected them with another, and to assume among the powers of the earth, the separate and equal station to which the Laws of Nature *and of Nature's God* entitle them, a decent respect to the opinions of mankind requires that they should declare the causes which impel them to the separation. . . ."

It was in this form, with two pointed references to God, that the Declaration was submitted to Congress. But Congress was not quite satisfied. Although they made many deletions from the final draft and a few other changes in wording, *they insisted upon two insertions.* In the next to the last sentence they made it clear that they were *"appealing to the Supreme Judge of the world for the rectitude of our intentions."* And, in the very last sentence of the Declaration of Independence, they strengthened their affirmation of our dependence upon God by adding the words, ". . . *with a firm reliance on the protection of divine Providence,* we mutually pledge to each other our Lives, our Fortunes, and our sacred Honor."

A paper appearing in the *Journal of the American Medical Association,* January 3, 1948, quotes Cardinal Bellarmine in 1576 (200 years before the signing of the Declaration of Independence) as expressing similar thoughts when he wrote:

"All men are equal, not in wisdom or in grace, but in the essence and nature of mankind. Political right is from God and necessarily inherent in the nature of man. . . . It depends upon the consent of the multitude to constitute over itself a king, consul, or other magistrate. This power is indeed from God, but vested in a particular ruler by the council and election of men."

This was no new doctrine either to the Founding Fathers or to Cardinal Bellarmine. They well knew it had come down through the long centuries: that for thousands of years, despite persecution, defection, and obstacles of every sort, the Jews had kept alive the sublime concept that man has an eternal destiny, that he derives his rights from his Creator, and that because of this he has solemn obligations to his fellowmen in each of whom he should see a child of God. Their view of man's spiritual nature had always been clear-cut. The author of *Genesis,* writing twelve or thirteen centuries before Christ, put it very specifically: "And God created man to His own image. . . . And the Lord God formed man of the slime of the earth; and breathed into his face the breath of life, and man became a living soul." (*Gen.* 1:27; 2:7)

God didn't have so to favor us. He could have formed us on the same level as the beasts of the field. Yet precisely because he did make us "living souls" with the gift of understanding and reason, He left us with an obligation to exercise our God-given rights BUT *with an equal responsibility to see that these rights are neither ignored nor abused.*

So far, unfortunately, too many of us have both ignored and abused them. A New York daily not long ago revealed its alarm over this apathy and abuse in words that should strike home to each and every one of us.

"Try this, if you will," it stated. "Go into any group—the more prosperous and fashionable the better the test—and speak of the 'self-evident truth that all men are endowed by their Creator with certain unalienable rights, that among these are life, liberty and the pursuit of happiness.' Say to this group that 'to secure these rights governments are instituted among men.' We venture that you will be startled by the number of people, particularly the younger people, who do not know that you are quoting the Declaration of Independence. And of those who know, a large number will not agree with the philosophy expressed. And of those who agree—and this is the most tragic thing—many will not have the courage to say so."

With this situation staring us in the face, is it any wonder, then, that the godless have taken on the job of rewriting American history to fit the doctrines of Karl Marx? And they *are* trying to do just that. The New York *World-Telegram* on April 20, 1948, quotes the Moscow radio as saying, "The U. S. Constitution is a fraud" and goes on to give the Red version of the classic boxing phrase, "We wuz robbed."

You don't believe that lie. I don't believe it. The mass of the American people don't believe it. But too many of us are lulled into a conviction that the problem will take care of itself.

It will not and it cannot. The only answer is to have more and more bearers of the *truth,* especially in those phases of life which, for better or worse, fashion the destinies of men—education, government, labor, and communications (newspapers, magazines, books, radio, television, and motion pictures). Put enough people who are fighters for the truth in each of those fields, and the rest will take care of itself.

THE CURE: MORE "BEARERS OF THE LIGHT"—MORE CHRISTOPHERS!

That is the answer, and there is nothing original about it. It is as old as the hills! As soon as there are more people turning on the lights than there are those turning them off, then the darkness disappears.

Some unknown author put it simply, yet so well: "Such is the irresistible nature of truth, that all it asks, and all it wants, is the liberty of appearing. The sun needs no inscription to distinguish it from darkness."

Even those who have little or no time for religion are beginning to see that now. They are beginning to realize that the evil forces that have risen up over the world in the last few years to crush them, have worked even more furiously to stamp out Christianity because it alone has *the light of Truth,* it alone is the one universal cause that champions man's dignity.

They are beginning to see the falseness of the subversives' claims of wanting to "protect the people," "to relieve oppression," "to provide freedom for the laborer." They are beginning to see these hypocrites just as Christ Himself saw them when He likened them to "whited sepulchres, which outwardly appear to men beautiful, but within are full of dead men's bones, and of all filthiness. . . ." (*Matt.* 23:27)

They are beginning to see that all the godless follow one pattern, namely, to deny or ignore the sacredness of the individual so that the State may become supreme.

What to do about it? It will avail us nothing merely to mumble "incredible," and blindly lash out against our enemies. That is like trying to fight *against* darkness when it would be much more constructive and effective to fight *for* light.

Neither should we think we are too few to make any real progress in solving the enormous problems now confronting us. Time and again throughout history a few have saved the many. If you recall, God Himself was willing to spare whole cities if a handful could be found who were filled with the love of God and the love of man. "If I find in Sodom fifty just within the city, I will spare the whole place for their sake." (*Gen.* 18:26)

Nor should we think that to be Christ-bearers we have to destroy. Emphasis should be on saving. "I am not come to destroy, but to fulfill." (*Matt.* 5:17) The words of Pope St. Gregory in A.D. 597 illustrate this point with all the keen insight of one who saw clearly the way salvation was to be shared with all mankind. Writing to St. Augustine of Canterbury, and instructing him how he was to approach the problem of Christianizing England, Gregory advised him to transform heathen temples into Christian churches rather than to destroy them, and, whenever possible, to adapt heathen practices to the celebration of Christian festivals. *"For,"* declared Gregory, *"he who would ascend a height must mount, not by leaps, but step by step."*

To bring Christ to the world we also must ascend "not by leaps, but step by step." Obviously, we don't have to possess all the saintly virtues to achieve that purpose. To refer again to the godless, the Reds don't ascend or try to ascend by leaps. They don't use only one-hundred-percent Marxists. They use anyone who is in any degree a fellow-traveler or sympathizer. They truly have adopted for themselves Christ's own admonition to the faithful. "Be wise as serpents," He urged, "and simple as doves" It is well to note that He stressed being wise first, not second. Unfortunately for the world's return to the Truth, *most good people tend more toward being "simple as doves" than toward being "wise as serpents."*

Furthermore, as encouragement to all in working toward a cure, it is no small consolation that to do effective good as a Christopher one does not necessarily have to be brilliant, well-trained, or in high position, for *"The foolish things of the world hath God chosen, that he may confound the wise; and the weak things of the world hath God chosen, that he may confound the strong."* (1 Cor. 1:27)

Today there are millions who would thrill to follow in the footsteps of the first apostles, to be twentieth-century apostles, no matter in how small a way. One girl, for instance, who works in a "five and dime" store in Boston wrote not long ago that she is trying to do her bit. All she does, as she modestly puts it, is not get "mad" at anybody. When her fellow workers try to taunt her with their disbelief in God, all she does is reply with some friendly quip, such as: "Sure you believe in Him! There's a lot of good in you." And seldom, if ever, has she received a harsh retort to this honest confidence in them.

In another instance, an older woman, who had little education and who made her living sweeping the floors in a department store after it closed in the evening, was so filled with the love of God that she decided to try and get another job where she could meet people and share that love with them; where she might serve, in her own small way, as an instrument of Christ.

With the wisdom which God invariably showers upon "little people" who are anxious to do His will, she transferred to a nearby women's college attended by young ladies from all over the country. She got a job sweeping and cleaning in one of the dormitories, and, as she goes about her daily chores, she makes it her business to meet as many girls as she can. Her whole approach is one of loving solicitude for each of them. She doesn't say much, but few girls are not touched by her deep faith when she says to any one of them, "I suppose lots of folks will tell you there is no God, but I tell you there is! And He loves you—and I pray for you every day at Mass."

These two zealous apostles—and thousands like them all over this land—have caught and are catching the Christopher idea, an idea which is basically *missionary*. This missionary idea, incidentally, is one which the Communists freely admit they "borrowed" from Christianity. The words of instruction continually repeated in one Red school which boasts of training 40,000 adults over a four-year period, is graphic illustration of that:

"What we give you doesn't belong to you! You mustn't keep it to yourself! Don't take *any* job. Get in where you can reach the masses. Get into a college, a government job, a trade union, or a newspaper."

With the very different purpose of spreading *light* where there is only *darkness*—those same words of advice, "What we give you doesn't belong to you! You mustn't keep it to yourself!" —can be applied to the whole Christopher movement. We must saturate our whole society with it, and, by so doing, we may easily change the whole course of history! God is behind us. He will supply His grace in abundance in what may be, for us, the most unusual opportunity since the creation of mankind to recapture the world for Christ. Far from being dismayed, we should realize it is a great time to be alive!

WE, THE ONE MILLION, HAVE THE ANSWER

In this land today there are probably a million lay persons willing and anxious to play the role of a Christopher in every and all walks of life. And although specially trained workers are essential for the more complex problems, the great pioneer work, the leavening of the multitude with Christian ideals, can be done in the same simple way it was by the early Christians of the catacombs. The one power that accounted for their tremendous success was their consuming love for *all* men, even their worst enemies, in each of whom they saw the image of Christ Himself.

And it is a power which the least of us can have. It is the *cure* for which mankind longs. It should not be forgotten, however, that we are followers of a Crucified One: as He suffered in His love for all mankind, so we must suffer likewise. Mary, His Mother, the *first* bearer of Christ, who brought Him into the world, suffered much. To be a Christ-bearer, a Christopher, must mean sacrifice, loss of time, inconvenience, suffering, misunderstanding, and countless disappointments that truly "try men's souls."

Still the answer is in our hands. For the next twenty or thirty years, or perhaps longer, this nation will play the leading role in world affairs. Which way it will lead depends upon us. If the Christian principles that make our country possible are reawakened in the One Hundred Million who know not the Truth, or have forgotten it, we can lead the world back to Christ.

It is a terrible challenge, but we must face the facts. There is no other way than the way of Christ. "I am the way and the truth and the life." (*John* 14:6) If we but strike a spark, that spark, in the Providence of God, may burst into a flame of love which will fire all mankind.

But there is no time to lose. We must show speed. The efforts of even the least among us will be blessed with results that will exceed our wildest dreams.

God willing, we may yet recapture the world for Christ! *It is a great time to be alive!*

III

PURPOSE MAKES THE DIFFERENCE!

"*To The Glory of God Alone!*" Such was the inspiring dedication which Johann Sebastian Bach, one of the greatest composers of all time, gave to each of the works which came from his generous heart and gifted pen.

For twenty-seven years he served as director of music at a church in Leipzig, Germany. If he had taken this post simply to earn a living, or to make a name for himself, he would have lived and died unknown, like so many of those who have no interest outside themselves. At best he would have been forgotten, good though his life may have been in its own small way.

But, filled as he was with the love of God and his fellowman, Bach had only one ambition. That was to serve as an instrument, however unworthy, to reflect the glory of the Most High into the lives of as many of God's children as he could. Little did he dream that because of this inspiring objective he was to draw out of himself a power of composition of such exquisite beauty that, instead of reaching only a few in Leipzig, or Germany, he would reach the world and generations then unborn. And to millions over the earth, he would bring through his magnificent cantatas and oratorios a fleeting glimpse of the majesty of the Creator of all.

That was his *purpose,* his motivation—to love God above all else and to love his neighbor because he saw in him the image of the Almighty.

Bach's whole life was a demonstration of the *power* of Christian love, and not a few people have recognized that. But, strangely enough, one of the greatest testimonials to the efficacy of that power came, not from an historian, a feature writer or an ecclesiastic, but from Anatole Lunacharsky, former Commissar of Education in the U.S.S.R.

> "We hate Christianity and Christians," this Communist proclaimed in 1935. "Even the best of them must be considered our worst enemies. They preach love of one's neighbor and mercy, which is contrary to our principles. *Christian love is an obstacle to the development of the revolution.* Down with love of our neighbor! What we want is hatred. We must know how to hate. Only thus will we conquer the universe!" (Quoted in *Izvestia*)

Note well the significance of that statement. *"Christian love is an obstacle to the development of the revolution."* It illustrates, as much as words possibly can, the undeniable fact that only those with a burning love, or a burning hatred, have a cause that is greater than themselves. They alone can change the world for better or for worse. The "in-betweeners" accomplish little or nothing.

For those who live only for themselves, even Christ Himself has small regard: *"I would that thou wert cold or hot, but because thou art lukewarm and neither cold nor hot, I will begin to vomit thee out of my mouth."* (*Apoc.* 3:15)

Each of us has to have a sense of dedication, a sense of sacrifice that will go beyond ourselves. That the godless realize this, even if too many God-fearing do not, is further emphasized by an editorial which appeared in a Communist paper a few years ago. "Men and women work for a principle on the *Daily Worker*," it reads. "Their salaries are not large. We deeply appreciate that our editors and columnists make real sacrifices, and that most of them could find ready employment elsewhere on the basis of their ability alone and certainly be paid far more than on the *Daily Worker*, especially if they would repudiate their principles."

More than anything else, this devotion to a cause, instilled so deeply into their followers, accounts for the untiring zeal of the disciples of Nazism, Fascism, and now Communism. They took it from early Christianity but they have brought it up to date, streamlined it, modernized it.

Motivated by a love of God and of our fellowman, we must take back that zeal—*with credit to the godless*—for, as Christ said, "And the Lord commended the unjust steward inasmuch as he had done wisely; for the children of this world are wiser in their generation than the children of light." (*Luke* 16:8)

If those who spread confusion have found in a method borrowed from Christianity a spirit of purpose, we have not the slightest excuse for neglecting that method a day longer. In every home, church, and school, in business, government, education, and the writing fields, our people must constantly be inspired to play a personal part as missioners in *changing the world for the better*. And in doing this, not only will the inspiration touch the best that is in them and strike a responsive cord, but it will render a tremendous service to humanity.

The genuineness and sincerity of our love of people is not measured by academic attitudes, by passing resolutions, by meeting once a month and complaining about conditions in the world and then coming back a month later to complain some more. Mere lip service is almost the equivalent of nothing at all.

PAUL'S DRIVING PURPOSE

To *love* thy neighbor as thyself means *doing* for others as we would *do* for ourselves, regardless of the time spent, inconvenience involved, even real suffering itself sometimes endured. In this, we might well take to heart the example of the Apostle Paul. Few in history have been driven more by this purpose than was he. Literally and figuratively, he was consumed with the burning desire to share his love of Christ with anyone and everyone. One of the most striking instances of his tender solicitude and of how tactfully considerate he could be in his approach, is eloquently evident in an account of an experience he had in Greece.

While waiting in Athens for his co-workers to join him, no one would have blamed him if he had taken time off to rest since he planned to be there only a few days. Yet he did nothing of the kind, because to give way to his comfort would have been to think only of himself. He felt an *obligation* to the Athenians and, as the Scripture narrates, *"His heart was moved within him to find the city so much given over to idolatry." (Acts 17:16)*

Even though it could only be a passing effort, he decided not to remain aloof. Making his way to the business center, to the market place where he would come in direct contact with the men of Athens, he began to strike up conversations with all whom he met. They regarded him as a meddler, but that didn't bother him for he was used to such a reception. One with the loving purpose which inflamed Paul pays little heed to any expression of disdain or contempt. He kept moving decper and deeper into their midst, until they *had* to pay attention to him. Finally, they decided to give him a public hearing and invited him to the Areopagus.

His opening words reveal the loving heart and soul of Paul. They are a masterpiece of tender regard for others who had beliefs very much opposed to his own, yet show that in no way did he compromise with them. One with less tact or less farsightedness could easily have upbraided them for being *"given over to idolatry,"* but not Paul! From the very start he wins them by saying, *"Men of Athens, wherever I look I find you scrupulously religious,"* referring to the idols which adorned the temple. Then quickly he gets to the point with another apt remark which distinguishes, yet neither cuts nor hurts.

Noticing one altar not erected to any god in particular but rather serving the purpose of being useful for new gods for whom no other altar could be found, Paul continues:

"In examining your monuments as I passed by them, I found, among others, an altar which bore the inscription, 'To the unknown God.' It is this unknown object of your devotion that I am revealing to you. The God Who made the world and all that is in it, that God Who is Lord of heaven and earth, does not dwell in temples that our hands have made. . . . It is He Who gives to all of us life and breath and all we have. It is He Who has made, of one single stock, all the nations that were to dwell over the whole face of the earth."

And he adds still another expression of His love for these men of Athens, so intent is he on emphasizing similarities, not differences. After saying, *"He is not far from any of us; it is in Him that we live, and move, and have our being,"* he concludes with the reminder that some among them have already said that very thing. *"Some of your poets have told us,"* he says, *"'for we are His children.'"*

THE AIM OF EVERY CHRISTOPHER

It should be the constant goal of every Christopher to follow this pattern of approach laid down by Paul in the first recorded talk on Christianity given in Europe. In the eleven sentences that make up his brief address are numerous lessons from which we can profit, but three in particular have a special meaning for one who is a "bearer of Christ":

(1) The whole of Paul's motivation was *love* of the Athenians even though they were "given over to idolatry." He felt that the love of Christ belonged to them as much as to himself. It was his job to adapt himself to them, not to expect them to conform to him. He strove hard not to offend. He was not merely trying to prove how wrong were they and how right was he. He was not out to "beat them down" nor to hurt them in any way. On the contrary, he went to extraordinary lengths to single out every possible point of agreement. He went to them—he did *not* wait for them to come to him. Anyone who has a true love of people will do just that.

(2) Another simple truth Paul stressed was *the existence of a personal God* Who has spoken to the world and on Whom the world depends.

That is the one immutable truth a Christopher who is steeped in a genuine love of people will strive incessantly to bring to all men. It is the truth upon which mankind must base all hope for a better world. It is the truth that the Founders of our country reverently and repeatedly affirmed in the Declaration of Independence.

In stressing this one truth, Paul did not intimate this was all of religion, but he did lay down most emphatically, though so simply, the fact that this was the one cornerstone upon which all else depends. And it is this cornerstone that all forms of materialism and totalitarianism relentlessly oppose and seek to destroy. Therefore, it should be the one truth above all others that a Christopher strives to carry into every phase of public and private life.

(3) While Paul made very few converts from this talk—only "Dionysius, Damaris and others with them," he was primarily interested in doing far more than winning a handful of followers. He didn't measure success by the number who went the full way with him. He was out to reach everybody, no matter how they received his message. He was doing exactly what Christ commanded. He was going to "all men," into the "highways" as well as the "byways." And he knew full well that he was planting seeds which would blossom later; that he was leavening the multitude; that, because he had taken the trouble to go into the market-place of Athens as the first Christ-bearer to enter there, he had brought countless numbers at least one step closer to Christ.

The true Christopher, motivated by love of all people for love of God, is continually trying to reach the many, not merely the few. The multitude, not merely a single individual. And that is why, like Paul, a Christ-bearer goes *where people are*—into the market-places, into the four great spheres that vitally influence, for better or worse, the great mass of humanity. He goes into *the educational field, government, labor-management relations, the writing field* (press, radio, television, motion pictures, books, and magazines).

In other words, the Christopher gets out of his own little world and into the big world, a world which will be run either by those who hate Christ or who know Him not, or by those who dedicate themselves to bringing mankind back to "the Way, the Truth, and the Life."

Every Christopher recognizes that fact. In their own perverted way, so do the godless. The "in-betweeners" apparently do not—those otherwise good people who, because of their apathy, are making a negligible impact on the basic problems that convulse our nation and the world. They pretend to be so absorbed in saving their own souls as to justify giving scarcely a passing thought to the salvation of their neighbors. They are solicitous for everything concerning their own personal security, but seldom lift a finger in behalf of the economic security of the hundreds of millions all over the earth who often turn in desperation, as to their only hope of securing social justice, to those who champion violence and even death.

Everyone should have a reasonable interest in good housing, good food, good clothing, and other personal advantages. The "in-betweeners," however, so distort this interest that they rarely get beyond taking care of themselves. Rarely do they devote time and energy to providing the personal leadership now so urgently needed to win for the great masses of mankind, not convenience or luxuries, but the bare necessities of life which God intends as their minimum right.

THE OVEREMPHASIS ON SELF

Parents, directors, and teachers too often are so preoccupied with protecting the young that they overemphasize self-preservation, self-sanctification, self-development, and self-enjoyment. Without intending any harm, they give their children the impression they have only one mission in life—to take care of themselves. Little do they realize this is only part of Christianity; that by failing to pass on the fullness of Christ's message they are clipping the wings of their own youngsters, fencing them in, depriving them of the more abundant and interesting life that God meant them to have. And in many instances they are heading for the monotony, the frustration, even the tragedy which is the inevitable result of concentration on self.

More often than not, they go through life hitting on only one or two cylinders when they could be driving ahead on all eight; they go through the years leading a drab, dull, even if harmless existence, scarcely conscious they have buried the talents God has given them. They live and die, never once realizing that Christ did *not* say to love God and self only—that is a primary and essential foundation, to be sure, but is only part of Christianity. The fullness of Christianity is to love others—*all* men. How much? Christ's standard admits of no evasion: "As thyself." The attitude of "God and myself," therefore, is not enough. It must be "God, myself, and everybody else."

The tragic story of Germany when the Nazis first began to come into power cannot be retold too often. If the *good* German people had followed that admonition of Christ and thought as much of others as they did of themselves, Hitler would never have succeeded in seizing power. But too few good folk wanted to be bothered with *teaching* because there was not much money in it; there was no glamor attached to the profession and it called for hard work. They didn't want to go into *government* because the salaries were low, and, in thousands of inconspicuous posts, the routine tasks were dull and uninteresting. Toward all the other vital spheres that touch the lives of every person in their country they had the same attitude. From a worldly point of view, such jobs didn't pay off.

Of course, all good Germans wanted good education, good

government, good relations between management and labor, good healthy writing in their newspapers, magazines, books, radio, and movies. But like the people described by the phrase, "everybody wants to eat but nobody wants to cook," they just couldn't be bothered.

As their apathy continued, so did the virus of totalitarianism continue to spread. In Austria, Czechoslovakia, Hungary, and the other countries the story was the same. The way was made easy for the disciples of hate since they went in as wolves in sheep's clothing. Their interest in social and economic problems could not readily be detected as sheer hypocrisy by the poor desperate people. In the name of Hitler—now Stalin—they promised better homes, more food, finer schools, bigger salaries, and improved working conditions. Again, the average people were fooled. *"These men must be good,"* they concluded. *"They promise so much!"*

They could not foresee that this was merely the bait hiding the hook of enslavement, that the totalitarians had not the slightest intention of seeing that their promises were fulfilled.

An object lesson in self-deception? Perhaps. The fact still remains, however, that the secret of totalitarian success stemmed from just one thing: the forces of evil and hatred went to the people with their false gospels, while those who knew better remained aloof, keeping the Truth to themselves. If just a small percentage of *good* people had possessed the ambition and courage to leave the narrow circle of their lives and work for the *light,* instead of leaving the field to those in the *darkness,* the whole course of history might have been changed.

Where Europe failed, however, we can succeed! For us there is still hope—*refreshing hope*—that it will not take much to rectify and remove the major ills that still plague mankind. And this can be done without tearing down or destroying anything.

All that is necessary is to extend, to continue, to develop, in each individual that fullness of true love, not only for God and self, but for others as well, that Christ laid down as the indispensable foundation of lasting peace. Moreover, it can be done quickly because this purpose taps a force for good that is deep within every human heart, a force that is ready and waiting to plunge in a practical, timely way into action capable of overcoming every obstacle.

There are numerous places to practice and perfect this love of others. One of the best places to start is in the home, especially when circumstances are difficult, perhaps even seemingly hopeless. Such action—Christopher action—will arrest much of the divorce, the juvenile delinquency, the general breakdown of morale that is creeping steadily into millions of homes as love of one another diminishes and the spirit of "every man for himself" begins to dominate with tragic results.

According to a recent newspaper report quoting a responsible government medical authority, at least eight million people in this country suffer from some form of mental sickness and another ten million now living will spend some part of their lives under mental care. The report goes on to say that these tragedies are symptoms of human, personal crises in the lives of millions of "little frustrated people whose daily paths are concentric circles."

Sometimes these tensions appear near the surface, reflected in quiet desperation, in accumulated failures, frustration and worry. But in numerous other instances, they break out violently, like flames from a smoldering pile of rubbish. To verify this you have only to pick up the daily newspapers and read the headlines of those extreme cases which are becoming more and more prevalent: "Torture Suspect Confesses," "Mother Stabs Infant to Death," "Despondent Couple Leap From Bridge."

In all these cases the background is the same. These are the unhappy mortals who are sick of their jobs, sick of their families and friends, sick of their very lives.

Yet the happy hope in all this dark picture is that millions of Americans who are on the brink of mental and emotional disaster can be guided toward self-salvation simply by convincing them to "wake up and live"—to use to the utmost the fullness of their lives which God intended to be their due. To get out of themselves and their real or imagined troubles by helping others to help themselves.

One mother instilled this love of neighbor into her children in season and out. But she went further. In her last will and testament she left far more than her worldly possessions. She bequeathed to them a priceless legacy that well sums up the Christ-like objective of her life:

"Love one another. Hold fast to that whether you understand one another or not. And remember nothing really matters except loving God and others over the whole world as far as you can reach."

TRUE LOVE KNOWS NO BOUNDARIES

It is of the essence of true love of others that it seeks to diffuse itself, that it knows no boundaries, that it stirs you to share it and spread it "over the world as far as you can reach." It is this all-inclusive love that sustains and furnishes the driving power for one who wishes to be a life-time Christopher. It is a constant reminder that the world itself will be better off because he or she has lived in it.

True love of others is the encouraging reminder to the Christ-bearer that he or she is working on the side of the fundamental goodness which the Creator of all has imbedded deep in the heart and soul of each and every human being.

The most hateful man in the world wants to be loved. The worst criminal often takes great pains to appear as a respectable citizen, insisting that others be honest with him. The most immoral of men cautiously guards the dignity of his wife and children.

No matter to what lengths people go to root out of their fellowmen that sense of decency which distinguishes man from the brute animal, they never completely succeed. Some remnants always remain, awaiting development. There is always hope, even in the worst of men.

All we need do to make that fact real in our lives is to conduct a little experiment in self-examination of our relations to the physical world around us. When we do, we will come to realize as did the American scientist, Steinmetz, that the Hand of God cradles the whole human race in loving solicitude.

> "I think the greatest discovery [to be made] will be along spiritual lines," Steinmetz wrote. "Here is a force which history clearly teaches has been the greatest power in the development of man. Yet we have been merely playing with it and have never seriously studied it as we have social forces. Some day people will learn that material things do not bring happiness, that they are of little use in making men and women creative and forceful. Then the scientists of the world will turn their laboratories over to the study of God and prayer and the spiritual forces which as yet have been hardly scratched. When this day comes, the world will advance more in one generation than it has in the past four!"

Anyone who is fired with a Christ-like purpose—a Christopher purpose—has already made this discovery. And, if they would reach *all* men, they will see the wisdom of using three methods recommended by our Lord Himself. If you love your fellowman, you will

(1) *Pray for them.*
(2) *Go to them.*
(3) *Teach them.*

Praying for All Men

This is an effective method of Christopher participation open to one and all. It is one of the easiest ways to grow in love of all men. Pray especially for those for whom few, if any, pray—for the confused, the evil, even the hateful. When you go into a bus or streetcar, into a theater or to a football or baseball game, or down to the beach, say a passing prayer for everyone there. Eternity has begun for each individual present, no matter how little they know or think about it. When you pick up the morning paper and pass the death notices, let them be a reminder to offer a brief prayer for all who have died the world over during the preceding twenty-four hours.

The tendency on the part of most of us is to restrict our prayers to our own selfish interests, overlooking the far greater needs of the hundred million in our own country, for example, who are drifting farther and farther away from Christ. "Love thy neighbor as thyself" certainly means to pray as much for others as one does for self. No matter how busy you are or what your position in life may be, whether you are old or young, with a college degree or barely out of kindergarten, you can get in a daily prayer for the billion and more souls throughout the world who have yet to hear that Jesus Christ was born, lived, and died for each of us, nearly two thousand years ago. You can pray for the millions who are hungry or starving and who are not allowed to exercise their God-given human rights and liberties.

Pray each day for your government. If enough Americans do this, it will be a powerful step in the right direction. One shopkeeper sets aside a portion of each day to pray that God may guide the Secretary of State in fulfilling his important tasks wisely and fearlessly. Such prayer will increase your interest in taking other positive measures to see that all of us have the best possible government. You will actively participate in saving your country (and the world itself) as others are active in attempting to wreck it. No matter how remote you may feel, even if you are bedridden, you can play a vital role.

By Going

Our Lord could not have been more insistent on this point. Over and over again He told His followers to "*go*" and keep "*going*," without ceasing, into the midst of all men the world over. And lest anyone think He was generalizing, here are His words, and they are most specific: *"Go ye into the whole world and preach the gospel to every creature."* (*Mark* 16:15)

Thank God this command was taken to heart by some, otherwise mankind might still be groping in deeper darkness than that which grips us now. The early Christians didn't sit in the catacombs, complaining about the ruthlessness of the Romans. They realized it was their one big job to go to them in every possible way, with the conviction that Christ died for them also and that His love belonged likewise to them. As slaves, into kitchens, onto farms, into trading houses and even into the army—in any and every capacity—they *went*.

They could easily have said, *"They don't want us,"* or *"It's too hard,"* or *"I must get paid more than that."* They did just the opposite. They continued to go in the face of the most frightful odds. In imitation of Christ's loving purpose, they endured imprisonment, scourging, ridicule, and death by the sword, by fire, by being thrown to wild beasts. And their terrible sufferings were not in vain. Without destroying anything they eventually won—won by "going" and by "loving" even those who drained the very life blood out of them.

Today the task is much easier; but the followers of Christ, while totaling hundreds of millions over the earth, have ceased to *go* except in far too few numbers. Once that trend is reversed and large numbers of people are once more *going* with Christ's love and peace into every phase of activity, into the highways as well as the byways, then and then only will there be a substantial change for the better.

In the four succeeding chapters will be found a detailed account of the four important fields into which Christophers are urged to *go,* because, through them, most of humanity is affected for good or evil, for better or worse. But no matter in what capacity he or she *goes,* any follower of Christ can do at least one of the thousands of possible things to bring Him into the market place. Where there's a will there's a way!

For example, a young mother, still suffering from the effects of tuberculosis, frequently manages to get over to any who chance to cross her path an understanding of and a sympathy for some Christian fundamental. A Wall Street broker has a special hobby of approaching individually any who belong to no church, tactfully discussing some basic Christian doctrine and then passing on a piece of literature for later reading. Nearly every one of the hundreds contacted on this person-to-person basis has been most receptive and even grateful that he bothered.

Others are taking literally the command of Christ to *go.* They are devoting any time they can spare from home or work to *going* with a Christopher purpose into clubs, parent-teacher associations, civic and welfare groups, food and housing movements, scout work, and any number of other endeavors that affect the general public and therefore need the leaven of Christ's Truth to keep them functioning for the good of all.

By Teaching

Christophers can do something to carry the teachings of Christ to the world. All of us at least have an obligation to offer to others and to share with them the truths given us by Christ. All we have to do is play the role of messengers. God could have arranged to have this done entirely by angels, but the fact is that He did not. He willed that men should be saved through their fellowmen. All He asks us to do is to pass along, to distribute, the simple, eternal fundamentals that are the basis of happiness for mankind in this life and in the life to come. He assured us He would always provide us with an abundance of help from on high, that we would not work alone. The more we fulfill this noble role, the more we can say with Christ: *"What I was born for, what I came into the world for, is to bear witness of the truth."* (*John* 18:37)

A young man doing excellent Christopher work specializes, as all Christophers should, in reaching those in whom no one else is interested—the weak rather than the strong, the spiritually hungry rather than those who have all the advantages of life at their disposal. In business, at parties, on trains, in taxis, on the street, with people in trouble, with the sick, the poor, with government officials, his every act is a prayer. He tries to fulfill the Master's command to "Love thy neighbor as thyself." And because he has such a zealous love for others, friendly, and hostile, he has drawn thousands a little closer to God. An acquaintance who leads a pagan life, recently confided to a friend, "I didn't know people existed with the love of God in their heart which that boy has."

In each of these instances and in thousands of others, truth, while it is divine, is dispensed in a *human* way, as it will always be. Academic theories leave most people cold. They are fed up with more and more housing plans. What they want are homes. Hungry people are not stirred up by recipes. They are looking for food.

Love of God as well as others is something active and dynamic, not a treasure to be hidden or discussed in vague terms. When each of us stands before God in final judgment, He will not ask how well dressed we were, how much money we made, how many trips we took, how much fame or glory we won for ourselves. But He will ask us—and our eternity will depend on the answer—what each of us did in His name for others.

THE SELFISH—AND THE SELFLESS

He who recognizes the Divine Image in his fellowman and therefore strives to help him, will find himself among those answering the eternal invitation of Christ: *"Come, ye blessed of My Father, possess you the kingdom prepared for you from the foundation of the world."* (Matt. 25:34)

But he who has lived only for himself will hear the very opposite: *"Depart from Me, you cursed, into everlasting fire which was prepared for the devil and his angels . . . for I was hungry, and you gave Me not to eat: I was thirsty and you gave Me not to drink. I was a stranger, and you took Me not in; naked and you covered Me not; sick and in prison, and you did not visit Me."* (Matt. 25:41-43)

To the protest that will invariably come from those so charged, that they would certainly have ministered to Christ if they had ever seen *Him* "hungry or thirsty, or a stranger, or naked, or sick, or in prison," the answer of Christ will be that sublime standard by which He dignifies *every* human being: *"As long as you did it not to one of these least, neither did you do it to Me!"* (*Matt.* 25:45).

Long before they die, those who disregard others in furthering their own selfish interests begin to pay the penalty. They are never completely at peace. No matter how much of this world's goods they may possess, they seem forever ill at ease, restless, dissatisfied never to have caught up with the rainbow they are pursuing. In their lives the lack of purpose outside themselves has a depressing reaction on all that is best in them. On their faces and in their eyes there is little lustre or gleam. Inside them, something seems to have died.

Those, however, whose lives are motivated with the vital purpose of doing all they can for others, actually begin to live some of their heaven on earth. Nothing daunts them. They develop a gaiety of heart that carries them through the most trying circumstances. They stay young in spirit. They quickly learn that thoroughness is the quality of true love, of true charity for others. With St. Paul they can say "Charity is patient, is kind; charity envieth not, dealeth not perversely, is not puffed up; is not ambitious, seeketh not her own, is not provoked to anger, thinketh no evil; rejoiceth not in iniquity, but rejoiceth with the truth; beareth all things, believeth all things, hopeth all things, endureth all things." (1 *Cor.* 13:4-7)

As you grow in this love for others, you will find your horizons expanding and your own power increasing. Even your sense of proportion will grow as you take yourself less seriously and others more seriously. You will learn how to disagree without being disagreeable. You will become more approachable. You will better understand why *all people* want to be truly loved, and not just tolerated. You will emphasize more and more the good side of even the worst of people; and you will recognize, as a result, the far-reaching significance of Christ's words: *"Love your enemies, do good to them that hate you, and pray for them that persecute and calumniate you."* (*Matt.* 5:44)

Christ doesn't want you to be a Casper Milquetoast, just realistic and appreciative of the simple fact that some hate only because they lack that precious quality of love. In true solicitude for them, as a Christopher, you can do something positive and constructive by supplying that lack, filling up that void, by sharing your own love.

You will be, in short, *another* Christ. And, more and more, you will be able to say with the Apostle Paul *"I live, now not I; but Christ liveth in me."* (*Gal.* 2:20)

This sublime motivation, this loving purpose will distinguish you who seriously strive to bring Christ into the marketplace. Because of this dedication to a cause, welling up within you will be a driving power which pushes through all obstacles, with patience and kindness. More and more you will be inflamed with a fire which warms but does not burn. Everything you say or do will reflect that devotion, loyalty, and quiet enthusiasm which is seldom, if ever, the happy lot of those whose only cause is themselves.

A remarkable transformation will take place in you, and often surprisingly quickly, once you make within yourself the simple adjustment from dull, narrow concentration on self, to the stimulating, vitalizing interest and concern in the general good of all. From having been unaware of anything beyond your own little, self-contained sphere, you will become a Christopher stepping out into the mainstream of life, into the thick of things. By God's help, you will be forever buoyed up with the knowledge that the world itself is at least a tiny bit the better because you are in it.

Where, in the past, your approach to life was one of selfish timidity and fearful caution, you will find yourself charged with Christ's daring, bold, yet prudent, "launching out," yet never reckless. From being half-hearted in most things, you will become wholehearted in all things. Instead of consulting first your own personal convenience before doing anything for anyone else, you will become lovingly absorbed in doing everything and anything you can for others. Where, previously, the slightest pretext could deflect or discourage you, nothing now will daunt your determination and sense of follow-through.

Invariably you will develop an inner warmth which manifests itself in an abiding sense of humor even in the midst of the most trying circumstances. You invariably will reflect in everything you do a Christopher concern for all. Naturally you will make mistakes. But you will always retain enough sense of proportion to laugh at yourself. Your never-say-die spirit will give courage to everyone you meet. Because you are eternally hopeful, you will often bring new light and new hope into the drab lives of those who have no cause beyond themselves—and who, consequently, have no sparkle either for themselves or for others.

And no matter what your limitations are, your noble purpose and your deep and satisfying conviction that, by God's grace, you can be an instrument in bringing Him to men and men to Him will develop in you an ever-increasing imagination and enterprise which constantly leads you on to new and greater heights. Too, this healthy, divine discontent will increase within you a growing resourcefulness, and alertness, a keenness of observation, and a capacity for work which might have lain dormant and undeveloped if the greater cause had not lifted you out of all the depressing smallness and self-torture of concentrating only on self.

More literally than anyone else, you will experience the real *joy of living*. Life itself will take on a new and exhilarating meaning. You will have the fun and thrill of knowing that, in however small a measure, you are building, not destroying; spreading love, not hate; light, not darkness. You will be fulfilling, in the most literal sense and to the fullest measure possible, the purpose for which you were created: *to love God above all things and your neighbor as yourself.*

IV

EDUCATION

Ideas Determine the Future

"ALL HE EVER TALKS ABOUT is learning enough to graduate so he can go out and make some money!" The speaker, a brown-eyed youth with a shock of bushy black hair, planted himself squarely in front of a dark-complexioned boy with serious eyes and a tight expression around the corners of his mouth. As he mentally gathered himself for another outburst, one of a group of boys standing outside a public high school in the heart of New York's East Side spoke up.

"Leave him alone, Al," he said, quickly. "Maybe he doesn't know any better."

"Maybe—maybe not," came back the disgusted reply. "But if he could see the letters my father gets from the old country, telling us what a break we've got living over here where we can do what we want without some Communist shoving a gun in our backs and stopping us, like the Nazis and Fascists tried to do, he'd quit that money stuff. Money isn't everything!"

"Cut it out, Al," the object of the outburst broke in. "Don't get sore."

"I'm not sore—just fed up, up to here." The first boy drew an imaginary line under his chin with a grimy forefinger. "The sooner you and others like you find out we've got to do like my father says—have God some place in our setup—the better off things will be around here. If you don't, the Commies'll be taking over and you 'n me 'n everybody else will be standing around, wondering what hit us!"

An amazing incident? Agreed. But amazing as it was, it actually happened. A Christopher, a public school teacher, was lucky enough to see and hear what took place from behind the wheel of her car parked a few feet away. As best she could, she jotted down what she saw and passed it on to us. What struck her, and us, more than anything else, however, was the one remark, ". . . have God some place in our setup." It was a surprising remark, and it is one seldom made by the youth in our schools. In fact, the typical reply to the question, "What are you studying for?" is usually summed up in the words, "To get a job and make some money." Nothing more.

It is the answer given by ninety-five out of every hundred of the best young American people, regardless of whether their grammar is all it should be or whether they use the language of the neighborhoods in which they live.

Of course money is needed to conduct normal lives, that is understood. But money is not the be-all and end-all of our existence. It is the overemphasis on money and on other material things that points up one significant fact that few people seem to recognize. It is that education in America right now is going through the same process of despiritualization which took place in Germany and, more than anything else, paved the way for Hitler. It is the despiritualization that the followers of Karl Marx work unceasingly to achieve in every country that their poisons can reach. It is the process that has one fixed objective: to condition youth to the idea that they are *animals*—nothing more.

"Look at these young men and boys!" wrote Hitler in his *Mein Kampf*. *"What material! I shall eradicate the thousands of years of human domestication. Brutal youth—that is what I am after. . . . I want to see once more in its eyes the gleam . . . of the beast of prey. With these I can make a new world . . . and create a new order."*

What Hitler plainly meant was that the Christian concept of the dignity of man made, as he is, in the image and likeness of God, must be forever banished. For spiritual values he would substitute the material. For love of God and the love of man for his neighbor, he would substitute the gospel of hate.

WITHOUT MORALITY, FORCE IS LAW

What Hitler knew—and Stalin knows—but which far too many good people do not yet realize, is that if there is no morality, there can be no law other than that of force. This was brought out most emphatically by Walter Lippmann in his address, "Education Without Culture," delivered in 1940 before the American Association for the Advancement of Science. Said Mr. Lippmann, "Modern education rejects and excludes from the curriculum of necessary studies the whole religious tradition of the West . . . thus there is an enormous vacuum where until a few decades ago there was the substance of education. . . . There is no common faith, no common moral and intellectual discipline.

"When one realizes that they [the graduates of our schools] have no common culture, is it astounding that they have no common purpose? That they worship false gods? That only in war do they unite? That in the fierce struggle for existence they are tearing Western society to pieces? They are the graduates of an educational system in which, though attendance is compulsory, the choice of the subject matter of education is left to the imagination of college presidents, trustees, and professors, or even to the whims of the pupils themselves.

"We have established a system of education in which we insist that while everyone must be educated, yet there is nothing in particular that an educated man must know. . . . By separating education from the classical religious tradition, the school cannot train the pupil to look upon himself as an inviolable person because he is made in the image of God . . . education founded on the secular image must destroy knowledge itself."

Proof that Mr. Lippmann had assayed the facts correctly is contained in the following instances of warped interpretations in the academic field. And these are examples that can be duplicated by the thousands.

In one textbook, *The Government of Modern States,* a well-known professor, W. F. Willoughby, states (p. 13) that, *"What we now speak of as individual liberties are merely the liberties which the state, as a matter of policy or expediency, determines shall be left to individual determination. . . . At any moment the state, acting through the machinery it has provided for itself, can enter this field and cancel the powers that it has granted or permitted."* This book also asserts the State is supreme, giving ultimate validity to all laws and the way in which they will be exercised. The State, according to another leading authority, possesses absolute and exclusive control over the legal rights and obligations of its citizens, *"individually considered or grouped into large or smaller associations."*

In one large city trade school for girls, with a student body of over 3,000, a biology teacher dogmatically teaches that there is no soul and advocates immoral practices.

In a graduate course in sociology in a large Eastern university, the professor asserted that it is not a crime to kill an imbecile, as an imbecile "is not a human being." The Nazis followed this same perverted reasoning and destroyed millions whom they considered undesirable in Buchenwald, Belsen and Dachau.

One professor, Harry Elmer Barnes, whose textbooks are used extensively throughout the United States, maintains the theory, as one observer put it, that "Christianity is the source of most of our social evils; that conversion to godlessness would make a better society; and that the ideas of soul, heaven, hell, immorality, sin, prayer, spiritual things and the notions of the sacred are 'cultural fossils in orthodoxy.'" This thesis is identical with the totalitarian philosophy. Hitler stated bluntly, "The Ten Commandments have lost their validity. . . . There is no such thing as Truth, either in the moral or in the scientific sense."

Contrast these aims of the godless with the words of the great poet, John Milton, three hundred years ago.

"The end of learning," Milton wrote, "is to repair the ruins of our first parents by regaining to know God aright, and out of that knowledge to love Him, to imitate Him, to be like Him, as we may the nearest by possessing our souls of true virtue, which being united to heavenly grace of faith makes up the highest perfection."

Then, again, compare his observations with that made a few months ago by a noted Protestant clergyman, Dr. Ralph W. Sockman, as he publicly deplored the increasing tendency to wall off public education as well as public policies from any concept of God. "We cannot preserve Christian democracy by training our children as pagans," this clergyman pointed out. And his conclusion is inescapable. The spiritual vacuum in America today is the fruit of an educational policy which for thirty years has ignored God.

If there is to be a clearer concept of morality, however, we must rely in most schools on literature, English, foreign languages, mathematics, natural science, and social science—in short, on *education*—to develop the concept that this is a universe founded upon law, *the law of God*! We must impress upon our youth that the violations of that law carry consequences quite apart from human imposition.

THE FUNCTION OF EDUCATION

Education must train the human will along with the intellect. It must produce a "free man." This is the basic education which our Founding Fathers urged as needed for the perpetuation of the Republic.

Education—*good* education—must point out, teach, and emphasize most convincingly that "man shall not live by bread alone." It must be dedicated to the proposition "For what doth it profit a man, if he gain the whole world, and suffer the loss of his own soul?" (*Matt.* 16:26)

Education must stress one fundamental fact which alone makes social living possible: man must be educated for his ultimate goal in life, the end for which he was created—to know, love, and serve God and to be happy with Him in the life to come.

Education must stand for liberty to exercise the rights God has given us, otherwise it will yield to tyranny. The truest education produces a self-disciplined individual, recognizing the existence of a personal God to Whom he will one day be accountable.

OUR OBLIGATION

The time has come—indeed, the hour is late, though not too late, thank God—to bring back once more into our classrooms these and other Christian truths which form the basis of our existence and of the existence of the United States of America.

Not for one moment should it be forgotten that a change for the better will take place only when, as, and if those who believe in God and therefore have a more serious responsibility—Protestants, Jews, and Catholics alike—really interest themselves in the 30,000,000 young Americans now in our schools. To abandon these, your very own, to the evil concern of those whose gospel is hate and materialism is to let go by default your children's future and the future of the greatest democracy the world has ever known.

Since the doers of evil concentrate, in a special way, on universities, colleges, and high schools, yet by no means overlooking the elementary grades or even the kindergarten. . . .

While they are highly selective in not taking any job but rather in specializing in philosophy, sociology, psychology, history, government, economics, and other courses where it is easy to weave warped interpretations into everything they pass on to our unsuspecting youth. . . .

By the same token, you people of strong, solid values—teachers, parents, and even students—must take back into your hands the positive conduct of sound education. As Christophers, you must seize the personal initiative which can restore to the market-place the Christian heritage of America.

You must no longer neglect to provide your share of good teachers. You must no longer give way to parental apathy but show instead an active and continuing concern in seeing that the policies and administration of all schools are strengthening America, not weakening it. You must not hide your *light* under a bushel while an energetic minority who deny God and the basic concept of American life are shouting their doctrine of *darkness* from the housetops, from the classroom and the campus, from the study clubs and the vocational guidance centers.

In short, as American citizens and taxpayers, not only do you have the right, but a serious obligation as well, to see that *all* schools supported by taxes, whether they be city, county, or state, are manned by healthy minded Americans, not by those who would destroy our very civilization.

CLASSIFICATION OF THE ACADEMIC FIELD

To help orientate those Christ-bearers who wish to do something as individuals in bringing education back to the original purpose for which it was intended—to train the soul along with the intellect—a very brief classification of the entire academic field is of first importance.

Education may be broken down in a variety of ways: elementary, intermediate, and advanced; parochial and nonsectarian; formal and informal; child and adult.

For our purpose of helping orientate Christophers who wish to do something as individuals in the educational field, the subject can be divided under three main headings: the teacher, the parent, and the student.

The Teacher

The teacher's main responsibility is in the classroom. He or she is one of the great channels whereby the heritage and traditions of a civilization are transmitted to the young whose habits, ideas, and way of life will determine the course of our national and world future. There can be no greater work for anyone for, as Cicero said, "What nobler employment or more valuable to the state, than that of the man who instructs the rising generation."

Man's ascent through the ages has been long and hard, and at each step he has accumulated new knowledge, about things, about people, about the relationship of men, one to the other, in accordance with the Divine Plan. This sum total of our wisdom is our world today. The teacher hands the keeping of this world to those whom he or she instructs. It is doubly important that those who guide the thinking of the carefree student of today and make of him the responsible citizen of tomorrow should be men and women of sound ideas. Never forget: what is in the teacher's head and heart passes into the minds of the young!

To be a teacher is to have a great mission in life. The instructor of mathematics who shows how to solve a simple equation or how to bisect an angle, the teacher of chemistry who explains how to break water down into its component parts of oxygen and hydrogen, the teacher of domestic science who teaches a girl how to make a home more attractive or a meal more edible—all these transmit certain branches of our accumulated knowledge.

Although none of these or allied subjects directly influence the moral and spiritual thinking, indirectly they can be a means of doing so. Just by being in any of these positions, a Christopher takes the place of someone who may be materialistic or subversive. This one fact is most important, for in after-class discussions when children mull over other subjects besides the one in which they have just been instructed, or in teacher associations and parent-teacher groups, the teacher can and should take a leading part in helping mold opinion on all phases of the educational field. This molding involves, as it should, the moral and spiritual side of education as well as the purely intellectual.

Right in the classroom, however, certain subjects do provide a direct opportunity for teaching youngsters how to live in accordance with the moral precepts which are based on the laws of God. The teaching of history offers an excellent chance to inform young men and women of the great struggles for those God-given rights that characterize our Western civilization in particular; in other words, the fight to preserve, as Lippmann puts it, "the religious tradition of the West."

In the study of literature, great writings can be traced to the growth of those selfsame ideas and ideals which helped make our democratic way of life and brought man from slavery to freedom.

Economics—the science that treats of the development of natural resources or the production, preservation, and distribution of wealth and methods of living well, for the state, the family, and the individual—provides an excellent background for the examination of a just economy based on God's commandments which apply equally to both employer and employee: to treat one another as you yourself would be treated.

The more advanced courses in civics, political science, comparative government, survey of civilization, philosophy, science, and social science can all serve a very positive purpose: to establish man in the proper relationship to his neighbor, remembering all men are children of God. If the courses fail to do this, or do it badly, the logical question to ask is why are they taught at all?

The very basis of our society involves the recognition and proper use of the rights and responsibilities we receive from God. And, as the Declaration of Independence points out, "To secure those rights, governments are instituted among men."

The greatest sins in much of our modern teaching are the failure, on one hand, to teach democracy as a creative and dynamic force; and the deliberate attempt, now too long prevalent, to weave warped interpretations into the original concept of what democracy means and of the Source—God—of its very existence.

Without a doubt, right at this moment the crisis in our education can be accelerated to continue our downward descent into the darkness of totalitarianism, or it can be stopped and turned upwards to reflect the will of our Creator by the action of those who have the *truth* and are willing to share it with their fellowmen; who are willing to help their neighbors and their neighbors' children become better citizens, worthy of the God-given heritage that was so dearly won for them by the founders of our country who pledged their all to make their dream of democracy come true.

George Washington in a letter to the Hebrew Congregation in Newport, Rhode Island, set forth a principle of which Americans in particular should well be proud, "a policy worthy of imitation," that shines like a beacon light of guidance and hope for all the peoples of the world to follow.

> "The citizens of the United States of America," he said, "have a right to applaud themselves for having given to mankind examples of an enlarged and liberal policy; a policy worthy of imitation. All possess alike liberty of conscience and immunities of citizenship. It is now no more that toleration is spoken of, as if it were by indulgence of one class of people, that another enjoyed the exercise of their inherent natural rights. For happily, the Government of the United States, which gives to bigotry no sanction, to persecution no assistance, requires only that they who live under its protection, should demean themselves as good citizens."

The first great responsibility of the Christopher who chooses teaching as a career is that of conveying these and other great American truths to the new generation of citizens. More than that, however, the teacher is, or should be, a community figure much respected by the young, a parent-substitute for many hours during the day, a counsellor, a companion, an individual worthy of the highest regard. For that reason alone the teacher becomes a figure to imitate and emulate.

By the same token it places on him or her a duty which involves personal deportment as well as civic interest. The voice of the teacher must be heard in the councils of the township, in the press, in public gatherings, in the various group institutions established for mutual help and improvement. In short, the teacher's day should not end with the classroom. People are guided, not only by what we say, but also by what we do. And the teacher is in an unusually opportune position to set a pattern of healthy behavior by his or her individual example.

Some teachers in this country are members of trade unions. Teachers who are members of unions must be something more than mere dues-payers: they must be active members. Because too many members of some of the locals of the Teachers' Union, for example, have merely affiliated and let it go at that, active minorities with strong subversive tendencies have been able to capture the leadership of the organization. Their strength, however, lies only in the weakness of those who have the *truth* but who surrender leadership by default.

What is true of some branches of the trade unions of which teachers are members, is true also of many branches of the Parent Teachers Association; and consideration of this group brings us to the second of the three main headings into which, as regards individual effort, the entire educational field is divided.

The Parent

Since both teacher and parent are interested in the development of the child, then both teacher and parent should have a chance to meet and jointly discuss the training of the child. But, again, this whole relationship can be twisted and perverted if the *good* people allow the *doers of evil* to do all the attending at PTA meetings, all the talking, all the organizing, all the directing.

That this unfortunate state of affairs has come to pass is borne out by reports coming in from all over the country of parents losing interest in PTA because those who live in the darkness have been more zealous in promoting their false doctrines than have the bearers of light in standing up and proclaiming the truth.

The Christopher—whether parent or teacher—belongs in the thick of things! Absence and apathy on the part of both teacher and parent merely increases the percentage of the irrational at PTA and kindred group meetings. Remember the words of Paul: "Be not overcome by evil, but overcome evil by good." (*Rom.* 12:21)

Another way the parent can exercise direct concern with education is through interest and action in the election of local school boards. These local boards of education help to select books, draft curricula, and supervise in many cases the choice of teachers.

A third avenue of parent participation is in classes for adults. Sometimes these are regular, formal classes; often they are just a series of lectures or an occasional forum. Yet every time, and in varying degrees, they all help to shape the attitudes of the community.

There is a fourth way parents can be extremely helpful in lifting the entire educational system to a higher plane. That is to leave no stone unturned in getting the better-qualified Americans (who, thank God, still constitute the majority of teachers) to reverse the trend away from a teaching career and get back into the thick of things. *This is most important.* According to recent surveys, during the 1946-47 school year more than 70,000 teachers' positions were unfilled. In the same period, 6,000 schools closed because of the lack of teachers. And it was estimated some five million students received an inferior education because of poorly prepared and inadequately trained instructors.

Every effort must be made to provide better pay for teachers, but millions of students must not be abandoned in the meanwhile. It must be possible—please God, it will be possible—to find enough men and women who, fired with the love of Christ, are willing to put up with all the self-sacrifice that a life of teaching entails—small pay, little chance of advancement, long, hard work, misunderstanding, disappointments—in order to restore to the market-place the Christian values upon which our country is founded.

It Is Being Done!

The best proof that this can be done is that many, given only the slightest encouragement, are taking up either teaching careers or positions associated with the educational field, not for what they can "take out," but for what they can "put in." They have caught the Christopher point of view!

One woman who had transferred from a teaching post in a high school to a commercial concern for higher pay, recently returned to the classroom because she came to realize that even though she was only one of hundreds of thousands of teachers, nevertheless she could, by patient persistence, do much that would leave the world better than she found it.

A man, with the encouragement of a parents' group, took a clerical position on a board of education which has been the special target of Communists. Even in his minor capacity he has helped check their inroads and promoted the very principles they strive to eliminate.

Another young man was so concerned, while in college, with the perverted slant being given to the subject of *history*, both ancient and modern, that after receiving his diploma he continued his postgraduate studies with a teaching career in this subject as his goal. He is now an instructor in his specialty in a large western university.

A young lady shifted from a secretarial job with a business firm to become assistant to the head of a department of a well-known university. All sorts of obstacles were placed in her path in an attempt to discourage her, but that only spurred her on the more. She became increasingly convinced that people like herself should forsake their own little worlds and petty comforts and get "into the fight" for *good* with the same determination that others were showing in the fight for evil.

She got the job. Now, in many different ways, she influences the teaching of thousands of students.

At one well-known boys' school there is a teacher who went there with a specific purpose in mind. Familiar with the background of the neighborhood in which the school is situated, he was painfully aware of the lack of spiritual concepts of the families in the area where education was concerned. This condition—passed on to their children—was brought home to him very pointedly one day in class when a young student, hearing him expound on the need for spiritual values in everyday living, exclaimed, "Gee, sir, don't tell us you believe in that tripe!"

It was a hard pill to swallow, but this teacher didn't lose his temper. Instead, kindly but firmly, he has kept hammering away at his beliefs and has had the satisfaction of having more than one boy come up to him and tell him they were beginning to see "daylight" at last.

A superintendent of schools in one of the New England states has remained at his post despite many flattering offers to enter business. "It isn't the easiest thing in the world meeting the expenses of a large family with what I make, especially when I could earn a lot of money if I got out of the educational field," this man told us recently. "But I've made up my mind to stay where I am. The good I can do in helping train young people in sound principles more than makes up for what I lose financially."

For people like these, and millions more like them, there are other tremendous opportunities to put into daily practice the Christopher ideal.

The Student

Individually, the *student* can find four different fields in which his or her chance to be a Christopher is unexcelled. They are the classroom, the school club, the campus (and campus activities), and the student movements.

IN THE CLASSROOM many subjects lend themselves to teaching through pupil participation and discussion. Student participation in shaping classroom opinion, however, should not degenerate into an endless and annoying repetition of hackneyed phrases because that, for a Christopher, will defeat your very purpose. The student must gain the respect of fellow classmates by his or her scholarliness. The healthy Christopher point of view must flow from the general discussion and not be stuck on to the end of it like a campaign sticker or an envelope. Once again, to repeat Christ's admonition: "Be ye wise as serpents and simple as doves."

THE SCHOOL CLUB. The student club is a regular feature of American educational life. Typical are sports clubs, language clubs, debating societies, and the like. For the young Christopher, however, certain particular clubs provide an excellent ground to sow the seeds of a democratic, God-fearing and God-loving way of life. In associations like a current events club, an historical society, a school newspaper or magazine, a literary group, a dramatic society, young people must inevitably concern themselves with ideas and ideals, with the spoken and written word. In addition, the public speaking class and the debating team furnish further opportunities to gather the "know-how" of presenting these ideas clearly, concisely, and convincingly.

Of late, many of these clubs have taken on increasing importance because they affect the total character of campus life and student movements in general. Incidentally, by the term *campus* is meant more than just the collegiate version. We refer, as well, to that of the junior high school, the regular high school, the junior college, in some cases even that of the business school—in short, wherever students gather for extracurricular activities.

Leadership in student life is first established within the various clubs and a candidate for school office is often judged by his activity in the smaller organizations. To the Christopher, who looks upon himself as a *lay missionary* among his classmates rather than a mere sponge absorbing facts, participation in these activities is of tremendous value because, in them, guidance can be offered, thought and action influenced —for *good*!

THE CAMPUS. More and more the campus, particularly as regards student elections, tends to reflect the currents in the outside world. Slates are put forward with such labels as "Progressive," "Liberal," "Independent," "Nonpartisan," "Militants," and so on. But if you search behind the labels, you will *sometimes* find that these catchwords partly conceal, yet partly reveal, the real forces behind the varying candidacies.

of your government, as has been pointed out previously. Without dwelling further on this particular phase of your participation, there are two principles which it would be well to bear in mind.

One is that a public position, from the lowliest civil servant on up to the President of the United States, is a public trust. If there be corruption in high places, there will be cynicism in low places. People will begin to look upon *all* government as rotten, will learn to look upon democracy as an ugly farce, will lose faith in democratic leadership. For you, as a Christopher, to hold public office, whether as a tax collector or as a Congressman, means that you will have to devote yourself to strengthening the belief of the common man in the efficiency and honesty of free, democratic government. In short, put public welfare above personal gain. Don't go in to do *well* for yourself but to do *good* for others.

A second principle for a Christopher is to prove to the people that they can be free and still be *fed,* that great liberty and good living can go hand in hand. Failure to meet the economic needs of the people through an intelligent use of government can create a loss of faith just as surely as corruption in government destroys interest in our free way of life. Economic chaos creates political chaos, and out of political chaos arise dictatorships and world upheaval.

If, however, you cannot go into the field of government yourself, you can still be listed in either of two classifications: the *electorate* or the *loyalty group.*

The Electorate

By the electorate is meant all those who are eligible to vote. To be part of the electorate is to be the inheritor of a great tradition, a precious, God-given right achieved after long struggle and much suffering. But just as man tends to neglect other aspects of his inherited rights, so does he tend nowadays to neglect his right to vote. *He abuses the privilege by neglecting it.* In the presidential election of 1900, for example, seventy-five percent of those who were eligible to vote, did vote. In 1944, however, only fifty-five percent voted. In 1946, only thirty percent made use of their ballot.

Realize what this means. If only thirty percent of the population votes, then it is possible for a body of human beings composed of only fifteen percent of the total electorate to elect its spokesman to *govern* the nation. That means eighty-five percent of the electorate would be taking orders from fifteen percent of the people. Anyone could hardly blame this fifteen percent if it were finally to conclude that a dictatorship would be as acceptable as a democracy since seventy percent of the people don't care to exercise their democratic rights.

The consequence of this abstinence from the polls is far-reaching. In the past it has made it easy for political machines to be set up that were little interested in the public good. Secondly, totalitarian elements find it not too difficult to slip their standard bearers into public office when the great mass of electors stays home on election day. And these totalitarians make their task even easier by using democratic lingo and democratic processes to subvert and destroy democracy. In short, failure to use your ballot smoothes the way for the corrupt politicians, for the selfish lawmakers, for the subversives to dominate the machinery of government *while they are still in the minority*—a condition which is quite contrary to the entire spirit of democracy where the majority decides public policy while still recognizing minority rights.

The Christopher, therefore, must be a voter. Too, he can get his family, friends, and neighbors to vote. He can become a canvasser on election day to help turn out the vote for the principles in which he believes, can carry his citizenship with a sense of genuine responsibility, can become a living part of his community.

The Loyalty Group

The loyalty group is a regular part of our society, as intrinsic to the making of public policy as are the various local assemblies or even the Congress of the United States. Such groups are merely combinations of persons banded together to affect popular thought by joint action. Some groups are good; some are bad—depending on your point of view and the moral worth of the issues involved.

They exist for two reasons. First, when we elect a candidate to an office, we do so because of a general attitude concerning him, such as his party affiliation, or his honesty, or perhaps even his looks. And once he is elected we seek openly to get him to favor some special piece of legislation which affects us deeply. Second, we may wish to educate or arouse the community on some issue so that there will be a constant pressure on all sections of society to swing into action.

Doing this takes many forms—letter writing and telegrams, meetings and parades, lobbyists and delegations, newspaper publicity and general advertising. Almost everybody is a member of *some* such group. It may be a trade union or a taxpayers' league or any of a whole host of easily recognizable gatherings. Here again a special duty falls upon the shoulders of the Christopher: the duty of acting in any such group with *purpose* and with *intelligence.*

A Christopher should ask himself or herself three questions when aligning with a cause. First, *what* is its purpose? Second, *how* does it intend to realize its purpose? Third, *who* controls the group?

Purpose should be examined closely. Too many people fall for a phrase. Sometimes the phrase is good, like "we want peace." But, as often as not, the supposed road to peace may be a road to war. A cliché is not a solution. The more dishonest a group is, the more cynically it will hunt for high-sounding phrases to catch the unwary.

How a group intends to realize its purpose is as vital a consideration as its aims. A foul means for an allegedly good end generally winds up as a foul end.

Who controls an organization is a matter which should be thoroughly investigated. Gullible citizens are too often tricked into joining a group, paying dues, lending a name to a letterhead, only to find out much later that the organization they support has become a loathsome thing in the hands of unscrupulous people who have *perverted* its original purpose. The Attorney General of the United States recently published a long list of organizations whose intent is subversive. An examination of their names or of their alleged programs would never, ordinarily, reveal the dangerous nature of these groups. Their real character can only be determined by the character of the men *in control.* Look particularly to see who is secretary of the organization to which you belong or which you intend to join. Check also on the editor of the group's official journal (if it has one), and investigate, also, those on the nominating committee who make the policy of the organization.

When these questions have been asked, and answered satisfactorily, the duty of the Christopher when he or she joins an organization is to participate *personally* in its activities. Go to meetings. Be alert. Know what goes on. Accept posts of responsibility. Vote in the elections. It is up to you, *individually,* to see that these pressure groups are utilized to *strengthen* your democracy, not to weaken it; that they are used to enrich your lives, not to impoverish them; that they are used to liberate each individual, not enslave him. Remember—to be a positive influence for good, you must be on the spot, meeting your fellow citizens and making your *living* presence felt.

THESE LEAD THE WAY—YOU CAN FOLLOW

The best way to show what *can* be accomplished in the field is to demonstrate by actual cases what *is being done* right now by some of those who have made public service their life's work. The old saying of the skeptics, "I'm from Missouri—show me," can most effectively be answered by *living examples.* Consider, then, the following, typical of hundreds of cases like them:

One man, motivated by the desire to *serve* his country as others were trying to destroy it, ran for Congress and was elected not long ago. One of his recent talks, according to those who heard it, figuratively "pulled them out of their seats" with the soundness and enthusiasm of his presentation of vital American doctrines.

A Seattle girl, a graduate of the University of Washington, came to New York after the close of World War II, uncertain as to what to make of her future. She finally decided to go down to Washington and try to get into some branch of government service, this on the advice of a Christopher friend of hers—*"the only person,"* in her own words, *"who ever showed the concern for me as an individual and with the fire of God's love which burned brighter than the zeal of the Reds who almost won me over."* When she realized how the subversives had "taken me for an ideological sleigh ride," her whole outlook changed. Her government job at the moment isn't too important, but the prospects are excellent for transfer to a more responsible position where she can do even greater good.

Not long ago 2,500 delegates of the General Federation of Women's Clubs, meeting in the East to consider the entrance of thousands of displaced persons, were persuaded to change their previous stand against the bill before Congress and went on record *in favor* of it. This turnabout was due to the never-say-die spirit of a handful of women whose courageous persistence continued through defeat. They never ceased working for a reconsideration of the measure. One delegate from Florida made a strong point by quoting to the assembly the words of Our Lord: *"For I was hungry, and you gave me to eat; I was thirsty, and you gave me to drink; I was a stranger, and you took me in."* (*Matt.* 25:35) Since the delegates represented some 3,000,000 women, the pressure their influence could exert on Congress can well be imagined. It was a wonderfully inspiring example of democracy in action and public effort for the common good.

A young man from Michigan, very much interested in the labor-relations phase of government, gave up a position in a manufacturing plant to go into Federal service where his zeal for good could be more widely felt.

A girl in Boston went to Washington, secured a position on a Senator's staff, and now is personally responsible for many important documents of factual data on one of the Senate committees.

Four young people, three men and one woman, gave up business careers to join the staff of the United Nations organizations. Two are interpreters, one a secretary, another a clerk.

Another Christopher, a man in his late thirties, resigned as plant foreman to run for office in his local community. Though without previous political experience, the soundness of his platform and the honesty of his approach helped defeat a small, well-entrenched political machine. "When I started out, people told me I was crazy—that it couldn't be done," he said. "I was polite and listened to 'em . . . then I went ahead and did it!"

A college graduate, after serving in the Merchant Marine during the war, has enrolled for an intensive training course with the view to entering the U.S. Foreign Service.

A woman, a former department store executive, has gone into personnel work in the government offices of her state where she is instrumental in seeing that only *loyal* Americans are put on the public payroll.

A lawyer in California offered his services and was accepted by the state Senate Committee on Education for the purpose of analyzing the *Building America Supplementary Textbooks,* volumes referred to elsewhere in this book as being considered detrimental to the best interest of this country and favorable to the slave way of life in Soviet Russia.

THE OPPORTUNITIES ARE BOUNDLESS

All these cases and numerous others paralleling them are tremendous steps in the right direction. Yet they are but a comparative drop in the bucket when the *vastness* of the field is realized. According to recent reports, including that of the Civil Service Assembly, some *5,900,000 employees* are on the public payroll. The Federal government accounts for 2,050,000, while state and local governments list some 3,859,000 workers. The opportunities to get into this vital phase of our national life are almost limitless. *It is up to you* to see that these opportunities are not wasted. When instances like those cited are multiplied thousands of times over, then much of the foreboding about how our government and nation may be misled will be dispelled.

SOME PRACTICAL SUGGESTIONS

To assist in this, here are a few tips which it might be well to follow:

(1) Know and make your voice heard by your local officials, councilmen, aldermen, etc.
(2) Know your Congressmen and make your influence felt by them, too.
(3) Follow the newspaper reports of how your Congressmen vote on various pieces of legislation.
(4) Keep abreast of the issues before your local, state, and national governments.
(5) Register and vote in primary, state, and national elections.
(6) Join civic groups (after proper investigations as to their purpose, methods, and personnel) and be active in such groups.
(7) Encourage others who can, to go *personally* into all phases of government work with the motive of *preserving* the God-given rights which the subversives are trying to uproot from our free way of life.
(8) Go yourselves—as *Christophers*—if it is humanly possible and in the spirit of *"Be ye doers of the word, and not hearers only."* (*James* 1:22)

Democracy's battle for existence is never finished.

In every classroom, in every government office, in every legislative and judicial chamber, the words of the Declaration of Independence should be publicly displayed and lived up to. And *in every heart* their meaning should guide every thought, word, and action. With our Founding Fathers you can defend these God-given rights and with them you can echo the words:

"We hold these truths to be self-evident:
(1) That all men are created equal;
(2) That they are endowed by their Creator with certain unalienable rights;

(3) That among these are life, liberty, and the pursuit of happiness;

(4) That, to secure these rights, governments are instituted among men, deriving their just powers from the consent of the governed;

(5) That, whenever any form of government becomes destructive of these ends, it is the right of the people to alter or to abolish it, and to institute a new government, laying its foundation on such principles, organizing its power in such form, as to them shall seem most likely to effect their safety and happiness."

As Raymond B. Fosdick, who retired recently after twelve years as President of the Rockefeller Foundation pointed out in an article in the *New York Times*, "Not Dollars Alone—Faith Is Also Needed":

". . . America has a song to sing that is not based on an economic creed or dogma and that has nothing to do with a catchword like 'free enterprise.' We were born in revolution and we are not ashamed of it. It sprang from a passionate belief in freedom and in the worth and dignity and creative capacity of the human personality. . . . This is the tradition of America, and we must not let the song die on our lips. The foundations of this country were based on moral principles that emphasized the rights of men everywhere to all that makes life satisfying and rewarding. To allow the Soviet Union with its totalitarian philosophy to appropriate for its own uses this promise of a better future is to betray the vision and greatness out of which we sprang.

"Our faith once captured the imagination of the world; it can capture it again."

Finally, to repeat the words the men who founded this Republic used in closing the Declaration of Independence:

"And for the support of this Declaration, with a firm reliance on the protection of divine Providence, we mutually pledge to each other our lives, our fortunes, and our sacred honor."

These men dared *everything* to win the God-given heritage which is yours today. You, as a Christopher, relying on the same Divine Guidance, can do no less than to work unceasingly to preserve this heritage for yourself and for posterity.

VI

LABOR-MANAGEMENT

Tremendous Issues at Stake

A SHORT TIME AGO in a large Midwestern city, I had occasion to visit a friend of mine, a vice president of a well-known manufacturing concern. He is a fine chap, what most people would refer to as a "nice guy," civic-minded, and a person anyone would be glad to know. However, in talking with him about the labor-management situation in general and the part of the individual workman in that situation in particular, he showed that he had a "blind spot" where his role in the business world was concerned. A "blind spot," incidentally, which you or I could easily have possessed had we been in his position, taken up as he was with the problem of running a very complicated industrial concern.

A long and costly strike had just recently been settled with his employees, and this executive, a ruddy-faced, extremely energetic man with a mind like the proverbial "steel trap" when it came to analytical figures and industrial problems, was anything but a cold, hard businessman when I saw him.

Pacing back and forth in his office for the better part of twenty minutes, he kept exploding about the ingratitude of people who were never satisfied with getting just treatment and fair wages. "They always want more," he almost shouted. "Give 'em an inch and they'll take a yard. Give 'em decent working conditions, paid vacations, health benefits—everything—and what happens? They go on strike because they say we're 'unfair to labor'! I don't get it. It beats me!"

I asked him if he really wanted to know the cause of much of his company's trouble. A sudden stop in his pacing and an incredulous "Now don't tell me *you* know!" was his only answer.

So, with this doubtful encouragement, I plunged in:

"Granting that you've done all you say you have," I told him, "you've still overlooked one very important item. You haven't given your employees *yourself*."

At that, the roof almost fell in. "Given them myself? Are you crazy? What do you want me to do? Go around the plant and play nursemaid to men who wouldn't appreciate it even if I were stupid enough to try it?"

"You miss the point," was my reply. "You don't have to be a nursemaid to anybody, but you do have to be a human being where your workmen are concerned. To you, your employees are just so many cogs in a wheel. You don't really *know* them, and they don't know you. Don't fool yourself—people resent not being treated as *individuals*. There's dignity in every human being and every human being likes to be treated as one. If you and your associates got out and made it your business to take a *sincere*, friendly interest in those who work for you (and I do mean a *sincere interest*, because people have a sort of 'sixth sense' about things like that; they can tell what is genuine and what isn't) I guarantee relations between you and them would be a whole lot better."

"Friendly interest, ha!" The reply almost blasted my eardrums. "That's so much twaddle! This is a business we're running, not a Sunday school!"

He was still muttering, almost sorrowfully, under his breath about people who weren't businessmen sticking to the things they knew something about, when we left his office that Saturday afternoon and got into his car to drive out of the plant. As we reached the main gate, a company policeman started to wave us through when this vice president suddenly stopped the car and stuck his head out of the side window.

"'Afternoon, Jim," he told the cop with a curt smile. "Have a good weekend!"

The look on the gateman's face was a picture no artist could have painted. From a sort of surly politeness, his expression changed to one of incredulous surprise, as much as to say, "What goes on here? He's never done this before." Then, quickly, he managed a grin and a "Thanks a lot, Mr. ——! Same to you."

When we were safely out of earshot, this executive turned to me with the air of a man who has made a startling discovery. "Darned if it didn't work!" was his amazed comment, and you could almost see the little "wheels" in his brain telling him, "This is good business. Friendliness really pays off."

To him his discovery was encouraging and, in a limited sense, it was to me, too. Yet, withal, it only scratched the surface of what was the cause of his, and of most human, troubles. If his friendliness had sprung out of a genuine *love* of his fellowman, of that gateman and of all his other employees, it would have furnished a solid beginning in eliminating the friction between management and labor. It would have paved the way toward better social justice on both sides:

fair wages and fair work, decent working conditions for employ*ees*; a decent respect for the rights of employ*ers*. This human recognition of the rights and duties of both capital and labor will prove, totalitarian propaganda notwithstanding, that the evils that afflict our human society *are not necessarily* inherent in our American economic system.

The solution is *not* to overturn our civilization as Communism would do, to take away property rights so man will no longer cheat or steal, to legalize the evil of class warfare and class hatred in order to arrive at the goal of a classless society.

The solution lies in the daily application of the Divine Law promulgated by Christ of Galilee. And this application will reform, not only our morals, but our institutions as well.

Every man is created in the Image and Likeness of God and, in that, *we are our brothers' keepers.* We are what we would have others be to us!

A well-known automobile industrialist, Henry Ford 2nd, is one of an increasing number of management executives who are putting this ideal into everyday practice. In talks given by young Mr. Ford all over the country in the past two years, he has stressed just one idea: industry would make a much greater contribution to humanity if it put as much time and thought into the human relations of its employees as it does into machines, buildings, and technological progress.

In a recent talk in Washington, D. C., he reproached his own company in the following words: *"It now seems clear that we have not kept the development of our human relations in industry in pace with the development of our production technology. Perhaps for every dollar we spent in scientific research for the development of better products and more efficient machines, we should have spent another dollar in research into the problem of people in industry."*

When ordinary folk all over the land read this in their daily papers, they sat up and took notice. This was something they had seldom heard before. It was an encouraging recognition of a very old idea: that each and every man counts as a human being, as a child of God.

An even more graphic illustration of how the man in the street received this news and, more particularly, the motivation which prompted its issuance, is expressed in the words of one Ford Company employee. Asked what he thought of young Mr. Ford, this worker replied, "Henry? He's okay. He's a *right* guy."

"Why do you say that?" someone insisted.

"He says 'hello' to you," came back the prompt answer.

"But what's so wonderful about that?" his questioner asked.

"He's the only 'big shot' who ever said 'hello' to me when he passed me in the corridor. Most of 'em don't even give you a tumble!"

So—people *do want* to have others take an interest in them. They don't want to be patronized. Sure, a man or a woman has to earn a living and wants to be decently paid; but he and she want more than money. They want to be treated in such a way as to be able to maintain the independent dignity which is their right—which is just another way of saying they want to be loved.

And they, in turn, do want to be their brothers' keepers!

THE RIGHTS AND DUTIES OF LABOR

On one hand, workers with a Christopher purpose should strive to carry out honestly and well all equitable agreements freely made, without violence, disorder, or outrage upon employers. They should accept just wages and not agitate for an immoderately higher rate of pay, which might imperil the economic soundness of a concern and bring about hardships for both employer and workers.

The Christopher-minded employers, on the other hand, should treat workmen as *free* people, as co-partners in ownership, profits, and management, and thus avoid extremes of both the left and the right. Those not possessed of considerable wealth—in short, the workers—are more defenseless against poverty and injustice than employers, hence an employer should, to quote Pope Leo XIII's great encyclical, *Rerum Novarum:*

> ". . . never tax his work people beyond their strength, nor employ them in work unsuited to their sex or age. His great and principal obligation is to give to everyone that which is just."

Thus, because management is in a more advantageous position, it has a greater obligation. In every country where it has failed to guard the security of the worker, it has prepared the way for its own destruction.

There is, however a *double danger* to be avoided—as another encyclical, *Quadragesimo Anno,* issued by Pope Pius XI pointed out. "On the one hand," to quote the encyclical, "if the social and public aspect of ownership be denied or minimized, the logical consequence is *Individualism,* as it is called: on the other hand, the rejection or diminution of its private and individual character necessarily leads to some form of *Collectivism.* To disregard these dangers would be to rush headlong into the quicksands of Modernism with its moral, juridical and social order, which We condemned in the Encyclical Letter issued at the beginning of Our Pontificate."

As remedies for the economic evils of the day, Leo proposed a return to the social and moral principles of Christianity and advocated *limited* intervention by the government as the guardian of public welfare and prosperity within the framework of justice. Workers were to be fairly paid, decently fed, clothed, and housed. Harmful child labor was to be stopped, workers' health protected, justice assured in negotiations and contracts. Finally, Leo concluded in his encyclical, which has come to be recognized by people of all faiths as a "Christian Manifesto on Labor," the state must remove causes of industrial conflict and control outbreaks of strife.

Leo was *far ahead* of his time, as Robert Wood Johnson in his book, *Or Forfeit Freedom* (Doubleday, p. 16-17) points out, since such ideas were "almost heresy" to the world of 1891. Since then others have likewise concerned themselves with social justice and, quoting Mr. Johnson: "*. . . when the Federal Council of Churches of Christ in America* [Protestant] *first met in 1908, it adopted a fourteen-point Social Creed which advocated such measures as abolition of child labor, reduction of working hours, adoption of a living wage 'as a minimum' in each industry, and suppression of the 'sweating system.' In more general terms, the Council also called for 'equitable division of the products of industry,' for abatement of poverty, and for protection of workers against the results of rapid economic change.*

"Christian leaders were joined by rabbinical bodies. Seeking modern application of Mosaic and Talmudic legislation, they supported bills guaranteeing workers the right to organize, outlawing child labor, establishing social security and old-age pensions, setting up fair employment practices, and so on. They also declared it the duty of society to use new machinery, skills, and productive power to banish hunger, unemployment, poor housing, and inadequate education from the social scene."

There you have the pattern for the position of labor in the

modern era, a pattern set forth by people of all religions and adhered to even by those with no formal religion but who do have a good sense of moral values. This unanimity of opinion in such a vital field is significant for *another* reason in addition to that of a desire for social justice, however. It emphasizes the fact that religion *and* labor *are the two greatest bulwarks against totalitarianism in this country.* The Rev. R. A. McGowan, director of the Social Action Department, National Catholic Welfare Conference, in an address before the convention of the CIO Textile Workers Union of America held recently at Atlantic City, New Jersey, pointed that out when he said:

> "American labor does not look forward to being superseded some time by an all-owning, all-employing, all-trading, all-governing government. American labor has thought of its own personal dignity and personal responsibilities. So I place the American labor movement along with religion in the first line of defense against a totalitarian America."

LABOR AND CAPITAL NEED EACH OTHER

By no means is it suggested now or ever that some of the evils in our economic life, about which totalitarians rant and rave, do not exist in this country. Sad to say, they do exist—*but* the elimination of these evils does not require the destruction of our economic system. Again, the fault lies not so much in the system *as in the greediness of man himself.* And, in attempting to resolve this condition, it must be realized very clearly that there will always be areas of difference between employers and employees. However, the Christopher point of view holds that these differences can exist without serious detriment to either side, *provided* honesty, decency, a sense of fair play, and acknowledgment of man's

God-given dignity, rights, and responsibilities are *mutually* recognized.

In other words, both sides must *play the game according to the rules.*

The Marxists violently insist that capital and labor are necessarily hostile to each other. Their great mistake (to quote again from *Rerum Novarum*) is "*to possess . . . the idea that class is naturally hostile to class; that rich and poor are intended by nature to live at war with one another. So irrational and so false is this view, that the exact contrary is the truth.*

"*Just as the symmetry of the human body is the result of the disposition of the members of the body, so in a State it is ordained by nature that these two classes should exist in harmony and agreement, and should, as it were, fit into one another, so as to maintain the equilibrium of the body politic. Each requires the other; capital cannot do without labor, nor labor without capital.*"

When this happy combination is "liquidated," economic chaos is the inevitable result. For example, in a press dispatch dated May 5, 1948, to the *New York Times* from that newspaper's correspondent in Vienna, there is given striking proof of how *accurate* such a statement is. Referring to the acquisition of Austrian industries, confiscated as German property by the Reds and undertaken by them to be run along Marxist lines, the dispatch goes on to say:

"*. . . The trouble is that these industries have begun to produce not profits but losses. . . . For a time the USIA industries, as the Russians like to call them, looked like a good investment since the Russians took them over in 1945 complete with large stocks of raw material. Seventy percent of their product was sold abroad for hard currencies or exported to the Soviet Union. The concerns were allowed to sell only 30 percent to Austria for schillings to pay their workers and to meet other overhead.*

"Evidently certain that capitalism was a simple process of profiteering, *the USIA administrators set aside no capital reserves, allowed nothing for depreciation, made practically no new investments, and increased wages for political purposes.*

"Then came currency reform, a general rise in wage scales and the present severe deflation. By this time the USIA industries were in debt from $15,000,000 to $20,000,000 to the Soviet military bank and, despite that bank's loans, were behind in their tax and pension obligations. Their raw material stocks were depleted and they were able only partly to renew them by compensation deals with Austrian concerns in the Western zones or by pressing the Austrian Government for allocations.

"Meanwhile, their overhead expenses increased, and Western occupation authorities had steadily forced down the Soviet bill against the Austrian Government for occupation costs. In an effort to get more schillings to pay their occupation army, which is larger than those of the three Western powers combined, the Russians opened a black market in Vienna. When this created a public scandal, they promptly closed it but instead began, through Austrian concerns, to sell USIA products in Vienna, Salzburg and Linz at 'grey market.'

"None of these expenditures has been successful and there have been purges in the USIA administration. It is reported Russian experts in Moscow who understand the capitalist economics are not heeded. Others are too good Marxists to make a success of the USIA, which must compete in a more or less free market. An attempt was made to use the Communist party in Linz to sell 100,000 pairs of USIA-made shoes at 200 schillings a pair, but the workers could not afford them.

"From the satellite countries, notably Hungary, comes the

same story that capitalism and Communism have not proved a good blend. . . ."

"IT IS BETTER THAT TWO SHOULD BE TOGETHER . . ."

So far in the United States, thank God, such a comparison —disastrous as such a comparison is to the godless totalitarian philosophy—has not been allowed to appear. And precisely because it has not been allowed to appear, capital and labor have been allowed the opportunity of ironing out their varied differences *within the framework of our democracy.*

In many respects they have been able to draw more closely together through institutions and organizations which, on both sides, are able to present their points of view intelligently and, generally speaking, express the majority viewpoint of each group as a whole.

In the field of labor, undoubtedly the most important of these organizations is the UNION. Operating on the Biblical theory that "It is better therefore that two should be together, than one; for they have the advantage of their society: If one fall he shall be supported by the other: Woe to him that is alone, for when he falleth, he hath none to lift him up." (*Eccles.* 4: 9-10), some fifteen million workers in the United States have organized themselves into trade unions.

These unions, and the labor field in general, offer a tremendously fertile field of activity for the Christ-bearer—the Christopher—who is aware of the necessity of bringing truth and its attributes to bear for the social justice of *all.*

The men and women in these unions look to their leaders, great and small, for guidance in many spheres outside their own particular activity. The nature of that leadership, whether it be for better or worse, for *good* or for *evil,* depends on the part that each and every one of the fifteen million members plays within his or her own group.

Modern labor organizations are more than just collective-bargaining agencies. They perform a variety of functions: economic, welfare, educational, community, and political. Considering these functions in order:

Economic

Within recent years particularly, it has become increasingly obvious that the *primary* purpose of any trade union is rightly defined as *economic*. It is the organization through which employees select their representatives who sit down with an employer or his representatives, to discuss and decide upon working conditions, hours of employment, wages, pension and retirement benefits, and other related questions. Through these trade unions it has been possible to establish working and living standards worthy of an American laborer, *worthy of a free man in a free democracy.*

Welfare

Although the economic function is the foremost function of trade unions, it is not the only function. Many unions are also welfare and benevolent organizations. They set up funds and committees to take care of their sick members, to give decent burial to their dead, to provide insurance for the family of deceased unionists, to provide vacations, to offer dental, medical, and optical care.

Educational

Many trade unions have extensive training and cultural programs for their members and for the families of their members. Such education is fairly inclusive, going far beyond simple classes on how to be an effective unionist. There are song and drama groups, classes in history and economics, bowling, basketball, and softball teams, literary societies, and public speaking forums. In short, trade unions seek to fill gaps in the formal education of their members.

Community

Many unions participate actively in the life of the community. They conduct drives to raise funds for the Red Cross, the Community Chest, and so on. They cooperate with other organizations and with local officials in sponsoring community agencies to care for the sick, the blind, the indigent, and the delinquent. Trade union members use these agencies, and trade unions often set up departments to guide their members in the use of such facilities. In some cases, trade union representatives even sit on the local or national boards of these community agencies.

Political

With functions as broad as those already listed, it is obvious that union organizations are more than casually concerned with legislation and government, since both these are directly associated with the civil and economic life of our country.

This being the case, unions have also a political function. They have urged, and continue to urge, certain legislation concerning minimum wages, child labor, limitation of working hours (especially for women), prison labor, and acts pertaining to the legal relationships between labor and management. In addition, they are intensely interested in other general legislation which touches on the everyday life of the American workman, such as housing laws, slum clearance, health services, and even foreign policy.

In a very real sense, then, unions may be the voice of the working class community; and, while they speak *for* the wage earner, they help also to shape the attitudes of the men and women who labor for a living.

Naturally, it is small wonder that the Nazis and Fascists tried—and the Communists still try—to penetrate the unions in order to dominate their functioning apparatus and thus determine their courses of action. Also, it is extremely enlightening to note that the Fascists, Nazis, and now the Communists, all of whom claimed and still claim to speak for the man in the street, immediately stifle free trade unionism as one of their first acts upon assuming ("seizing" would be a better word) power. The totalitarians may allow the trade union forms to exist, but they destroy their several functions because they know that the unions can be a powerful and effective force in upsetting tyranny. That is why the enemies of democracy immediately outlaw the right of the workman to strike and to bargain freely for higher wages and better working conditions.

Those courageous enough to attempt to do either of these two things, promptly find themselves ticketed for the salt mines, the concentration camps, and even the terror-filled "ride in the night" from which there is no return—merely a notice to the victim's family that he or she has conveniently committed "suicide."

Striking proof that this is happening, and happening almost every day, is contained in a United Press release from Berlin on May 6, 1948. With the caption above the release reading "STRIKE BROKEN, RED STYLE," the dispatch goes on to say:

> "The newspaper *Der Tagespiegel* reported today that the Russian management of a Soviet corporation at Espenheim offered German workers a free trip when they threatened to strike for more food.
>
> "Workers who wanted to strike were advised to report for a journey to Siberia.
>
> "There was no strike."

That last sentence bears repeating—"*There was no strike.*" Short, snappy, almost anti-climactic. Yet the totalitarians in our midst, especially those who have fallen hook, line, and sinker for the party line, without themselves actually being card-carrying party members, would do well to ponder over those few words. For those who would substitute for our free way of life, even with its imperfections, the terror, violence, and death of the godless, here is actual proof (and just one of countless instances) of what happens when the God-given rights of man are trampled under by the hobnailed boots of a tyrannical, so-called classless, State.

A FIELD FOR POSITIVE AND CONSTRUCTIVE ACTION

Precisely because trade unions in a democracy such as ours are so influential a force in the basic segment of American life (the wage-earner), the possibilities for positive and constructive action, particularly by the Christophers in such groups, are almost unlimited.

Almost from its beginning the trade union movement has had its wings. Some of these favored radical action; others a more conservative approach. Some wanted a greater emphasis on politics; others abhorred political action. Some preferred the craft form of organization; others, the industrial form of groupings.

To understand the situation completely, however, the Christopher must fully understand the part the American Communists have played within the labor movement. Communism introduced a new element into the trade unions. Its disciples did not look upon the union primarily as a means of meeting the day-to-day needs of working people. They viewed unions as means toward the seizure of political power and the establishment of a proletarian dictatorship over all of society, including the unions. And to accomplish this, they brought into the different groups of organized labor the concept of the "fraction," a body of disciplined and trained Communists inside a trade union whose purpose was to "bore from within" with the aim either to *rule* the group or *ruin* its effectiveness for good.

And, through these "fractions" or "cells," they tried, and still continue to try, to do both. In the middle 1920's, they set up their Trade Union Educational League to start their process of infiltration. When they subsequently failed, they decided to pull out and put up counterunions in opposition to those existing among the rank and file of American workingmen. These countergroups were known as the Trade Union Unity League, although its objective was anything but unity. Again having failed to meet with any degree of success, they returned to the fold of organized labor around 1934 and under orders from Moscow began anew the process of boring from within.

Often concealing their identity and subversive affiliations, they offered themselves as *organizers*. They plunged into the thick of things. They didn't sit on the sidelines and hope to revolutionize by wishful thinking and inaction. In this work of organization they showed great courage, vast skill, and endless zeal. And they were rewarded for their "apostolic" efforts. They won leadership in many labor groups simply because they came in with a fixed purpose and worked unceasingly and devotedly to reach their goal.

Their success, incomplete as it is, has been out of all proportion to their members. This organized minority has gained key positions and helped swing many labor policies to the left, mainly because they have had the zeal for spreading the darkness of subversion, while those possessed of the light of truth have, so far, not made their voices and actions felt in sufficient volume.

If ever there was a challenge to good, sound-thinking

Americans to regain the initiative out of the hands of these godless—and out of the hands of the unscrupulous and dishonest who may not be totalitarian-minded—this is it!

To be effective, however, the Christopher must not rush pell-mell onto the scene, expecting to turn the tables overnight. A careful study of the entire field of labor, *organized labor in particular,* will give him or her the chance to decide upon the job for which he or she is best suited.

First, there are the regular, *full-time administrative positions,* such as the walking delegates and the business agents, the presidents and the managers. These are men whose primary concern is hearing grievances and settling them and, in addition, shaping the general policy of the organization. In some instances these posts are elective; in others they are appointive. In most cases they are filled by men and women who have worked their way up in the union from the ranks; in some instances, however, outsiders hold these positions.

Second, there are the *field men,* usually referred to as the *organizers.* These people have a hard assignment. They are trade union "missionaries," carrying the union gospel to the unorganized. They must have imagination, determination, and courage. So arduous are their tasks that very often after they have organized some corner of the nation they settle down to become administrators, delegates, or agents.

Third, there are the *labor lawyers.* These men are generally much more than ordinary attorneys. They help negotiate agreements, advise unions on legal matters, guide administrations on political and legislative policy. In many unions the lawyer is the dominant figure behind the scenes.

Right now, and in the foreseeable future, there is a very great need to get more Christophers into this particular phase of the labor field.

To illustrate this need: not so long ago at a diplomatic reception in Washington, D. C., one of the guests overheard a young Jewish lawyer discussing with some friends the labor situation and its effect on our national life. And as this lawyer continued to talk, it became increasingly evident that his views almost paralleled those of the Christophers in the economic field.

Curious to know the reason for these opinions, the guest made it his business to take the lawyer aside after the discussion had ended and politely question him. The answers he received were enlightening, to say the least!

"*I can understand your curiosity,*" this Jewish gentleman told him, "*but to give you the whole story I'll have to tell you what happened when I first began to study law. It was up at Harvard and the opening speech that our professor—a non-Catholic, by the way—gave us has stuck in my mind ever since. He told us if we wanted to do our country a real service we ought to concentrate on labor, not corporation, law. Most of us had intended to do just the opposite, for the very commercial reason that there was more money in corporation practice. But what that professor said changed the minds of quite a few of us.*

"*He pointed out the need for men with sound American doctrine to get into organized labor with as much enthusiasm as those with vicious and totalitarian ideas had done, so far. He finished with the words, 'If you want the best background for labor law, study the Papal Encyclical,* Rerum Novarum, *of Leo XIII. Read that and you'll never regret it. I gave that same advice last year and the year before to the Catholic students especially, but they didn't see fit to take it. All of them took up corporation law instead.*' "

"Yet you didn't?" the guest interrupted, admiringly.

The Jewish lawyer smiled. "*Not only I, but six other Jewish boys in the class as well. Maybe some of the other students went into labor law, too, but I couldn't vouch for it. I do know we seven Jewish lads took the professor's ad-*

vice. We keep in touch with each other fairly often and I can tell you one thing. None of us has ever regretted making the decision we did!"

When more and more Christophers echo those words, the tide will begin to turn away from the godless and back to the God-given tradition upon which America was founded.

But to continue the discussion of the positions that an ordinary Christopher can fill:

Fourth, there are the *labor educators.* This category includes educational directors, librarians, teachers, group workers, dramatic directors, athletic coaches.

Fifth, there are the *labor journalists.* Every national or international union puts out a magazine or newspaper. In addition, many local unions do the same. Modern unions have press agents, publicists, pamphleteers, reporters. There is a job for the man or woman just out of college and for the newspaperman with a generation of experience.

The sixth classification covers *labor political organizers.* Almost every major union group has its political action committee or its league for political education. Many individual unions even have their own political departments.

Labor research and statistical personnel are included in the seventh classification; generally speaking, these people are economists. Often they are men and women with high standing in their profession. Sometimes they are assistants with a secondary school background.

In the eighth, last, but not least effective, group are the *administrative staffs* of the trade unions: clerks, typists, secretaries, and accountants.

These are all full-time jobs. They compose the paid apparatus of the union. However, there are other jobs that are not full-time paid positions but which offer, in some cases, an even greater opportunity for a worker to be effective in shaping *for good* the character of his or her own union.

For example, there are the shop stewards, men and sometimes women generally elected by the workers in an office or factory, or in a section of some branch of a particular industry. Their duties are to handle grievances at the plant or office level, to collect dues, and to transfer the policy and plans of the union to the rank and file of its members.

Shop stewards are the equivalent of the noncommissioned officers in the army or navy—except for one very important detail. Very often they are the *makers of policy* as well as its executors. Usually they enjoy the confidence of their fellow wage earners and, because of this confidence, can be an extremely powerful force for good. They can be real leaders, not only in handling grievances, but also in shaping the general thinking of the people in their office or plant. They can guide their fellow employees in their voting when the time comes to choose union officers. They can keep their associates alerted on what is happening inside the union as well as give advice on different courses of action to be taken and the methods to be used in pursuing those courses. In short, the shop steward is the backbone of the union.

In addition, there are the board members of local unions. These are generally men and women who, while they work all day, serve on the executive board of their local union group on free evenings. They are not paid officials, but are regular workers who hold elective positions. Such men and women are usually highly respected members of their union and, by and large, have risen to their positions from out of the ranks of the shop stewards. Board members hold policy-making posts. As such, they can either make or break a union.

Then again there are special official groups in offices and factories, such as grievance, legislative, political, organizing, and entertainment committees. In all of these posts, rank-and-filers first assume the responsibilities of group leadership. The Christopher worker must look upon such posts, not merely as routine positions, but as tremendous opportunities *for doing good.* By doing this, he or she can be the most effective single force in molding the thought and action of his or her co-workers. On the one hand, any individual who gets a group of close companions to vote him into a position and then proceeds to forget his responsibilities would do much better not to get himself elected at all. His indolence will soon discredit him. He will harm himself and any cause or group with which he is affiliated. On the other hand, the Christopher worker who aspires to a union position, full-time paid or part-time voluntary, *must be ready to do the job!*

Finally, at the base of the union is the individual worker. He or she does not stand out, as do those who hold paid positions or those who hold prominent nonpaying posts. The individual worker is just another "soldier in the army of the working people," yet, in the final analysis, he or she is the *most important* person in the organization.

For a Christopher, this is a most significant fact. Realizing it, he or she must constantly work toward persuading others of its fundamental truth . . . and then follow up such conviction with *positive action.* It is the ordinary member who elects the shop steward, the executive board, the union officers. It is the individual member who *really* makes the union policy. For a member to be unaware of his or her power, is to be the kind of member who will not attend union meetings and will not vote at labor elections. He or she will allow unions to be taken over by gangsters, whether they be strong-arm underworld characters or politically subversive dupes. *When corruption and Communism move into unions, it is due primarily to the fact that the rank-and-file member has neglected his or her duty.*

Just as it is extremely dangerous for the average citizen to stay away from the polls at election time, so it is equally, if not more, hazardous for the ordinary worker to stay away from his or her union meetings. To know what is going on and to take a hand in the proceedings, a person has to be *on the spot*—at the scene of the action.

You may be sure that the enemies of freedom and democracy are always there. By concentrating, for example, on trade unions, they are able to lay hands on a tremendously powerful weapon with which they can paralyze industry and commerce in times of national crisis. By capturing control of labor unions, the godless subversives give the impression that the voice of labor and the voice of totalitarianism are one and the same. That is why they seek to convert what is one of the greatest forces for liberty and national good into a force for evil and dictatorship.

A LITTLE WORK CAN ACCOMPLISH WONDERS!

To give one striking example of that missionary zeal for evil and how influence for good took the play away from the godless and brought Christian ideals back into one phase of the labor movement:

For the better part of a decade one powerful local branch of a newspaper union in the Eastern United States was the target—and a vulnerable target, at that—of intensive subversive activity because of the union's influence all over the country. It had always been populated with hard-working, self-sacrificing fellow-travelers and equally zealous misguided liberals, who were rightly impressed with the wages and hours improvements which had been gained by the left-wing administration.

There was an opposition group, too, but until recently it was largely ineffectual. The people in this latter group knew what they wanted, but lacked the necessary "know-how."

The missing links were *organization, inspiration, and man-power.*

A couple of years ago, prodded by some good, hard-working unionists, this group began really to do something. Meeting monthly, it brushed up on trade union practices, social action philosophy, and parliamentary procedure. It acted as a sort of clinic to thrash out various important labor problems and so became conversant with the entire labor picture in that particular locality. It studied the subversives' techniques, among them the contact method that the godless have exploited to the best possible advantage. It got as many union members on the various committees as it could, in order to silence the leftist administration's claim that the opposition did much talking but little union work.

Motivated by a sincere Christian love of their fellowmen, they copied the subversives' tactics of interesting themselves in *every* union member, especially those who were uncertain or on the fence as regards being morally right or subversively wrong.

Not long ago, the development of this approach won a complete victory. From an overwhelmingly leftist administration, the scales swung decisively in favor of the sound, God-fearing majority which, for too long, had been unable or too apathetic to make its wishes heard. But the crux of the whole victory for the forces of light was *activity*. The actions of the well-informed, intelligent rank-and-file members helped mold the future of this union. And, of course, self-sacrifice in attending union and committee meetings, helped, too. It was a tough battle, but it brought results.

In practice these unionists put into action the principles for *good* economic living. The application of those same principles, as applied to the whole labor-management field, has been summed up very concisely in the "*Code for Industrial Peace*," published by the Institute of Industrial Relations of East St. Louis and Belleville, Illinois. Quoting briefly from this *Code:*

"We acknowledge the Brotherhood of Man under the Fatherhood of God. Hence we recognize in every man, whether manager or laborer, the dignity, the sanctity and the eternal destiny of the human person. We further recognize that all men as human beings and as members of civil society have certain inalienable rights, which no one, however powerful, can violate without injustice.

"Management and Labor both perform essential functions in society, the one complementing the other in the production and distribution of commodities and services necessary and useful for human living. They are inter-dependent units of the same organic whole; therefore, what is good for one is good for the other, and what hurts one hurts the other.

"Management and Labor have the solemn duty of mutual cooperation towards achieving an economic structure in which each individual will be enabled to fulfill his obligations of Social Justice, that is, of making his proportionate contribution to the general welfare.

". . . the sincere application of justice, good faith, and fair dealing . . . is the indispensable means of securing an equitable working out of the natural rights of man embodied in the Declaration of Independence and the Bill of Rights. Only thus can America's future as a free nation be assured."

It is up to the Christopher—the Christ-bearer—to bring this glorious concept of the dignity of both the workingman and the employer back into our economic life. A comparative few, working in the spirit of Truth, can bring sanity and decency back into this vital phase of our national life—where these virtues rightfully belong!

In doing this, they will be one with the Carpenter of Nazareth, Who Himself knew what it was to toil and labor. In doing this, they will literally be helping to carry Christ into the market places of our country—and eventually into the whole world.

VII

WRITING

The Power of Words

BEFORE ANYTHING in this world is ever done, *thought* precedes the *act*. From the time Gutenberg first invented the printing press and in increasingly higher proportion ever since, thoughts have nearly always been inspired by what someone put down in writing in a newspaper, in a book, in a magazine, or in modern times, in motion pictures, radio, and television, as well.

Centuries ago the chief means of spreading a thought, an idea, was by word of mouth, from a merchant to a customer, from a soldier to his family, from a trader in the market place to those grouped around to haggle over the quality of a piece of rare silk or a cannister of precious oil.

But what a contrast today! In the newspaper field alone, the daily pronouncements out of Washington, London, Paris, Rome, or Moscow reach the ends of the earth within the space of a comparatively few minutes. Such has been the magic of modern science in multiplying the power of the miraculous *word.*

Words can be a power for *good*—or they can be a power for *evil.*

No more striking example of the truth of the second part of that statement can be found than the fate of Germany in the years immediately following the end of the First World War, when it began to forsake its struggle for democracy and to turn to the blandishments of Adolf Hitler. Right there the world witnessed one of the most terrifying demonstrations of the power of propaganda.

In newspapers, magazines, books, pamphlets, over the air, and in motion pictures, the German people were swayed, cajoled, perverted, hardened into an evil pattern of global conquest. Force of arms followed later, but ideas preceded the first putsch, the first territorial annexation, the first shot of World War II.

Today, the virus of materialism, of totalitarianism, of Communism, of perversion of all types, is literally being forced upon us here in the United States—forced into our lives, our thoughts, our business, our homes, our families. And, to an astonishing degree, it has met with a favorable reception by those in our midst who are not basically bad but only gullible and unthinking.

Those behind this drive, those doers of evil, have a purpose, a goal. All their efforts are directed toward it. All their energies spent in the cause are just so many paving stones in the road to the conquest of "light" by those who live in the "darkness."

That we have similar means at our disposal to fight for what is right, is our hope, however. Yet it is a hope we must still fulfill, for, up to now, our efforts have been meager in comparison with those who would destroy our way of life, our freedoms, our very civilization.

THE WRITING FIELD IN AMERICA TODAY

Conveying ideas is one of the biggest industries in America today. We are influenced by the books, magazines, newspapers, and advertisements we read, by the sounds that come over the radio from a script written in advance, by stage plays, by motion pictures, by television, by newsreels.

All of these leave their imprint on us as individuals. They help influence our thoughts, mold our tastes, determine our judgments, control our actions.

In radio there have been outstanding examples of magnificent entertainment—splendid dramas, grand variety shows, brilliant musical presentations—which reflect the American public's innate good taste.

In many magazines and newspapers, in instances too numerous to mention, good writing and good, honest news coverage have helped to keep these two phases of the writing field relatively free and unfettered and a credit to our literary discrimination.

But in the motion picture industry, in radio, in the book world, in magazines and in newspapers, too much that is cheap and tawdry, too much that is immoral, too much that is materialistic and profane, have caused a lowering of literary standards at a rate that is truly alarming.

We do not expect all "cream" in our entertainment, but we do expect that the "milk" will not turn sour.

Most of us, for example, do not object to an occasional story about crime. We are not prudes. We are healthy-minded and decent. But we do resent a continuous and deliberate appeal to our baser instincts.

We resent in current literature, on the screen, over the

radio, all that is not merely subversive or obnoxious but actually dreary, repetitious, and decidedly unentertaining, because the writers are appealing, not to most of the people, but to the *few* who prefer depravity and perversion.

Yet, while they may be appealing to a few, the effect on the general public is so far-reaching as to amount to a national tragedy. As J. Edgar Hoover, head of the FBI points out, "Filthy literature is the great moron-maker. It is casting criminals faster than prisons can absorb them."

An exaggeration? Hardly. An all too tragic incident illustrating the truthfulness of Mr. Hoover's statement happened not long ago in Washington, D. C., when a fourteen-year-old boy armed with a German pistol killed a policeman and then tried to end his own life. The boy was so obsessed with stories of crime that the neighbors had refused to let their children play with him. Reporters discovered that he had stacks of gangster fiction and crime comic books hidden away, and that he saw three or four movies a week, mostly gangster films. Cornered by the police, the boy was reported to have put the pistol to his head, yelling defiantly: "You'll never take me alive, coppers!" En route to the hospital, he expressed no feeling of remorse for what he had done. Instead, he was quoted as asking, "Did I kill the cop?" An American tragedy if ever there was one, whose cause, in national terms, has been the expressed concern of many responsible men and women.

Recently, the head of one of the largest bookshops in the country confessed that she was ashamed to sell many of the books published today. Even keeping them in stock, she said, seemed like cooperating in the collapse of moral values.

To say that the public demands such stockpiles is only a half-truth. A short time ago, Mr. William S. Paley, chairman of the Columbia Broadcasting System, referring to the "growing volume of criticism of American broadcasting," said, "First we have an obligation to give most people what they want most of the time."

Since most American people are decent-minded and decent-living, if every writer, producer, and publisher were to follow Mr. Paley's standard, all forms of information and entertainment would immediately become, not only interesting and highly enjoyable, but sound information and wholesome entertainment as well.

SOMETHING TO DO ABOUT IT

There is some value, of course, in refusing to buy offensive or indecent literature, in turning off vulgar, boring, or subversive radio programs, and in abstaining from cheap movies. But the cure does not lie there, for it is like objecting to bad food without providing anything better. Good cooks must replace the bad ones, and in this case the cooks are the *writers*. They are the people who directly or indirectly prepare a movie or radio script; the newsmen who "talk" to millions; the authors of short stories, serials and articles; the novelists, the biographers, the playwrights.

And new and better writers can be found.

They will come from among *you*, the people of substance, of sound, healthy values—the vast group of Americans who constitute the backbone of our nation and of our Christian civilization. From among the tens of millions of you who are decent, honorable, and law-abiding. You who have your feet on the ground, who are thoughtful and generous, genuine and stimulating. You Americans of every race and color can make a substantial contribution to the well-being of our country if, fortified with truth, you will go in large numbers into the writing field. It is one of the main fields in which the Christopher can work to change the world, to bring back integrity instead of untruth, individual responsibility instead of mass hypnotism, thought instead of mere sensationalism.

Words are the coinage of the world of ideas. It is even more important that words be honest than that money be honest. As the mind of the Christopher centers itself on Truth, his words will take on the simplicity and clarity of his purpose. He will be an island in which words that are clear and honest shine like a beacon through the prevailing fog of doubt and illusion.

In our world of mass communication, professional writing is one of the most important links joining man to man or skillfully separating them (as do the godless) by planting doubt and hate. In the field of professional writing the Christ-bearer can find a wide scope for his or her work, provided, of course, that he or she has the talent for it. And that talent, incidentally, is much more generously distributed than most people realize.

We of the Christopher movement know from experience that this is so and it is of no use to protest, as some few do, "Perhaps you're right, but they still don't want worth-while people in the writing field."

That is neither fair nor accurate.

Many with godless leanings have succeeded in infiltrating the writing sphere, of course, and have secured editorial and executive positions. To this group also can be added secretaries and readers of manuscripts who make every effort to keep good, healthy literary works from reaching the proper authorities. Seldom, however, do these godless aim for the top jobs in the writing field. They find it more to their advantage in poisoning the minds of the public to have genuinely respected men and women at the head of publishing concerns, people who, unwittingly, serve as "fronts" for their behind-the-scenes activities.

In contrast to these godless, there is, fortunately, a far greater number of sound, sensible Americans who still hold similar posts. And these men and women definitely do want *good* material to be submitted for publication. Multiply their number, particularly of those who are articulate in supporting their beliefs, and the whole trend toward materialism in this field can not only be stopped, but changed for the *better*.

An editor of a motion picture magazine recently remarked, "In my opinion it is the failure to realize the message of interest and value they have for the modern world that keep the majority of potential writers away from successful writing." And, a few months ago, the editor of a leading house which publishes "pulps" of wide distribution and low quality remarked, "We want stories of better quality. But we find that too few better-quality people are interested in writing!"

In Hollywood alone, one major studio found only *six* manuscripts out of *two hundred* submitted to possess "screen possibilities," and these six were reported as none too good themselves.

So the opportunity and the need for new writers with good ideas are there. Apart from the numerous possibilities in screen and radio writing, in the publishing end of the field alone there is scope enough for everyone with sufficient talent and perseverance to make a place for himself or herself. According to a recent survey, roughly 2,000 magazines are printed and distributed throughout the United States each month; and this total does not include trade periodicals, house organs, and others of strictly limited circulation.

Of this 2,000 the first 130 magazines have a combined circulation of more than 200 million copies each month! *This means more than one magazine for every man, woman, and child in this country*. In just five classes of publications alone there are circulated:

3,223,000 detective story magazines,
9,263,000 love and adventure "pulps,"
7,976,000 "true confession" magazines,
10,755,000 movie magazines,
25,215,000 adventure "comic" books.

CERTAIN LAWS OF WRITING

We do not claim that a person of substance and integrity can sell to these magazines after ten easy lessons. Let's make that clear. There are certain laws of writing. The fundamental principles may be learned with comparative ease, but each branch of literature has its own special rules. "It takes years," said one of the nation's top writers, "to learn the wisdom, to acquire the experience that a writer must have. As far as the *craft* goes, you never learn it. Each piece of writing presents its own original problem of craftsmanship. Not every violinist can be a Heifetz or a Kreisler, but there are plenty of places for musicians outside the concert stage. Most of us want to start out as vice-presidents, when we should be content to begin as office boys."

There is room for thousands of good writers. Out of these thousands, it is certain that a few will rise to the top of their professions, as cream rises to the top of milk. But, famous-to-be or not, everyone counts.

WHICH BRANCH OF WRITING SHALL IT BE?

Some of you will find your particular talents better suited to one type of writing than another. Some of you will like to work only with facts; others, with imagined situations that are "dreamed up," in the language of the trade.

In other words there are two main divisions to which all writing belongs: fiction and nonfiction.

The former deals with invented circumstances, like those in stories and fantasies. The latter deals with facts or alleged facts or interpretation of facts. Of the two, the latter is the more simple and more direct way of putting over an idea, of "selling" a thought, of proving a point. But it does not follow that nonfiction is the only method or even the most effective. Fiction, because it is more subtle, can often be more potent.

Fiction—and in a more restricted sense, nonfiction as well—can again be broken down into two further categories: stories (articles, feature columns, or editorials) with a "moral"; and just plain stories. In the first instance, a novel, short story, or article is clearly intended to convey some purposeful thought. As such, the writing very directly affects public thought. In the latter case, however, the object is simply entertainment, or amusement, or perhaps the building up of excitement, whether it be pleasant or stimulating or, too often unfortunately, horrifying.

For one who has a purpose, a *good* purpose—in short, a Christopher—the following branches of the writing field offer a tremendous opportunity to spread *light* where there is *darkness*. To furnish entertainment as refreshing as it is wholesome.

First, there is the world of . . .

Newspapers

In motion pictures, over the radio, in feature stories, much of the emphasis on the news we get and the people who prepare it, has been dramatized along "big" lines. Film, magazine and radio heroes are nearly always star reporters, columnists, press executives, or managing editors. Always they are alert, aggressive, very much "on the ball." In most cases this is true and only serves to point up the fact that in the press field, as in other phases of writing, specialization by trained experts is the rule rather than the exception.

To break into the newspaper field, the question of age is a vital factor. To learn the trade you will have to start at the bottom of the ladder and work up. Managing editors and feature columnists and city desk men don't, like little Topsy, just grow. They have to start out as copy boys or cub reporters or secretaries. Newspapers want young men and women to train because the training takes some years to complete. Yet the newspaper field does offer inexhaustible opportunities even to the more mature, since the number of metropolitan dailies is very small when placed alongside the total number of newspapers of all kinds published in this country. (There are, at the moment, nearly 2,000 dailies, and some 15,000 weekly newspapers.)

There are the small town and county weeklies. There are the newspapers put out by occupational groups, by those interested in the theater, advertising, hardware, men's and women's clothing, or by the trade unions and social welfare, fraternal, and religious groups. And in these latter fields there are great opportunities for the beginning or semiprofessional writer.

Breaking them down systematically, there are:

(1) The national publications put out by such groups as veterans organizations, by national and international trade unions, by business associations, by fraternal orders, by church and religious groups, by women's societies, by political parties.
(2) The parallel publications by state and county organizations (of groups similar to the above).
(3) The local periodicals, sometimes put out for one company, one plant, one veteran's post, one chapter of a society, one church, one small community.

These publications are of dual character. Some are addressed to the public at large. Others are what are commonly referred to as *house organs.* These latter have a limited reading public since they are intended only for the members of a particular organization, for the people employed in a particular plant, or for the adherents of some religious, business, or political group. These periodicals are not listed in any of usual press directories, yet their circulation runs into the *millions.* They spring up spontaneously wherever a group of people with a common background or objective get together.

And these house organs wield unbelievable power. Their readers will often give their editorials more attention than they will the editorials of the metropolitan press. That they should do so is quite understandable since these small publications represent an interest that is direct and personal.

Speaking of these house organs (some in this group are newspapers, others are magazines, but for practical purposes we list them here in the general press field), an active Christopher who edits a periodical published by a large corporation, wrote:

"Most of the big companies put out industrial publications, and more and more of them are going into it. A few years ago there were over 5,000 industrial periodicals on record, but the number has grown a lot since then . . . it is this field that I think offers the greatest opportunity for doing good.

"The circulation of employee magazines . . . is particularly important because so many of the mill and factory workers who read them read very little else. Big companies are willing to spend a lot of money on them to promote good industrial relations, lessen friction, get a bigger return on their wage dollar.

"The editors are about evenly divided between women and men, with most of the big magazines edited by men, but a lot of important ones, also, handled by women. The average editor's pay varies from $2,500 to $6,000, but the large publications go all the way up. However, other angles to the job are more important than pay. For one thing the editor and his staff act as go-betweens for management and labor. They go around the mills and factories talking to the workers and get a lot of valuable sidelights on how they feel about things. And they are also pretty close to the top management of their company, because they have to know the inside story on company policies to be able to interpret them correctly in what they write. For these reasons, they have a good chance of taking leading parts in employee relations problems.

"As far as the qualifications for the jobs are concerned, a good knowledge of English and an understanding of human nature are the chief requirements. You have to like people and have a real respect for the people you are writing for. If editors think they are different kinds of human beings from the workers . . . then they'll never be good editors. Most editors have assistants and an inexperienced person may start in at that position while getting experience. Some colleges give courses in industrial journalism that are wonderful foundations for the job, but that training is not half as important as being the *right kind* of person.

"In short, the employee magazine can have a good deal of influence on a lot of people, and that is why I think the field is a 'natural' for Christophers, a good one for people of high principles to get into."

Everything this editor writes is only too true. Yet it must be added that not in all cases will such publications offer a full-time job. Sometimes they pay for part-time work, especially where the publication comes out monthly or bimonthly or even quarterly. Frequently the publication will be issued by a voluntary worker. More often than not, the person chosen is the one who *volunteers.*

This point cannot be emphasized too strongly. In clubs and factories, in student, veteran, employer, employee, fraternal, religious, and community organizations, it is possible for one alert person to propose the issuance of a publication and then to handle the publication himself. The audience may be small, but it is intimate, tied together by common interest. If every person with good ideas, and in a position to do so, takes over a little responsibility in the conduct of these organs, he will end by helping to shape the habits of tens of millions.

Closely related to the field of newspapers is that of . . .

Magazines

What has been said of newspapers is equally true of magazines. There are in the United States literally thousands of such publications. Periodically there are lists published of all these magazines with statements on the kind of material they want and the prices they pay. Such lists can be found in special writers' journals on almost every newsstand.

Roughly, magazines are broken down into the *slicks*, the *semi-slicks*, and the *pulps*.

A *slick* is a magazine conspicuous for its glossy or coated paper, its expensive art, its nationally known writer-contributors, its top-grade advertising. A *semi-slick* is a periodical which follows fairly closely the style and format of a *slick*, but which does not quite duplicate the expensive layout, does not have as many "big name" writers, and uses less elaborate advertising.

A *pulp* is a magazine which uses a lower grade of paper, has less top-grade advertising, features quite often a garish cover display, and uses story or article material by writers other than those in the top brackets.

For every one of the slick or semi-slick magazines, however, there are dozens of pulps. And among the readers of the latter are precisely the people who should be reached by wholesome, positive, and creative ideas, by Christophers who can turn their hands to perform a great service to society without impairing the interest in the material they write.

To sell to any of these three branches of the magazine field, requires a reasonable amount of technical knowledge of the writing craft, of course. It requires a painstaking study of the type of writing each periodical regularly features. It involves, if possible, the placing of your material in the hands of a reputable agent who will know far better than you where a particular story or article should be sent, and can advise you how to "smarten up" your material or change the format to suit editorial needs.

If a writer has never sold to any great degree, even the most reputable agents charge what is known as a *reading fee.* This is done to pay for the time and energy spent by an agent or his staff in analyzing the possibilities of a particular story or article since there is no guarantee that such a story or article will be suitable for publication. Once you begin to sell regularly, however—and you can sell if you have a certain amount of talent and a somewhat greater amount of perseverance—the reading fee will be dropped and a percentage basis arrangement made between the agent and the author. Twenty-five hundred editors throughout the country are searching for new material; one thousand Christophers with a purpose can supply that demand.

In the past few years there has sprung up an entirely new type of publication known as the *comics.* By a *comic* is not meant something necessarily funny, although the cartoon strips which compose them were originally intended to be humorous.

Modern comics can be quite serious. An increasing number feature crime or adventure stories. A lesser number are aimed at direct education of the reader. Labor unions and religious groups publish comic books whose purpose is as serious as life itself. And this medium has been chosen because it reaches a section of the population which is able to follow a presentation much more easily if put forth in illustration form, especially in the form of colored pictures.

Nor are these comics aimed only at children. They are read almost as widely by adults as by youngsters. Witness what happened during the recent war when comic books were the fastest selling literature among GI's in army PX's and navy ships' stores.

Comic magazines, as such, have become highly specialized since the first cartoon book "hit" the newsstand. Writing for them calls for a special technique, for what a comics writer puts on paper must be as visually acceptable as it is correct from a literary standpoint.

In a few cases the writer both pens the script and draws the cartoons, but the majority of strips are handled by *several* people—writer, cartoonist, inker, letterer, and so on.

If you feel your particular talents lie within this field (and there is a definite need and opportunity for people with good ideas—for Christophers), once more will it be necessary for you to consult the *good* comics now being published. Learn their format, their taboos, the things they stress, amount of dialogue, transition of action from one cartoon blurb to another. And also consult the market publications which will list the needs of the various publishing concerns which put out these comic books.

Next to be considered is the world of . . .

Books

Many people, when they think of books, think of the novel. Actually, it is but a small portion of the book world. Textbooks are turned out annually by the millions, often written by nonprofessional writers such as teachers, college professors, specialists in one field or another.

There are technical books on a variety of subjects, from "how to play bridge" to "how to build a house." There are books for children—and this is a great and expanding market—with books aimed at youth of all ages. There are books aimed at special occupational groups or at people living in some particular community or part of the country.

Again, as in other branches of the writing field, authoring a book requires a special technique, a special talent either natural or developed. Some people are born with it. Others, and these are in the majority, come by such skill only after careful preparation and hard work.

Many of you have the native ability to acquire such skill if you will only get into some branch of the writing field, working for small-town newspapers, house organs, veterans' publications, business trade journals, and so on. But always you must keep on *writing . . . writing . . . writing*. And, as you write, so will you learn to get the feel of words, the technique of plot construction, the best methods of developing an idea.

If you have this talent, again you will have to consult the periodicals of the writing trade to learn what books are in demand, what the technical requirements are, word-length, factual data, and so on. Consulting such journals, you will come to have a working knowledge of publishing houses, how to approach them, how to market, and how to sell. You will get, too, some idea of how wide and varied is the field, how many opportunities there are for the hard-working, creative author with good ideas—the Christopher author.

Radio

Although radio is a comparatively recent creative medium whose career covers just over a quarter of a century, yet, in the course of any single day, many people pick up more ideas "out of the air" than they do from the pages of a book or a magazine or newspaper.

Radio work is varied. The number of people who hand out ideas directly as news commentators and interpreters is comparatively small. But there are many other aspects of radio work.

There are the script writers who pen everything from detective dramas, adventure serials, human interest playlets, on-the-spot interviews, to the much-discussed soap operas. There are the playwrights who prepare the more pretentious radio drama shows. There are the staff writers who fill in the dialogue "breaks" between orchestral or vocal interludes on all-musical programs. There are the comedy scripters and "gag" men. There are the announcers and the newscasters who give routine reporting on the significant events of the day.

For you, the beginner, who wants to get into radio, the same preparation must be made as for the other writing fields. You must have or at least acquire a working knowledge of the craft. You may have to start out at the very bottom, perhaps as a receptionist in the offices of some broadcasting studio, or as a secretary or as a clerk, in order to learn your way around. If you have some writing background, however, there is always the possibility of getting into the field and of developing a new type of radio program, a new format, a different kind of ether character.

As with small-town newspapers or small publications, there is a better chance of starting out on some small radio station where conditions will not be so hectic as they too often are in the major broadcasting chains.

By surveying the field, following the market through radio trade publications, and developing your writing skill at every opportunity, you who make the world of words your career will acquire a fairly good working knowledge of where you can best fit into the broadcasting picture. You will also have the technical equipment to make good once you get your chance.

And speaking of getting your chance, just recently has been opened up a brand new phase of the entertainment business—*television.* It is still in its swaddling clothes, so to speak, and the people who are in it at the moment usually confess that they are only feeling their way around, learning all the "angles" just as they and their predecessors had to do when radio first became popular. If ever there was a field which, both literally and figuratively, provided a chance to "get in on the ground floor and grow with it," that field right now is television.

And when the people with good ideas do get in, another tremendous step forward will have been taken in shaping our society to the pattern of a better world.

An ever-closer relationship is developing between television and . . .

Motion Pictures and the Theater

Years ago when motion pictures were first made, the problem and the opportunities fairly closely paralleled those which confront the television industry today. But the film business has come a long way since the first nickelodeon had people whispering excitedly about the pictures that actually moved!

The motion picture industry today is a field of specialization, from script girl to film cutter to top-flight director. For an amateur writer to break in with a bang, to take the film capital by storm, is a rare exception. And, unless you have an agent, if you attempt to crash filmdom's gates by long distance via an unsolicited movie script, you will find that all the major studios return such manuscripts unopened for fear of lawsuits involving a charge of plagiarism.

Yet you can make a place for yourself in Hollywood if you are willing to start low and work up. To get any job in any field you have to be on the spot, you have to be *there* where people can personally evaluate your ability and potentiality before they hire you.

And, just as a person who wants to be a cook has to start to work in the kitchen, doing any one of a variety of lesser tasks, if you want to make motion pictures your field, you will have to get into the industry first and go on from there. With God's help, your own natural or developed talents will provide the impetus to further advancement.

If you were a fisherman you would have to cast your bait into the water to catch fish. If you want to break into motion pictures, you will have to put yourself in a position where your skill can eventually be recognized. Not every fisherman —or writer—will be successful; but if you don't make the attempt in the proper place, you'll never have even a chance of reaching your goal.

With an estimated 80,000,000 people paying to see motion pictures every week, the field is large enough for many with sufficient talent and an equal amount of perseverance. Add to this the growing number of concerns which produce low-cost movies for industrial and educational purposes and the scope of the field is widened to an even greater degree.

Certainly, if the field is large enough for subversives to set up a school in Hollywood itself—as they have done—and train, since 1943, some 10,000 men and women technically qualified for positions in the film world and other branches of communication, the field is big enough for you with good ideas to get in and make your presence felt.

You who have the "light" must become as keenly aware as those who spread "darkness" that the motion picture industry is a natural for spreading ideas, because it plays a greater role than any other agency in fashioning the morals of millions in this country and throughout the world.

There is no reason to have an exaggerated fear of competition from the big names in the motion picture writing craft. As a leading editor in the monthly field told us recently, "It is no longer true that people buy a certain magazine because of the 'big names' on the cover. That day is past."

And that day is past in Hollywood, also. If you feel movies offer the best scope for the exercise of your literary talents, by all means try them. Get a job, any kind of a job—stenographer, clerk, office assistant, studio policeman—in order to be where you can see enough to learn the ropes. Don't be too proud to start at the bottom. And while you are learning, keep writing and perfecting your skills. There is no better guarantee of success in any field.

The world of the *theater* is much more limited than the movies since the number of legitimate theaters in America does not even begin to compare with the number of motion picture houses. Yet, in other respects, the stage is a far more adaptable field for the Christopher.

Amateur and semiprofessional dramatic groups can be set up with limited funds. And such groups have been systematically developed by the doers of evil in the United States. They have not only served as a means of drawing young people into their orbit through providing an interesting and entertaining activity; they have also been used to present unpalatable ideas in a palatable way, to "pep up" meetings, to stimulate rallies, to peddle unpleasant notions wrapped in pleasant tunes and terms. These amateur groups have also become training grounds for young people who have graduated to semiprofessional and professional status in the theater.

Broadway and Main Street want good plays, good comedies, good musicals. There is no reason under the sun why you people with good ideas—you Christophers—can't provide them. The "vineyard" of popular demand is there. You can see to it that, instead of the "laborers" being the few, they will become the "many!"

HAVE A PURPOSE

So there you have it. If you want to be a writer, there are your opportunities. But if you want to be a writer of *substance,* you must be inspired by higher ideals than merely making a living. The writer whose only object is dollars, will turn out trite, lifeless material. While money is necessary, you will need a more dynamic motive if you are to survive the long, slow, often painful process which leads to success.

A far more vitalizing reward must inflame you with the ardor to keep on even in the face of difficult obstacles—the knowledge that you will be serving your fellowman. Like a doctor whose chief objective is to relieve suffering through the experience he has gained, the worth-while writer is eager to share with others the ideals which dominate his own life as well as to interest and entertain. As one great editor says:

"Writers come from persons who have a story to tell or who are imbued with a desire to cause others to think as they think."

If you have a purpose, therefore, you have strength.

Set your standards high; you will find deep satisfaction in work well done.

You will be thrilled to explore and master new techniques, and possibly to start new trends in the craft of writing. As a Christopher writer you can bring the basic principles of Christ into literature with the same zeal, the same skill, the same perseverance which His enemies use to exclude Him.

And because you are a Christopher, you can interpret human existence more faithfully.

You will have the satisfaction of knowing that the world is better because you have lived, have been useful, have played a part in "renewing the face of the earth." *A writer who has the lofty desire to serve the common good inevitably rises above that frustration characteristic of those whose purpose is only their own private good.*

Writing can become a labor of love, a living prayer, a work which will ennoble and sanctify both you and all who read what you have written. You will be more interested in "giving" than in "getting." You will think less of "taking out" of the world, than of "putting in." *Hope* will carry you high over the disappointments, the rejections, the heart-wrenching failures which even the finest writers must suffer at first. You will know the deep and lasting joy of creative work; and you will play a real part in bringing to your fellowmen some of the true, the good, and the beautiful that the Creator of all intended for all.

WRITING IS WORK

Good literature does not consist of 2,500 words dashed off in two hours. It takes time to write well. To become proficient in any art requires long practice.

But if you use the self-discipline which most successful writers find indispensable—that is, if you force yourself to write a certain minimum each day—you will make progress. (Incidentally, learn to type well. You'll find it a priceless asset.)

And just as important as writing is reading. A famous writer once said a good author reads six hours for every hour he writes. Read first-class literature, both the time-tested classics and the best work of modern authors. Read attentively, absorb the spirit and the tone of good writing, learn its structure and techniques.

Technical excellence ordinarily comes from practice. As Helen Magaret, novelist, biographer, and teacher, told us, "It has been my experience as a teacher that literary talent is not rare but common . . . we do not need more *skill;* what we need is more *will!*" And in the words of one of the editors of *The Reader's Digest,* "There are a lot of people in the world who can write but lack the courage to keep at it; there are a lot of people . . . who have the courage but can't write. When you have the two together, the ability to write and the courage to keep at it, nothing in this world can stop you from succeeding."

WRITE FOR EVERYBODY

Most beginners write to please themselves, not others. This can be a serious handicap. Try to key your stories to a mass audience, to the *many,* not merely the *few,* since the foundation of writers is actually twofold: (a) having something to say, and (b) having acquired through much practice the ability of saying what is to be said, to say it in a way that can be understood by most readers.

This can be done without compromising the content of your piece, for it is primarily a technique. The greatest exponent of the art of appealing to *all* was Christ Himself. He had the common touch. Normally, He spoke in words which all the people understood. Those who imitate Him in style as well as in content are well on the way to success. For example, many books have been written on Bernadette of Lourdes, but scarcely one had a circulation of more than a few thousand because all were "slanted" for five or ten percent of the faithful. Then a Jew, Franz Werfel, saw in Lourdes a tremendous story. He keyed his presentation to everyone, not just to a few. As a result, *The Song of Bernadette* has moved millions. And though Werfel had exceptional talents, at least in one respect you can equal him—that is, in writing for *everybody*.

DEEPEN YOUR SENSE OF VALUES

Contemporary literature is often unsubstantial, artificial, hard-boiled, and cold-blooded. It deals with petty people and petty problems. And it emerges as petty writing simply because too many writers, having neglected to develop their spiritual nature, are destitute of strong values.

To achieve magnitude in your stories, you must first deepen and strengthen your own sense of values. A writer must *be* something. A great heart and an understanding mind can be developed through daily reflection or meditation, prayer, intimacy with the New and Old Testaments (from which the greatest writers have drawn much of their inspiration).

Even fiction should communicate an idea, a philosophy. Although the author's purpose is not to teach but to tell a story, into that story he inevitably will put what he believes, what he is. He must see reality *whole,* instead of ignoring great fundamental actualities, instead of concentrating on the superficial and accidental. Among those misleading the world are writers who believe and affirm that life ends with death, that the flesh is to be served blindly, that one's own gratification is the highest law of life.

STRIVE TO INTEGRATE THE HUMAN WITH THE DIVINE

As a Christopher writer of fiction, you can do something few others are doing consistently today: not merely can you tell people how life should be lived—you can show what life really *is*. Like the manufacturer's book of specifications and directions found in the glove compartment of a new car, you can show the Creator's rules which are necessary for a whole and complete existence.

You must know the basic laws of human life before you can authentically depict character, the reaction of character to situation (source of dramatic conflict), and the enrichment or impoverishment of character wrought by dramatic conflict.

You must show through *action* how happiness or misery inexorably results from certain modes of action, how particular characters motivate specific kinds of action which change their lives and the lives of others for better or for worse. Truly realistic writing, in which the protagonists themselves push the action forward, is characteristic of great novels and stories. We associate this method with Thackeray and Dickens at their best, with Undset, Tolstoi, Dostoevski and others. It is in the best works of Grahame Greene and Richard Sullivan. Many of Willa Cather's novels are Christian, not only in outlook, but in characters, theme, and background. Even in such a nonreligious book as *A Lost Lady* is this Christian point of view evident.

Writing in *Life Magazine* some time ago, Evelyn Waugh nailed his own colors to the mast: "I believe you can only leave God out by making your characters pure abstractions. So in my future books there will be . . . a preoccupation with style and the attempt to represent man more fully, which, to me, means only one thing, man in his relation to God."

If you agree that writing should be deeply significant but still doubt whether editors will buy such work, listen to what one of the most eminent editors in the country has told us:

"What makes quality in a piece of writing? The thing that makes pieces of writing dry as dust is lack of faith. Whenever a thing with faith, written with talent, is printed the public will buy it. Excellence in writing comes from a reaffirmation of universal truth. The reason there is special hope for the

Christian writer is that he has faith, the element that is missing in other writers."

But, he warned, this does not mean you should simply write *about* religious subjects. "Many writers write about religious themes, but with merely the intellectual approach. They give the impression perhaps that these things do not really mean much to them. That kind of writing does not attract readership. You must write *with* faith, a spirit of faith, not merely *about* faith, and then your writing will be avidly read."

LEARN TO LIKE PEOPLE

The more you move among people, the more inspiration, warmth, and compassion will characterize whatever you write. You will be convinced of at least the potential dignity of every man, of a lingering nobility in even the so-called dregs of humanity. You will know that every man, no matter how mean or hateful, remembers real love and craves it from others.

If you have a consuming love for *all* men and not for just a *few,* if you are writing for *everyone* and not for just *some,* your writing will have warmth, friendliness, and humanness which will appeal to all. Each time you find yourself stretching to the measure of Christ's sympathy and affection for all, you, too, will glimpse God's image in every person you meet —and reveal that insight in the things you write.

FOLLOW THROUGH

Expect difficulties. Booth Tarkington wrote for years before attaining recognition. Jack London had to sandwich his writing in between income-earning hitches at sea. Many a contemporary "big-time" novelist or Hollywood writer began by slaving at half a cent a word for the pulps. The few writers who have hit big success on the first try are the exceptions.

A doctor doesn't attain skill and reputation in a year or two. He must go through college, medical school, and internship. Avoid extremes of optimism or pessimism. Most beginners make the mistake either of underestimating their own buried talent or of expecting to write a best-seller or Hollywood smash hit the first crack out of the box.

Finally, perhaps you are not an exceptional writer. You may never be at the top of the list. But if you can write at all, you can be one of those *five million* American newspaper, book, magazine, radio, television, and movie rank and file writers who, besides earning fair incomes, influence the thoughts of others.

If you can't take up writing on a full-time basis, write as a sideline. Many housewives are selling successful articles and books. If you know how to take care of a home, why not share your experience with others through the home and family magazines? No matter what your work, you may be able to turn out something the public is hungry for. This would be doing your part in bringing Christian principles and ideals into the market-place. And it would mean a little extra income, too.

Profit by rejections; they show the detours to be avoided. *But* don't take them too seriously. Editor A may reject a manuscript which Editor B snaps up with enthusiasm. And always—always—keep writing.

Remember—quitters never win. Winners never quit!

Writers should cherish that motto. Christopher writers should make it their special slogan in carrying Christ's truth not to just a *few,* but to *all* men!

VIII

THE LIBRARY

Arsenal of Ideas

In the United States today, approximately 12,000 librarians are needed to provide the proper library service to which the American people, young and old, are entitled. According to the American Library Association, 70,000,000 of our citizens are now either partially served or are not served at all.

Looking into the future, it has been estimated that in the next six years 18,000 more professional librarians and about 50,000 clerical assistants will be required to fill posts in public libraries throughout the country, to staff the libraries of colleges and universities, and to administer the special libraries which serve business and industrial concerns, government agencies, professional groups, and institutions. But most of all, they will be needed to run the libraries in the 28,000 secondary and 225,000 elementary schools which train millions of impressionable young Americans, the youth of today who will be the adult citizens of tomorrow.

The power of the librarian to assist in this task should not be underestimated. Contrary to the belief of many, a library is no mere storehouse of printed volumes. It is an arsenal of ideas. It is, in fact, the very battleground where truth and falsehood struggle fiercely for possession of the human mind. Again, contrary to popular belief, the librarian doesn't escape from life; he or she helps to mold it for good or for evil. Any incompetence can serve as well as ill will in stunting the minds and warping the souls of those who come to the library to be remade. An otherwise good book in wrong hands, a bad book in any hands, may do tremendous damage.

PRINCIPAL FUNCTIONS OF A LIBRARY

The varied functions of an average library make equally varied demands on the intelligence and training of its personnel.

(1) For example, selecting and ordering books and other material is within the province of the *order department.* From any standpoint, the success or failure of any library depends upon the proper selection of the printed matter which goes on its shelves. The standards of any library will be the standards of those men and women who compose the order department. Since most libraries usually operate on small budgets, the book selectors are in a position of particular power for good or evil. All too often an individual can use his or her position in this section to purchase books that will do untold harm and refuse to purchase books with sound values, giving as reason for such refusal the excuse, "no funds."

We have been informed that in one of the leading universities of our country, which has in its possession millions of bound volumes, there exists an occasional discrimination against sound religious books and those which contain reference to the basic principles upon which America is founded. Atheists and agnostics are able to keep from the shelves books of genuine value simply by disapproving their purchase on financial grounds.

On the other hand, however, a person with a Christopher purpose, who is qualified to work in this field and in this department, can do much to change, for the better, the selection of reading material for the general public. As one West Coast librarian writes: "The head librarian here is a fine-living man and quite prominent in civic affairs. Whenever I hear of books with good Christian principles, I put in an order for them—and most of the time the library buys them."

It might be well to point out, in this connection, that libraries make it a practice to order books which seem to be in demand—a fact of which many library users are not aware. If your library does not have a copy of a particular good book, you and your friends, with a Christopher purpose, can bring friendly pressure to bear upon the order department simply by putting in a "reserve" for it.

(2) Those who *catalogue* books perform the second function of the library, that of organizing and interpreting collections after they have been purchased, so that the readers may benefit by the fact of having a wide variety of volumes accessible. The Christopher cataloguer has opportunities every day to highlight the more worth-while material by simple technical devices.

(3) The third function of the library is to *advise* readers. Reference librarians, who help people to locate information, have it in their power to assist in the building of a better world, or to help in the destruction of the liberty and free, God-given rights we now possess. By person-to-person contact with readers these librarians can shape the thinking of thousands, since people frequently recommend to their friends the books which they have been advised to read.

(4) The *circulating librarian* performs the fourth function of this arsenal of ideas and has tremendous power for evil or for good. One young man still remembers that when he was in his teens such a person advised against his selecting a certain book on psychology. Had he read that book, he admits today, much of his outlook on life might have been distorted. Circulating librarians are continually asked about reading material, "Is this good?" With a Christopher motive, they can easily discourage an individual from selecting a worthless volume simply by replying, "I read it and I don't think there's very much in it." This approach is far more effective than a condemnation because, for some curious reason, many people seem to want to read books about which others are outspoken in their criticism.

In this connection, some libraries have even organized special departments to prepare special courses of reading for people such as outlines of study, programs for study clubs, group projects, and so on.

(5) The fifth function of the library is to extend its operations through branches, traveling libraries, and like facilities, especially in rural areas.

ADDITIONAL FUNCTIONS OF A LIBRARY

Included under the general listing of all these functions there are several additional phases of this increasingly important field which should be mentioned briefly.

First, librarians in adult education, including readers' advisers, community workers, and group leaders, perform a much needed service, since they are in close contact with the millions of adults who turn to the libraries for *special* services. (The greatest demand for these services today exists in the fields of science, technology, and social studies.) A leader in an adult education discussion group has perhaps the best chance of all to further the Christopher idea. Such a group usually meets to read and discuss outstanding books of every age and in a wide variety of subjects. An able leader can point out what is truth and what is error and, somewhere along in the schedule, will find an opportunity to show the necessity for a belief in God and in religion.

Second, *institutional libraries,* specifically prison and hospital libraries, offer rich fields of endeavor for the Christopher. Here the librarian must see to it that the physical institutional routine does not create institutionalized minds. He or she corrects and eliminates dangerous mental attitudes, and creates good ones, by judicious prescription of books. The prisoner must be made a law-abiding and useful citizen again; the hospital patient must forget fears and anxieties for the sake of the cure and regain self-reliance during recuperation. The librarian with sound principles is not only vitally important to these processes, but is strategically placed to direct the thoughts of many who, with the preoccupations of daily private life interrupted, have just begun really to think for the first time. Since World War II, the number of these positions has increased greatly.

Third, there are splendid opportunities open at the moment for *army librarians.* Many calls for candidates have frequently gone unfilled. With a Christopher purpose, such librarians could do a magnificent job of spreading *truth* by proper selection and featuring of reading material at military posts scattered all over the world. Many librarians during the war were particularly good on personal advice and counsel, and made it a point to keep on hand appropriate books to fill the needs not ordinarily met by the regular collections of volumes allotted to them.

Public relations (which actually is library advertising) offers additional chances for work with a Christopher motive. The library has a good collection of books for children, for example. It may have a special display on sources of spiritual help in the face of the atomic threat. It may even sponsor a lecture on religion in twentieth-century literature. If the public relations officer is Christopher-minded, he or she can so present this material that the spiritual concept is faithfully and convincingly brought to the attention of the reading public.

Finally, because of the recent development of such new resources as motion picture films, microfilm, visual aids, sound recordings, music scores, maps, and pamphlets, there is an expanding field for those who wish to work in these new media.

QUALIFICATIONS FOR LIBRARIANS

For those who may want to enter this field as *general* librarians and whose duties will be very broad—selection and ordering of books, cataloguing, reader guidance, adult education, etc.—the following itemized qualifications will give some index as to the type of men and women needed:

> Interest in *books* and in *people;* business and administrative ability; pleasing personality; courteous and responsive manner; keen intelligence; quickness of perception; accuracy; tolerance; adaptability; resourcefulness; good judgment; persistence; common sense; neatness.

> As regards educational background, there are required:

> Four years of college and one year of library school; emphasis while in college upon physical or social sciences, history, American and English literature, a working knowledge of French, Spanish, or German.

The qualifications for *children's librarians* vary somewhat from those for general librarians. To summarize them briefly, however, they should include:

A liking for children and young people; respect for their ideas and interests; a belief that good books should be a vital part of their lives; adaptable personality; good health.

Further, they should include:

A knowledge of children's books and an ability to evaluate and select new volumes; a reasonable degree of proficiency in public speaking, to include story telling, oral reviewing, radio talks, and instruction in the use of library facilities.

Concerning education, it is necessary to have:

Four years of college, plus one year in an accredited library school; wide experience in reading children's literature.

The average number of hours worked weekly in most libraries is between thirty-six and forty-four. Annual vacations of three to four weeks are customary. In university libraries, vacations are usually one month; in school libraries, two or three months.

There are other professions with higher incomes, but for the alert and able worker progress is comparatively rapid. The great shortage of librarians has resulted in sharp salary increases. Capable young persons have risen to responsible administrative posts within five to ten years. Even so, those who wish to become guardians of these arsenals of ideas and who expect to be heavily repaid financially will stand to be disappointed.

Those with a Christopher purpose, however, who wish to become librarians and are willing to make sacrifices—and sacrifices some must make, if this important sphere of influence is to fulfill its democratic function—will find that there are tremendous opportunities to do much good. To their credit, many have already realized this and done something about it. One man, who received his master's degree in library science, recently took a job at the bottom of the ladder in the library field just to be able to become a part of this sphere of ideas. His is a deeply spiritual motivation and he fully expects to have to spend eight or ten years in varying posts, until he can reach a more responsible position where his influence for good may be felt in an ever-widening circle of library users. In the meantime, he has written a number of articles on various phases of his chosen field for the purpose of interesting others with sound ideas to become librarians. At every opportunity he points out the danger of allowing those with "erratic" tendencies to take positions which can just as easily be filled by those with a deep sense of truly American principles.

Not all who want to enter the library field, of course, possess the requisite academic training to qualify as full-fledged librarians. Still, they can serve a most useful purpose as subprofessionals and clerical assistants, performing a variety of library tasks, in which their influence for good can be felt by those in more responsible positions.

A HIGH VOCATION

The librarian has a high vocation. With a new age coming to birth, it would be unfortunate indeed to close one's ears if a call to that life should come. To one imbued with the Christopher idea this applies especially. Such a person should experience the added realization that being a servant of the people, in the capacity of librarian, does not call for a person to be prejudiced or obscurantist. He or she should be mainly concerned that those who employ his or her services receive the sound nourishment and wholesome refreshment they seek in books, and that, *before* taking what is unwholesome, they should at least be made to recognize the specious poisons which often lurk on library shelves.

To fail in this task is little different from putting deadly drugs in a medicine cabinet within the reach of a child. A pharmacist would know how to use chemicals, however deadly. What is more, he would have the right to use them. A child would not, and his parents would certainly have no right to place them within reach of his inquisitive hands. In one of the largest mental hospitals in the United States something very much along these lines recently took place. A doctor—a subversive—got on the medical staff, and one of the first things he tried to do was to order questionable books for the hospital library. He demanded that they be bought at once. When told he would have to take the matter up with the hospital board, he promptly set to work to bring as much pressure as possible to bear on the authorities by encouraging others of his twisted mental persuasion to apply for positions on the hospital staff.

On the other hand, and on a brighter note, in one of the leading Eastern cities the chief of the children's and young people's section of one of the metropolitan libraries has always made a point of personally and individually selecting each and every book which goes into the children's and young people's collection of some twelve thousand volumes.

She makes sure every single book is unobjectionable and uses great discretion in permitting any sort of questionable book to get into the hands of young people. For example, certain art books are kept on a shelf for reserved books behind her desk. If any student wants to see one of these books, she questions him or her and ascertains if the intention to use the volume is a legitimate one. Only if and when she is convinced that the latter is the case, will she let the boy or girl have the material requested.

Of this woman can be said what one parent wrote about a certain other librarian in her own community.

"I have always been impressed," the letter read, "with the

fact that Miss —— is not merely a 'custodian of books,' as many librarians are, but a person who makes the students and the teachers alike aware that books, like food, have to be used wisely."

THE LIBRARIAN'S STOCK IN TRADE

God's influence in every human being is nourished on truth, and truth is the librarian's stock in trade.

The *true* librarian is the scholar's ready reference, the teacher's right hand, the bosom friend of youth, the staff for troubled parents, the guide to well-spent leisure, a beacon of truth in a twilit, stormy world.

When he or she is the opposite of these things, he or she represents an active menace to everything for which our civilization stands. For example, in Washington, D. C. there are no less than *three hundred* libraries, a fact the godless have been well aware offers a fertile field for their activities. Since the members of Congress and other branches of government frequently have recourse to these libraries in preparing legislation or furnishing data on a variety of subjects for Congressional consideration, it is not hard to imagine the harm that can be done by those who purposely provide "slanted" reference material to an unsuspecting applicant.

The risk to readers is acute, also, when many of those who pass for librarians are semi-literate but quite uneducated, tolerant but not informed. It can be a case of the blind leading the blind. One cannot safely traffic in ideas without first having a firm grasp of their history and without making a sincere effort to see them in their true light. Even facts must be fitted into a background. Nor are they always equipped to distinguish fact from fancy, when both come couched in the same terminology. As for tolerance, that cardinal virtue of undisciplined minds, one cannot be tolerant of falsehood and likewise tolerant of truth, for *to tolerate* means *to put up with* something one may not like. No public servant, especially no sound-thinking librarian, has a right to put up with untruth—or to dislike truth.

You who have the Christopher idea firmly implanted in your minds and hearts should not be content that young Americans sometimes find it difficult to discover the truth they seek in our libraries. Instead, you should be concerned that our rich heritage of scholarship and genuine literature is often being overlooked in favor of much that is pagan and materialistic. If sanity is to emerge once more and soon, more librarians are needed who have a real, God-fearing grasp of the intellectual content of our civilization, who have some realization of the importance of preserving it in living minds.

In America, the vast majority of our citizens read books. You, who cherish truth and reverence human dignity, ought to be intent that they do more with books than waste their time, becloud their imagination, and confuse their minds.

And, if charity be more than a meaningless word, you should dedicate yourselves to this task—even if it involves some measure of sacrifice.

There is a nobler service to humanity than the saving of human lives, great as this latter task is. It is the preservation and increase of God's own life in the lives of all mankind. If you believe this, if you wish to live sanely in the world that can yet be changed and brought back to Christ, then you should earnestly and sincerely try to encourage at least one other person to enter the library field with a Christopher purpose if you yourself cannot make it your lifetime career.

IX

SOCIAL SERVICE

Man's Welfare Here as Well as Hereafter

A STUDY WAS MADE in 1942 of social, industrial, and economic conditions in Syracuse, New York, considered to be an average, fairly well-to-do American community. According to the survey, nearly everyone in the city had a job at that time, with the total weekly payrolls amounting to some $900,000. Despite this prosperity, however, during the course of the investigation it was discovered that seventy percent of the families in Syracuse received services from social service agencies.

Of the 60,000 family groups living there, seven out of every ten used an average of two units of social service apiece out of the city's 114 welfare, health and recreation agencies. This figure, furthermore, does not include persons admitted to hospitals, the beneficiaries of social insurance programs, the users of public playgrounds, nor the services rendered by agencies which failed to report. The final cost of all services combined was approximately $9,000,000 a year, or about ten weeks of payroll income.

This one instance alone gives some idea of the extensive scope of social work, a field which seeks to meet four general problems—economic need, health, behavior, and the use of leisure time—through the use of scientific knowledge and methods. It gives, too, some idea of the frequency with which the general public calls on social service agencies for assistance and counsel.

The pressing problems of the present with regard to this field are twofold. One concerns the lack of sufficient trained, sound-thinking men and women to handle the increasing volume of social service work. The second is concerned with the materialistic approach used by many officials and social case workers in their conduct of social service affairs. It is an approach that considers each person, not as an individual created by God, but as an animal whose instincts are little different from the Marxist idea of a human beast of burden in a collectivist State, or (as Hitler put it) a potential "beast of prey."

By no means are all social welfare personnel subversives. Many of them are urging needed reforms in business, government, social relations. But no matter how good their suggested reform programs may be, the fact that they omit any reference to the Creator, to any secure basis for human rights, makes their program dangerous. It eventually heads them for the collapse that dooms all materialistic endeavors. The Christopher, on the other hand, who has that clear-cut concept of the Origin of all human rights, who has a firm belief in the sacred worth of every human being, could do much in this field to ensure more lasting blessings to many here, and over the world, who are finding the battle of life ever more difficult.

Without that emphasis, without that clear-cut concept, the best of social reforms programs becomes but another potent weapon in the hands of those who would wreck our country, instead of a means by which we can build a better world. T. S. Eliot put this thought quite clearly: "This is the last and greatest treason," he wrote, "to do the right deed for the wrong reason."

DIVISIONS OF SOCIAL SERVICE WORK

In the United States today there are 72 national and 576 state governmental organizations whose functions are within, or closely allied to, the field of social work. In addition, there are 442 national and international and 59 state voluntary organizations dealing with social and welfare work. In this country there are 100,000 social workers, classified under 108 different titles.

Generally speaking, social service agencies are divided into governmental services (federal, state, and local) paid for by taxes, and private or voluntary services supported by contributions, bequests, or part-payment fees. The private agencies exist, of course, because communities find a need and try to meet it. The public agencies exist by virtue of an unquestionable moral truth: *"The duty of rulers is to protect the community and its various elements; in protecting the rights of individuals they must have special regard for the infirm and needy. If, however, private resources do not suffice . . . it is the duty of the public authority to supply for the insufficient resources of personal effort. . . . Hence, in making laws and in disposing of public funds they must do their utmost to relieve the penury of the needy, considering such as one of the most important of their administrative duties."* (Pope Pius XI)

In the *Social Work Yearbook, 1947*, put out by the Russell Sage Foundation, there are listed eighty different divisions of social service work. To give but a few, there are:

> Administration of social agencies, adoption, adult education, adult offenders, the aged, aliens and foreign born, the blind, boys' and girls' work organizations, Catholic social work, child labor and youth employment, community chests, crippled children, day care of children, disaster relief, education for social work, employment services, and and so on.

As is obvious from this partial listing, social services deal with a much wider range of problems than just those of poverty and need. For example, there is the enormously important field of crime prevention and juvenile delinquency. Among the federal agencies dealing with this problem are the Children's Bureau, the Department of Labor, the Federal Security Agency, the U.S. Office of Education, the U.S. Probation System, the Bureau of Public Assistance, and the Social Security Board. State agencies include youth commissions and public welfare departments. Other groups in this field are the churches, the Boy and Girl Scouts, the Junior Red Cross, the 4-H Clubs, the Congress of Parents and Teachers, the General Federation of Women's Clubs, labor auxiliaries, women's church councils, and various other Protestant, Jewish, and Catholic organizations.

THE NATURE OF SOCIAL SERVICE WORK—AND ITS DANGERS

Activity in this field today is largely of two kinds: social *group* work and social *case* work.

Social *group* work involves such spheres as:
Americanization; community organization; club activities;

neighborhood work; recreation; civic activity; housing; legislation; publicity; public health.

Social *case* work is concerned with such fields as:

Child welfare; family welfare; medical social service; probation, parole, and protective care; psychiatric social work; school visiting, school attendance; social investigation.

Those who have made a study of prevailing theories and practices in this field state that social case work is primarily a matter of personality analysis, utilizing an approach based on ideas and techniques which, on the whole, are materialistic and pagan. Social workers learn a great deal of their required knowledge of sociology, economics, government, psychology, and other social studies from many godless-minded professors and their viewpoint is shaped accordingly. These professors doubt or deny the existence of a Supreme Being, the essential worth of the individual human soul and the freedom of the will. And much of the teaching of these men logically leads to the acceptance of the totalitarian state, even though they themselves may not carry their theorizing to its final conclusion.

For many of them, the only source of human rights is society itself. What society gives, it can take away. And since the organ through which society enforces its customs is, in their view, the State, then the State can take away any and every right we now enjoy. To paraphrase the words of one of the founders of American sociology, custom is king and custom finds its way into law. If, for instance, society adopted the custom of putting aged people to death, then—in the opinion of these men—this custom would be perfectly acceptable. All right and wrong, in their view, is relative to the society in which people live.

The danger to our Christian civilization inherent in such

a philosophy is becoming more and more apparent to sound-thinking Americans the country over. As one distinguished professional man, Dr. F. L. Feierabend, writing in the *Journal of the American Medical Association,* pointed out so clearly:

> "Physicians must reject the teaching of the materialist sociologists and return to the teachings of the moral law. They must reject completely the doctrine of the materialist, which teaches that religion, and morality, is the opium of the people and that man is motivated entirely by instinct. Doctors must avoid this materialistic doctrine or by their acts they will be promoting regimentation. Neglect of social responsibility invites the State to take over with coercion and regimentation."

Emphasizing the seriousness of Dr. Feierabend's warning, it may surprise many to learn that a great number of states have sterilization laws (at present there are thirty-one sterilization statutes with sixteen of them obligatory, that is, they do not require the consent of patients, parents, or guardians).

Social workers cannot avoid involvement in problems created by these laws, when, for example, they place a client in an institution for the feeble-minded when there is a state law or an institutional policy providing for sterilization of patients before discharge.

Social workers often handle cases in which the doctor has advised therapeutic abortion, sterilization, or artificial birth control. Highly complex divorce cases requiring sound moral judgment, proper placing of children, and so on, also come within the scope of social case work.

Since the social worker comes into close person-to-person contact with clients, his or her ideas on these subjects will inevitably pass over to their minds, much as what is in a teacher's head is transmitted to the students in the classroom.

This is especially true when it is recognized that the client frequently relies on the case worker for advice and a sympathetic, favorable handling of his or her problems.

When the case worker's ideas are warped or colored with a godless philosophy, then the client receives distorted impressions which he or she frequently is in no position to judge as to their inaccuracies. Often such a person has no defense against a case worker's continual emphasis that man is but a creature of passion, has no free will, is dominated by unconscious impulses of a lustful nature, and so on. From this pagan concept, it is but a step to the acceptance of the notion that man is but an economic animal and that whatever rights he has come from the State.

This acceptance is further hastened when it is remembered that the people with whom the social worker comes in contact are often emotionally unsettled because they are improperly housed, inadequately fed or clothed, without proper medical care and advice, and lacking any real economic security.

For the Christopher entering this field, convinced as he is of his own essential dignity and of the intrinsic worth of those whom his profession serves, his is the vocation of putting an individual back on his or her own feet and giving that person the opportunity of better working out his or her eternal destiny.

One social worker (a woman, by the way) with Christopher purpose and possessed of great gifts of mind and heart, started at the bottom in the field and because of her ability, devotion, and hard work over a long period of years, has risen to a high-level position in federal government. There she has a direct, almost daily, effect upon the lives and security of nearly every one of our people. Finding that the trend of thought in this particular social service agency was toward the forgetfulness of sound Christian values, this

Christopher almost single-handed has changed the policies and the thinking of the agency personnel by emphasizing the sacredness of the home and family, justice in administration, and genuine charity for the poor and needy. She does this in the spirit of Christ: "Amen, I say to you, as long as you did it to one of these My least brethren, you did it to Me." (*Matt.* 25:40)

EDUCATION AND PERSONALITY REQUIREMENTS FOR WORKERS IN THE SOCIAL SERVICE FIELD

Generally speaking, to be accepted for social service work, a man or woman must have:

A master's degree from a recognized school of social service. With current shortages in social service personnel, however, some persons with only one year's work in such a school are being employed at present, but, in the majority of cases, there will be no promotions available without a master's degree. Undergraduate preparation should emphasize such things as biology, psychology, sociology, and economics. Then, too, such subjects as political science, history, and English should not be neglected. A well-balanced, rather than specialized, undergraduate preparation is considered by most leading authorities to be the best means of entering a field which employs social workers in bad times as well as good.

As for *personality requirements,* the prospective social service worker must:

Like people and want to work *with* and *for* them; must possess intelligence, courage, and optimism (the latter tempered by a firm grasp of reality).

WHERE SOCIAL WORKERS ARE MOST NEEDED

The particular fields of social service most in need of trained, sound-thinking men and women are those of:

Public welfare
Parole—state, federal, municipal
Probation—adult and juvenile—also state, federal, municipal
Board of education attendance officers—these are not merely truant officers but investigators of home conditions as well.
Child guidance
Recreation
Boy and Girl Scouts
Girl Guides
Psychiatric social work

Men are especially needed to fill responsible positions in such branches of social work as:

Parole
Probation
Social service instruction, i.e., professors competent to teach courses in this subject, with particular stress on adult and juvenile delinquency.

Penology and prison administration
Criminology—as scholars in the field of the scientific study of crime, its causes, conditions, symptoms, and possible cures. Men in this field must have a practical background in parole or probation work.

THE CAUSE OF MOST SOCIAL ILLS

All that we have so far written about the social service field has dealt with *effects* rather than *causes.*

The root of most of our social ills today—economic insecurity, inadequate housing, insufficient wages for the present high cost of living—is not so much material as spiritual: the eager pursuit of worldly goods, the desire for possessions, the ambition for more power, the striving for outward success. A sociologist who works for social reform, while neglecting this widespread disease of the soul, is only treating the symptoms: he is not getting at their causes and may even be aggravating the malady.

If people today lack many things they need, this is not basically to be charged to any "system," but to the avarice in the souls of so many others, to the fact that too many think in terms of the good of the *few,* rather than of *all.* Whatever they call themselves, such people are materialist in their thinking. And it is this very greed for material things which lies at the root of current social ills. There is no doubt that social reform is needed: but even more, and as an indispensable foundation, there is need for a return to fundamental principles.

Strangely enough, the one thing so many who earnestly desire to help humanity forget is man himself. They forget he is something more than an animal to be fed, housed, clothed, and amused. They forget he is a person with spiritual needs which far surpass in importance any of his material wants, important as those things are.

The very concept of social service for all men regardless of race, color, or creed owes its origin to Christ. It is the privilege and task of the Christopher to restore that concept since he knows there is as little chance of most of the beneficial effects of social service work continuing without it as there is of keeping a house warm after the fire has died out in the furnace. For a time the house still feels warm. But this is because of the left-over heat that was generated while the fire was burning. When that lingering warmth vanishes and the furnace is cold, then suffering is bound to follow until the source of the heat is once again rekindled.

In the same way social service work will defeat the very purpose it aims to achieve as it rejects more and more the only Source Which has ever had complete and practical "compassion on the multitude."

It is nothing short of tragic to continue to allow the management and staffing of the social service field to slip into the hands of those enemies of Christ who would use it as a stepping-stone to the enslavement of the very ones they temporarily help.

There is an extraordinary opportunity for the Christopher to recapture and restore the divine inspiration which is the very foundation of social work. He should lead the way as a champion of the one great essential for social work: that God in heaven is solicitous about even the least of His children.

One of the most powerful reminders for the Christopher of this earnest concern of God for man's welfare in this life is contained in the unusual answer Christ gave to the messengers of John the Baptist who were sent to find out whether or not He was the true Messiah. "Go and relate to John what you have heard and seen," Christ declared, almost abruptly. "The blind see, the lame walk, the lepers are cleansed, the deaf hear, the dead rise again, the poor have the gospel preached to them." (*Matt.* 11:4, 5)

As you will notice, only the last point of the six mentioned in Christ's statement dealt with the strictly spiritual: "The poor have the gospel preached to them." But even in that there was a reproach to those who should know better than to neglect to pass on to the poor of the world the Truth intended for *all* men.

The other five points Christ mentioned concern the *physical* sufferings of mankind. What a strange, yet wonderful, proof to give of His Divinity! He could have given a hundred other testimonies instead of choosing this one. He didn't refer to Himself directly. He spoke only of the effects on others of the flow of God's Love in heaven through Him to afflicted man on earth.

If God is so solicitous for humanity in their afflictions, what a stimulating inspiration it should be for anyone and everyone in the social service field to strive to be Christ-bearers from God to troubled mankind—to be the human instruments through which the divine compassion is channeled to their fellowmen who need and want it so much.

THE RARE PRIVILEGE

The zealous social worker with a Christopher purpose, who has the opportunity of seeing how the "other half" of the world lives, has the rare privilege of sincerely trying to help those in need while still seeing that human dignity is not sacrificed in the bargain. As that great humanitarian, Jacob Riis, so well put it:

"The social worker sees destitution and disgrace, depravity and degeneracy, but also he sees courage exhibited by those of the 'underprivileged' group in the face of seemingly insurmountable obstacles. He sees faith, hope, and charity expressed in the daily lives of those in whom economic, educational, cultural, and social background is woefully lacking. He has the privilege of seeing personalities, cramped and hidden by barriers that sometimes are not of their own making, trying to reassert themselves. His may be the privilege of helping that personality to a better understanding of its own possibilities and to the attainment of its 'summum bonum' (highest good).

"The social worker is not content to 'sit in his house by the side of the road, while the rest of men go by,' but rather he is in the midst of the maelstrom of life, trying to understand the viewpoint and the troubles of others so that he can better help himself and his fellowmen to a fuller life, a realization of the Master's formula 'to have life and to have it more abundantly'."

The social worker who is fired by the Christopher purpose, who is concerned with man's welfare here as well as hereafter, can help bring to suffering humanity the world over a little of that peace and comfort which the Creator of *all* meant to be the lot of *all* mankind.

X

PERSONAL POWER AND SOCIAL RESPONSIBILITY

A FEW MONTHS AGO while hurrying to keep an appointment in New York, I noticed, vaguely at first and then more consciously, that a small crowd had gathered in front of a shop on Park Avenue near 54th Street. Curiosity prompted me to stop and see what had caused such a show of interest. Peering over the heads of the crowd I saw attractively framed and exhibited in large, bold-faced type, of all things, *a prayer*—a prayer that was all of 700 years old! Its author? St. Francis of Assisi.

Pleasantly surprised at the setting, I read through those exquisite lines that flowed like some long-forgotten litany:

Lord, make me an instrument of Thy Peace!
Where there is hatred . . . let me sow love
Where there is injury . . . pardon
Where there is doubt . . . faith

Where there is despair . . . hope
Where there is sadness . . . joy!
O Divine Master, grant that I may not so much seek
To be consoled . . . as to console
To be understood . . . as to understand
To be loved . . . as to love, for
It is in giving . . . that we receive
It is in pardoning . . . that we are pardoned
It is in dying . . . that we are born to eternal life.

Why those lines were put into that shop window, I never found out. Yet, because of the setting, the words seemed to radiate a special warmth and meaning. That simple prayer written by the Little Man of Assisi, sums up freshly and perfectly the great need of our day: that each of us acknowledge his individual power as an "instrument" of peace; that each of us show individual initiative and assume personal responsibility in restoring to the world the love and the peace of Christ.

No matter who you are or what you are or where you may be—you can do something to change the world for the better. You are important. You count!

One of the most poignant yet dramatic illustrations of that belief in action is contained in the story of Ah Chai, an eight-year-old leper girl in South China. Hungry, alone, and wasted away with the disease which gnawed at her young flesh and bones, Ah Chai's life reached its supreme tragedy, so she thought, one hot summer's day when she was driven out of the village that had been her home by the villagers who hoped thereby to rid themselves of her pollution. So heartless and cruel was the fury of the mob which, armed with sticks and stones, shoved and pummeled her, that leprosy seemed fated to be cheated of its victory.

And then it happened.

A missioner approaching the village from the opposite direction saw the commotion and quickened his pace until it became a trot and then his trot a run. Into the center of the crowd he went. A glance told him the child's condition, yet he didn't stop. Bending down, he picked up Ah Chai in his arms while the crowd fell back shouting in warning, "Unclean . . . unclean!"

Cradled in the missioner's arm, the child stopped crying, but only for a moment. Then the torrent of tears began anew, yet this time they were tears of happiness, tears of gratitude that someone cared.

"Why . . . why do you bother about me?" she asked between sobs. The priest swallowed hard and answered:

"Because God made you and made me." And he continued, "That makes you my sister and makes me your brother. I'm going to take care of you. You'll never be hungry or homeless again."

"But how can I pay . . . ?" Ah Chai started to ask, but the missioner smilingly shook his head for silence.

"All you have to do—all God wants you to do—is to return His love by showing that love to as many others as you can. Promise?"

A nod of a tear-streaked face was the eloquent reply.

That was when Ah Chai was eight. She died three years later, not long after her eleventh birthday. But in those three years she did much to bring the love of God and His Peace into the lives of all the other lepers with whom she had to live and who were given to the missioners' care. She sang to them, she dressed their sores, she fed them, but most of all, *she loved them.*

When she died, they expressed their gratitude, and thousands of other Chinese from the surrounding countryside echoed their feelings in these simple words: "Our little bit of Heaven has gone back to Heaven." And they would point upwards.

EVEN THE "LEAST" CAN AFFECT THOUSANDS

If Ah Chai's story ended there, it would be inspiring enough. But it didn't. She is still doing good. Her life and what she did has been spoken about, told and retold, in countries all over the globe. Hearing it, people are deeply touched, yet the effect on them is invariably more than that. It gives them courage and hope. Once she realized her divine worth, this "least" of God's children was important, after all. She did count on earth . . . for eternity.

And just as she thought with the vision of Christ, in terms of herself and of the world, so you can do likewise and your power for good becomes more effective and far-reaching. Once a person gains even a partial comprehension of the rôle he or she can play, personally and individually, everything takes on a new and hopeful aspect. The account of the three laborers who were working on a cathedral illustrates this.

The first man was a colorless-looking individual. When asked to define his job, his bored reply was that he spent all his time in cutting blocks of stone. And he added, "If I didn't have to earn a living for myself and family, I'd quit in a minute!"

The second man's job was to cut the timber that went into the building's construction. He, too, went about his work in a listless way, and in his continual complaining there was proof aplenty that his heart was not in his work.

The third laborer possessed none of the manual skill of the other two. He merely carried the stone and wood the others prepared. But he sang and whistled as he trudged back and forth with his heavy loads. To all appearances his work was the least attractive, the most monotonous and uninspiring, yet he went about it with zest and spirit. None of his fellow workers could understand it; and one day a newcomer who didn't know him very well asked him, point blank, the reason for his good humor. "What kind of work do you do?" was the way he put it. "What is your job?"

The cheerful laborer's reply was short and simple, yet it stressed the true perspective of all his toil. "What do I do?" he repeated. "Why, I'm building a cathedral!"

In a very real sense he *was* building a cathedral. While his rôle in the whole project was menial and insignificant, still he was a vital factor just the same. The structure couldn't rise without him—or someone like him. And because he had a big perspective, that perspective gave a big meaning to his little job.

In the same way, no matter how insignificant you may be or feel, you can still do something to change the world for the better. For those who try to be other Christs, there comes an understanding, experienced perhaps for the first time, of that real zest of living that God intended for all who are intent on using the talents entrusted to them for His glory and the good of others. Even if they possess only one talent, they do not bury it like the servant in the Scriptures who told his master, "And being afraid I went and hid thy talent in the earth: behold here thou hast that which is thine." That man received the stinging and justified rebuke, "Wicked and slothful servant," (*Matt.* 25:25, 26) for his failure to put that talent to good effect. Ordering his other servants to take away that which had been freely entrusted to him, the master then concluded, "For to every one that hath shall be given, and he shall abound: but from him that hath not, that also which he seemeth to have shall be taken away." (*Matt.* 25:29)

For those with the ambition really to do good, ringing constantly in their ears is the challenge of urgency so well expressed in the words: *"I shall pass through this world but once. Any good, therefore, that I can do, or any kindness that I can show to any fellow creature, let me do it now. Let me not defer it or neglect it, for I shall not pass this way again."*

Not for a moment should a Christopher forget he has his own destiny to work out here and hereafter. Yet neither should he ever lose sight of the fact that he has a like obligation toward others. There is specific definiteness on this point in the command of Christ. While He said, "Thou shalt love thy neighbor," He was very careful to give the measure of how much that love should be. "As thyself," He said. There is no contesting that.

One of Christ's own apostles, St. James, seems to be even more emphatic on this point. "Religion clean and undefiled before God and the Father," he says, "is this: to visit the fatherless and widows in their tribulation, and to keep one's self unspotted from this world." (*James* 1, 27) Note the emphasis he put on solicitude for others. Even if a person with weak faith starts to share with others the Truth he possesses, his own strength is thereby increased. He is like a run-down person who begins to exercise: the more he does it, the stronger he becomes.

DESPITE MISGIVINGS

This opportunity—unfortunately, in some cases, the failure to realize such an opportunity exists—calls to mind an instance of a young man just out of the army after the close of World War II. He'd heard of the Christophers, so he informed us, and he came to us with this question: Did we think it worth while for him to take up work in one of the vital fields into which we are trying to direct a million Christophers in order to bring the world back to Christ and thereby insure peace.

The mere fact that he was undecided as to his future potential for good stressed the plight of so many people with fine ideas who underestimate their individual power to help return the world to Christ. Without putting it into words, this young man was saying, in effect, "Everything you say is okay, but what can a guy like myself do to push those ideas along? These days the ordinary person hasn't got a chance!"

It was explained to him, and he had the common sense to appreciate the truth of what was said, that peace is achieved, not through government decree, but through the conscious, personal striving of the individuals who make up society. When it was pointed out that the great source of strength of one who works as a Christopher is the fact that he does not work alone, that Christ works with him and through him, a look of reassurance came over the young man's face. At the final words, "It comes down to this, Tom. God works through you—isn't that something?" with an amazed shake of his head he replied, "Gee that *is* something, all right!"

That he was convinced God can and does work through ordinary mortals like himself, despite human limitations and weaknesses, is evidenced by the fact of his applying, and being accepted, for a post in the federal government where his influence for good, expressed in his enthusiastic adherence to sound, fundamental, God-given American principles has been a source of inspiration to all those around him. Literally, he is putting into daily practice the meaning of the words "For this was I born . . . that I should give testimony to the truth." (*John* 18, 37)

AN IMPORTANT DISTINCTION

There are many basic reasons justifying consistent and continued emphasis on individual responsibility and participation in shaping the destiny of mankind.

First of all, the teeming millions of humanity are nothing more than you—one person—multiplied over and over again.

While it is almost impossible to overstress individual responsibility, it must still be pointed out that one extreme should be avoided. It is the exaggeration of the "individuality" of the individual to such an extent that the social nature of man is lost sight of and the dangers of "rugged individualism" allowed to step in and cause considerable harm. Each human being, while he comes into the world as an individual, is likewise born a social being as a member of his *own* family and of the *whole human* family. He must live as an individual, true, but he also has obligations as the social being God intended him to be. When he renders an account of his stewardship after death, there is a social as well as an individual consideration. For each of us there will be a particular judgment at which everyone is judged individually as to his own personal life. Then follows the general judgment in which all participate as members of the human race.

Therefore, while you can exert power for good, individually and personally, you must ever be mindful that it should be exercised in terms of society and not in any isolated, antisocial sense. We are, as St. Paul reminds us, "everyone members one of another." (*Rom.* 12:5) And again, "for none of us liveth to himself, and no man dieth to himself." (*Rom.* 14:7)

TO BEAR FRUIT

Insofar as a person fulfills this role, he or she enjoys peace and happiness both here and hereafter. Yet constantly before one's mind's eye should be the eloquent reminder contained in the Scriptural parable of Christ and the fig tree. While beautiful in appearance and pleasing to the sight, Christ cursed it and it withered away. Why? The answer lies not in the fact that it was doing any harm, but only that it was doing no good. It produced only foliage, not fruit. And the latter was the purpose for which it was created. ("*And seeing a certain fig-tree by the wayside, he came to it, and found nothing on it but leaves only, and he said to it: May no fruit grow on thee henceforward for ever! And immediately the fig tree withered away.*" (*Matt.* 21:19)

INDIVIDUAL EFFORT WITH SOCIAL EFFECTS

There is no special "product" that you have to "manufacture." Goodness is within each and every one, and all one has to do truly to bear Christ is to be a messenger, a distributor of that God-given attribute. Countless people all over the country, and indeed all over the world, have come to realize this.

Nothing is as convincing proof of the success of that "distribution of goodness" as are actual examples of people who have become Christ-bearers in their daily lives. One man, who as an individual feels a sense of responsibility to society and is doing something about it, wrote us as follows:

". . . Many times I have heard how fortunate it would be if enough persons with Christopher ideals would enter the teaching profession. I have finally decided to do that very thing and am going into the government and international relations field in the graduate school of ——— University. I can see the importance of bringing the right values into the fields of government, politics, history, and labor. Perhaps as a teacher I can help others see this necessity also. I am resigning a position in business that pays quite well, but feel so strongly about the crisis in which the whole world is becoming so deeply involved that I cannot have peace of mind if I do not do all in my power to help. . . . I'm 34 and have a family to care for . . . but God will bless our little attempt and all will come out well, I know."

In Boston one lady started a now-recognizable trend toward bringing the Christ Child back into Christmas greetings cards. Year in and year out she had listened to people complaining that most Christmas cards were too pagan. Determined to do all in her power to bring a religious note into the greetings being prepared for the birthday of Our Saviour, she got a job with one of the largest greeting card companies for that very purpose. From the start she met with cooperation on all sides and, since this one pioneer Christopher sparked this trend, it has grown and is still growing. Her resourcefulness as an individual is certainly acting as a leavening force in our society.

Another zealous Christopher, very much in the public eye, is Fulton Oursler, a senior editor of *The Reader's Digest* and originator of the new radio triumph based on the life of Christ, "The Greatest Story Ever Told." Mr. Oursler, anxious to bring the story of Christ to the millions, struggled for four years to get "The Greatest Story" on the air. Many said it couldn't be done, but he had the faith that it could. Today he sees that program acclaimed all over the nation. Commenting on this stirring presentation, Mark Woods, president of the American Broadcasting Company which airs the production, stated not long ago:

"In these critical years, people throughout the world increasingly have turned to religious precepts for guidance. From time to time demagogues and leaders of evil intent have endeavored to use the powerful influence of radio for the realization of their goals. In America, however, radio has proved itself a potent influence for the inspiration, education, and enlightenment of peoples in all walks of life. We believe that 'The Greatest Story Ever Told' is unsurpassed in each of these categories."

INDIVIDUALS LEAD THE WAY

On a large American passenger liner whose crew had allowed themselves to be led by a handful of Communists, one straight-thinking seaman single-handed brought his crewmates back to positive American principles. Every chance he got (and where there was no opportunity, he made one) he talked up all the freedoms that the Declaration of Independence, the Constitution, and the Bill of Rights guaranteed. When a few others were impressed, he got them to do the same. In a short space of time he had won a sizable group, the grip of the subversives was broken, and godless totalitarianism lost sea-going allies. It took just one individual to spark this reverse trend.

A girl at Wellesley College, who confessed in the beginning that she belonged to "no church," heard a Christopher talk and found something in it which was to influence her life. The speaker's *"you count!"* stuck in her mind and stayed there even after graduation. She came to New York and got a job, not a very important one, in a radio station. Because of the knowledge that she, individually, mattered, all her better instincts soon rebelled at the actions of two subversives who blue-penciled references in scripts to God and American ideals.

At first she tried, on her own, to get the deleted references back into the scripts. However, when the leftist activity increased, she went to the head of the department and respectfully suggested she thought it good business to keep the mention of God and democracy in the scripts instead of taking them out.

The department head, unaware of what had been going on, agreed. More than that, he personally made it his business to check the scripts for any blue-penciling from then on.

On a widely circulated magazine read by millions, another girl has done, and is doing, equally effective work. She makes it her business to attend every union meeting of her craft and sometimes she is the only non-leftist present. "I feel like I'm in a room with 65 horse thieves," is the way she puts it. "But one little person like myself can accomplish something just by being there. They feel uncomfortable having someone present who knows they are horse thieves!"

A Christopher was instrumental in getting off the air a well-known news commentator who trod the leftist path in analysis of each day's events. The broadcaster was employed by a large corporation which didn't realize that the program it sponsored was being used to undermine the freedoms and opportunity for a profitable livelihood which our God-given liberties make possible for all. When this Christopher spoke to a member of the executive board of the company, things began to happen immediately. Company officials began to listen in on this commentator and had their worst fears confirmed. They were being made the distributors for subversive propaganda and were paying hard cash for the privilege. Luckily, since they employed the newscaster they could also release him. And they did just that in short order—all because one Christopher was on his toes and had the courage to make his voice heard.

Proof that Christopher action is not confined to the United States alone, but is world-wide, is found in the example of a woman-Christopher in South America. She made her field of Christ-bearing that of her national government, particularly the effort being made to pass a law erasing all reference to God from her country's schools. Personally undertaking a campaign of visiting every one of the one hundred and twenty-five legislators in the government, her reception was usually anything but pleasant. She was snubbed, ridiculed, given the well-known "run-around" from one official to another. She was threatened with violence and several times even physically ejected by those who wanted no part of a bearer of Christ and who hated the very mention of His Name.

But still she kept on until they finally consented to see her. When the final vote was taken some weeks later, sixty-three voted to keep the idea of God in the schools while sixty-two were opposed. *One* vote made all the difference. And one woman who suffered more than a little was personally responsible for a victory that touched the lives of every person in her country.

You, whose light may have been temporarily dimmed by what the world has to offer in all that is material, can take heart and hope from the story of St. Francis Xavier. At the University of Paris, Xavier was very much the young sophisticate. He loved the things of this world and was little interested in those of the next. The warning of "what doth it profit a man if he gain the whole world and suffer the loss of his own soul?" (*Matt.* 16:26) was not unknown to him. But for too long he saw its meaning, if at all, as only "through a glass, darkly."

And then one day, in a brief, suspenseful moment of self-examination, he finally caught the overwhelming significance of the words. If he, one individual, was worth so much, so then was *every* man. He was consumed with a burning desire to share that knowledge with *all* mankind. He felt he had to get that idea across somehow to people wherever and whenever he could. How much of his life remained to him to complete this task he naturally didn't know. But it really didn't matter. Whatever he could do, he would do, to bring the knowledge of Christ to all men. In ten years—the sands in the hourglass of his life ran out at forty-five—he reached, personally, nearly a million men, women, and children!

EXCLUDE NO ONE

You, as an individual, can walk in Xavier's footsteps if you will also try to reach *everybody,* even those who hate you and all you stand for. You must be like the Christopher who made it his business to talk to a notorious woman Communist in a large Eastern city not long ago.

This Red was only twenty-one years old, but already her fire and zeal for the godless "crusade" had made her name a byword in subversive circles. Perhaps because she was flattered that any God-fearing person would come to see her, or possibly because, in her egotism, she thought she held the whip hand, she consented to talk to this Christopher. And her greeting was not surprising, "Now listen. I don't believe in God! Before we get into any discussion, I want you to understand that."

"I do believe in God," the Christopher answered in a calm, friendly way. "And because I believe in God, I believe in you. You were made in His image and likeness and all humanity is you, over and over again."

The Communist said nothing to this at first. Finally she bit her lip, then burst out, almost pleadingly:

"Why don't you . . . you Christians tell that to the whole world instead of keeping it to yourselves?"

There isn't much more to tell. The interview ended soon afterwards. But the thing that impressed this Christopher—and has since impressed all who have heard what happened—is that there was a Communist *begging* the followers of Christ to bring the message of His love to all mankind!

This is a challenge you must meet and, with God's help, will meet.

ONE SMALL VOICE

You who may feel you do not "know enough" to be of use as effective Christophers, remember—one small voice which makes itself heard on the side of truth is often like a clarion call to action to those who can do something. A man out in the Midwest not long ago was chosen as a delegate to a widely publicized labor convention. The appointment, instead of flattering him, flustered him, especially in the face of some advice as to his responsibility in watching out for the best interests of his fellow workers.

"I . . . I'm afraid I don't know enough about policy to be much help," was his bewildered argument.

"You know the difference between right and wrong," came back the heartening reply. "If you think anything is wrong, get up on your feet and say so!"

The convention wasn't long under way before a well-thought-out and carefully executed program of an anti-Christian minority group in the convention had progressed so far that its final adoption seemed a certainty. While most of the 1,600 assembled delegates (representing some 700,000 workers) sat back unaware that this small but influential bloc in their midst were on the brink of success, at the eleventh hour our friend—the man who didn't think he *knew* enough—got up from his chair.

He addressed the chairman, and was immediately recognized.

His mouth opened a couple of times to speak without giving forth a sound, but finally he managed, in a half-frightened voice, to say, *"I'm sorry, Mr. Chairman, but this whole thing doesn't seem honest to me!"*

Then he sat down quickly, mopping his forehead, feeling the blood pound madly through his veins, and waiting for the roof to fall in on him.

It fell in, all right—but not on him—because the effect of his simple statement on the rest of the gathering was electric. Up to then they had been quite passive, but now they came to life as if awakened from a deep sleep. A heated discussion followed. Eventually, realizing they had almost been railroaded into serious injustice, the delegates adopted a sound policy which was just the opposite of what the anti-Christians had cleverly proposed—and had almost got away with.

One man did all this, and one seemingly insignificant effort won a resounding victory.

Your individual power for good is no less than his, but you must not keep it to yourself. You must be honestly concerned about the salvation of all mankind, not merely absorbed in saving your own soul. You must fight where you can for the economic security of countless millions who can't fight for themselves. You must no longer remain aloof, utterly preoccupied with getting more and better food, housing, clothing, comforts, and pleasures for self.

When a million like you do the same thing individually and collectively, it requires no great stretch of the imagination to realize what a far-reaching transformation can take place, not alone in America, but all over the world.

G. K. Chesterton spoke truly when he said that in spite of *all* accusations to the contrary, Christianity has not failed the world. The tragedy of our times is that too many have failed to try the truths of Christianity. Yet it is in *your* power to bring Christ back to the world and the world back to Christ. *You* have a touch of divinity which will begin to blossom into completeness here on earth, even before you hear those final words of eternal benediction:

> *"Come, ye blessed of my Father, possess you the kingdom prepared for you from the foundation of the world."* (Matt. 25:34)

XI

INFLUENCING THE WORLD FROM THE HOME

On a street corner of a northwestern city, just over a year ago, a newsboy stood hawking his papers, one grimy fist holding up a copy of the evening edition for the passers-by to see. His hoarse-voiced, solemn chant "Getcha papers here. Read all about it—Reds lose control of labor union" mingled with the roar of speeding cars and trucks and the thin clang of bells as the traffic lights changed from green to yellow, then to red, and repeated the procedure over and over again.

A man, passing by, paused for a moment to scan the newspaper headlines. The newsboy eyed him expectantly until the man, with a faint smile, reached into his pocket, took out a coin and dropped it in the youngster's outstretched hand, ignoring the folded paper which was offered him. "Keep it for yourself, son," he muttered, quickly. "Read what it says about the Reds losing out in that union. It's a little over your head now, but read it anyway and remember it. It'll show you what REAL Americans can do once they put their minds to it. I know—I found out the hard way!"

A moment later, as he hurried away, conscious of the newsboy's puzzled stare which followed him, he found himself wishing he could have explained himself a little better. Especially would he have liked to tell him—to tell everybody—about Helen. For Helen was his wife, and it was she who deserved the credit for the full-streamer headlines which shouted their message of victory for the democratic God-given way over those who had used their liberty to try to destroy it.

It hadn't looked that way at first, though. What was it she'd told him, when he'd complained about the Reds taking over and he had wanted to pull out? "You stay clear of that crowd, Walt," she said. "Don't get mixed up in their underhanded tricks. It'll only mean trouble, and the children and I don't want anything to happen to you."

But that was before she'd found out that getting decent people to quit the union was just what the Reds wanted. When she finally realized they could only be defeated by having men like himself go back in and work for what was right, she'd reversed her stand. She'd persuaded him to stick it out, urging him to attend every union meeting, even though it meant the same old story of being shouted down every time he tried to do anything constructive. Then she'd come across with her second bit of advice: get others, who thought as he did, to follow his example. And, thank *God,* he'd done just that. It wasn't long before the rank and file of decent "Joes" began to prick up their ears and take notice. And, as they did, the Reds had found the going that much tougher.

Finally, Helen had capped her triumphs with, "Why don't you get Harry or Fred or some of your other friends to run for a place on the executive board next election?" Little dreaming—or was she?—that they, in turn, would help vote *him* in as president of the union!

The man shook his head admiringly. What a terrific sense of direction, what resourcefulness that woman had! It was more than her feminine intuition that made her see how well he and the others would succeed just by *going,* just by *being,* where they could do the most good. Even though they'd barely held their own at first, they'd kept on until the tide gradually swung in their favor. And, finally, a whole new slate of men besides himself had been elected, men who thought America was pretty much okay, men who didn't want a bunch of subversives plowing under everything America stood for.

In substance, that is the history of how the control of a fairly large labor union right here in the United States was taken away from an organized minority of leftists. The newspapers gave the electrifying results, but they didn't tell the whole story behind the headlines—of how one ordinary labor union member, because of the influence of his wife at home, helped bring back to his union administration the God-given concepts on which America was founded and which make all our freedoms possible today. From her kitchen a housewife had helped change for the better the whole trend of a vital phase of our national life! She had clarified for thousands of workers the difference between Christian democracy in action and the tactics of pagan totalitarians.

But she had a Christopher purpose—remember that. Remember, also, that what she did, in the home and from the home, others with the same motivation can do as well.

The home is the most vital social unit in any democracy. It influences the actions of all society. But goodness must not only be cultivated in the home, it must be carried far beyond its doors. In this the man of the house must play his part, not only in helping to formulate and direct family policies, but in seeing that these policies are executed. Primarily, however, on the shoulders of you, the woman in the home, falls the responsibility—to your children, to your husband, to your neighbors, and to yourself—of keeping the mainstream of life ever conscious of the great truths upon which civilization rests. For you, this is not merely an ideal. It is a solemn obligation.

When all you fine women in our country realize this and make it your business, in one way or another, to bring Christ into the market-place, a fresh, purifying wind of lasting peace will sweep across this land. And, eventually, it will sweep on across the world! It will help everyone, even those extremists who are caught in the current widespread epidemic of sleeping powder overdoses and lost weekends. There will be far fewer closet hangings. Those sick with a nameless sense of guilt will want to keep on living, because from the home good women with a Christopher purpose will have made life worth while for the whole world.

When this comes to pass, Communism or any other form of subversion will disappear, because Communism—like Nazism and Fascism—is a disease that feeds on evil conditions and sick-hearted despair.

WOMEN HAVE THE POWER

Since woman's influence for good can be so great, it is logical to seek the reasons why so few, to date, have caught this idea.

One reason, perhaps the most important one, is that you women underestimate your own power. You argue that you feel so helpless, so inadequate, so bound down by the circumstances of everyday life. Too often you think you must be highly trained, have prominent positions, or be gifted with genius to do great things. Well, those may be your ideas, but they weren't Christ's! The woman of Samaria at Jacob's Well possessed none of these qualities, yet in her and through her Jesus brought untold numbers closer to His side. Peter and the other apostles and disciples were only ordinary men, usually unlettered and, more often than not, poor. Yet Christ said to them, *"Come ye after Me, and I will make you to be fishers of men."* (*Matt.* 4:19) And these common folk went on to revolutionize the entire world!

In every human being God has implanted, personally and individually, a special power to influence mankind for *good.* You good women, once you realize this, will become Christophers—Christ-bearers. And recognizing that same power in your husband and in your children, you will inspire them to become Christ-bearers, too.

GIVE YOUR FAMILY A PURPOSE

Then you will be less concerned that your sons and daughters choose profitable careers and more concerned that they find for themselves a sphere of influence for good. And insofar as you see them as instruments of God, you will automatically avoid that inclination of so many parents and teachers to overemphasize self-preservation, self-sanctification, self-development, and self-enjoyment—as if one's only purpose in life were to take care of his or her own soul and his or her own body, letting the rest of the world, literally and figuratively, "go to the devil." You will not imitate the wealthy parents of one young girl who taught their daughter from her earliest years to save every dollar she got her hands on, themselves matching every amount she so miserly amassed. These parents were not teaching her thrift. They were teaching her selfishness, a fact which showed itself later on in the girl's life. A grown woman now, she is one of the most self-centered persons one could possibly meet.

It's a fine thing to have security. But once that is achieved, then the first concern must be the food, housing, clothing, and education of others. It's a wonderful thing to know the truth. But you who possess the truth dare *not* leave the world in error. When true vision—Christ-like vision—is given to your children as they reach manhood and womanhood, they will not retire into their own insulated "hothouses," into the cubicles of their faith, leaving the running of the big world to those who either hate Christ or who know Him not. They will not devote themselves entirely to self-preservation, for any animal can do that. They will, instead, become other-Christs, eager to help feed a hungry world, eager to help bring peace to a world divided against itself, eager to speak the truth to a world which has been too often listening only to lies.

You have a life ahead of you and, over the years, a thousand opportunities to train your children to be leaders, not followers; to choose a life's work, not for the salary alone, but for the influence which that work affords. You cannot and dare not delegate that responsibility to others. The classroom cannot take the place of the home. As an Episcopalian professor, Bernard Iddings Bell, pointed out in the New York *Times Magazine* not long ago:

> "One of the chief hindrances to decent education in America today is the overloading of our schools by placing on their shoulders responsibilities which, in other times and countries, have as a matter of course been assumed by the home."

For this overloading, Dr. Bell goes on to state, those who are in control of the schools are partly to blame, since they have only been too willing to assume the task of total development of growing boys and girls, believing that they can do a better job with them than their own mothers and fathers can possibly do. And he continues with the thought that anyone who listens to current school pretensions and knows the facts is bound to conclude that American schools and colleges for a long time have been biting off more than they can chew. The results are bad, because overworked and unskilled instructors (and we might add, subversive teachers, too) are experimenting with attempts to integrate the characters of our youngsters by nursing them into social maturity —and failing miserably at it!

But, as Dr. Bell emphasizes, "the parents, lulled into a sense of security, have largely abdicated; the schools cannot take over; the progeny is not much fun to look at. Because it is undisciplined, it becomes irritable, unruly, unhappy, frequently a general nuisance, sometimes definitely antisocial and occasionally criminal." Finally, Dr. Bell concludes ". . . unless we know how human beings must live if they are to acquire a sense of significance and self-respect; unless we discover and live by man's true relationship to the totality of things, to God, to the Ultimate whose purpose sustains the universe—unless we have learned these things, which can be taught nowhere so easily or so competently as by parents to their own offspring, our civilization will continue to disintegrate, even as now it plainly has begun to do."

In short, your youth is largely being trained to demand only these things: big money, short hours, long vacations, the easy job, the "soft snap," the employment that can provide the maximum of material comforts and the minimum of that which pertains to the Creator Who made the world and everyone in it.

The subversive—the Communist (like the Nazi and Fascist before him)—has different ideas, however. He'll let you run that shiny new, white-walled convertible, while he runs the city council. He'll let you take that trip to Florida, or Bermuda or Timbuktu, while he works unceasingly to reach the greatest number of people with his poisonous doctrines. Why? The answer is simple. All the shiny new convertibles, all the luxurious vacations, all the wealth and comforts in the world, count not one iota in swaying the destinies of mankind.

Jobs with a purpose, the subversive knows, pay little, demand long hours, and offer few natural attractions. But in the home and from the home your children—your husbands and your neighbors, too—must be influenced to take these self-same jobs, to take them as other-Christs, or the day may come when there will be no jobs for decent, God-fearing people at all!

HIT FOR THE BIG MARKET

It's a big job, make no mistake about it. It's a challenge to all the best that is in you. But you can meet it, you must meet it, you will meet it. Unlike the woman in Washington, D. C., who listened to a Christopher talk and, while deeply impressed, still couldn't realize that she, personally, was capable of tremendous deeds, you will not ask as did she, "But couldn't you tell us some *little* thing to do?"

Good as she was, this woman was still thinking, as do too many otherwise fine people, in terms of little things, little projects, little spheres of influence—while the godless think in terms of the world!

The answer given her, however, opened her eyes to the breath-taking possibilities for good around her. "Here you are, living in the most important capital on the face of the earth," she was told, "with a thousand and one opportunities for doing something big, something worth while. Don't you see that? Don't you see that subversives who are out to wreck our country are getting into every branch of our government? If a woman with your fine ideas were to spend a whole year getting just one decent, God-fearing person into some government job, you'd be doing a wonderful service to God and to your country! And remember this—even though you may think that you're just a little person, still you're important. You *count*!"

How well another woman, Mrs. Charlotte McDonnell Harris, realized the truth of this is evident from one very effective thing that she did. Some time ago she had read and been disturbed by an article in the *Ladies' Home Journal*. This article, one in a series entitled "Letters to Joan," dealt with a so-called modern outlook on "sex freedom in a changing world," with the implication that morals change with each generation. Others who read it may have shaken their heads, muttered to themselves, and then done nothing about it. But not Mrs. Harris. Her reply, "A Letter to Joan from a Catholic," appeared in a subsequent issue of the *Journal* despite the fact that she had never written for the general public before. She might easily have said, "Oh, but I can't. I'm no professional writer. Send it to the *Ladies' Home Journal*? Don't be silly. They wouldn't even read it, much less accept it!"

She might have said all these things, but she didn't. By her very silence she would have helped foster the continued publication of false concepts. And the significant thing about the whole affair is that the editors did read her article, sent her a nice check, and published what she had to say. As a result, her vital Christian message went out to some four and a half million homes. When it is remembered that not one of Christ's twelve apostles had the means of reaching any like number of people, then must come the realization of what wonderful things you women with good ideas can do with the marvelous facilities of communication at your command. As the Washington *Post* pointed out not long ago, "The weakness of public opinion is that so many people express it only privately."

If you would be a Christopher, you should see to it that such an observation cannot be made of you.

FROM THE HOME INTO THE IMPORTANT SPHERES

In the home and *from* the home, you can influence your husband and your children first of all, and second, the world outside. If there was a steady stream of young people from the average good American home entering the four great fields of education, government, labor-management, and writing, it wouldn't take long to restore a healthy, wholesome tone to these important spheres of influence. In these spheres the bearers of Christ are most urgently needed, since the atheists, materialists, and many others with abnormal and dangerous outlooks, are most active there in spreading their ideas to reach all mankind.

Into Education

For all you women who have children, surely there is no greater privilege than that of helping your own flesh and blood to devote their lives as other-Christs in the lay apostolate of, for example, teaching. In many ways teaching is the greatest of all professions. It was the one Christ chose, because through it He could do the greatest good.

You will want to avoid the tragedy of one mother, a good woman in many, many ways, who summed up in these words her failure properly to guide her children, then long since grown into manhood and womanhood: "You know, I'm afraid to face God!"

"But you've led a good life," someone interrupted. "You've always been generous to worthy causes . . ."

"Yes," came back the disconsolate reply. "But I've failed to give the most important things to my children. I've failed to give my time and I've failed to give myself."

Two million students in our secular colleges are today yearning for the truths of Christian doctrine; and at this very moment the enemies of Christ are everywhere, using the high school and college classroom as a dispensary of poison. To bring light where there is only the darkness of error, you must first see to it that only the right things are taught in our educational institutions. This is most important. In any community where parents do not interest themselves in what is being taught their children, the godless subversives and the promoters of perversion invariably seize the initiative in worming their way into the school with their harmful doctrines. A recent report in the Los Angeles *Times* quoted the California State Senate Investigating Committee on Education as stating that the American way of life "gets the worst of it" in the *Building America* series of textbook supplements being used in the state's schools. American culture and achievements are talked down and the progress (?) of Communist Russia talked up. The report summarizes references to the United States: ". . . the class struggle is highlighted by contrasting the silk-hatted capitalists with the ill-clad sad-faced workers—not just once, but over and over again."

In a seventh and eighth grade volume which discusses Herbert Hoover, the report goes on to say, "The man who later became President of the United States (a fact not mentioned in the text) is portrayed as a 'mining engineer who had spent most of his life outside the country,' and as a 'food dictator.' Nothing is mentioned of Hoover's achievement of seeing that the United States was able, not only to feed itself, but to save the hungry peoples of Europe, of his later becoming Secretary of Commerce and then Chief Executive."

Continues the report: "Under a photograph of President Wilson drawing the first draft numbers in World War I runs a caption to the effect that 'Although the Constitution prohibited "involuntary servitude" the draft laws were upheld by the courts.'"

In Volume 30, "Seeing America," "the last and certainly one of the worst," according to the account, there is continually portrayed before the eyes of a typical pair of young people "the seamy side [of American life] with nowhere a picture of a beautiful park or other abundant examples of healthful, happy life."

"And so the young . . . have seen 'America'?" the report concluded. "They have seen its slums, its expropriated farms and drought victims, its hot dog stands, and the shanties of miners and steelworkers. They have seen its mules, its jackasses, and its jobless. They have been shown the class struggle through pictures and the wording of captions."

Finally, the article pointed out, regarding the volume on Russia, that the pictures of that country "have been explained as showing plump, well-fed people, fertile farms, and a general air of well-being and prosperity. They were obtained from Sovfoto, an official Soviet agency. . . . These pictures should be contrasted with the Farm Security Administration illustrations in 'Seeing America.' When the two volumes are placed side by side, the contrast is striking. This, too, is propaganda of the most subtle and vicious type."

Is there reason, then, for parental concern as to what is being taught their children in our schools? After reading the above (only one of many examples from all over the country which could be listed) you can supply the answer!

Into Government

Then there is the field of government. If you have read Chapter V, "Government—Your Job to Make It Good," you will understand why every one of the millions of jobs in our national, state, and local administrations should be manned by the best products of the best American homes. True, we need good doctors, lawyers, engineers, merchants, bus drivers, dry cleaners, and butchers. But there is a far more urgent need of getting better blood in every artery of governmental life.

A sound-thinking young man in San Francisco, who recently took a minor post in state government, gives special credit to his Christopher wife who enthusiastically backed him up, particularly when he passed up a better-paying opening in the law field.

If you would be a Christopher, you will also take to heart the example of another woman, a mother who encouraged her son to take a government job. "If he does no more than carry wastebaskets, at least he will be there," she said. "And he can work into something better." When her husband objected to such a humble beginning, she answered, "If boys like ours, with normal, sensible ideas, don't go into government work, we'll be letting it fall into the hands of those who are out to wreck America!"

Into Labor-Management

You can do much to influence your husbands and your grown-up sons and daughters to participate actively in the labor-management field, one of the strongest forces for good or evil in the United States today. Whether it shall be a force for evil or a force for good depends, to a great degree, on you. Like the unionist at the beginning of this chapter, more and more men, with the cooperation and help of their wives, have acquired the vision to see how dangerous labor power may become unless it is also Christian power.

Not too long ago a large corporation offered a union official, a remarkably brilliant and efficient man, a position at double his salary and—note this—a home and a car besides!

The man turned the offer down. He was satisfied to remain with his labor union, where the income was smaller but where the opportunity to do good was so great as to defy imagination. And in this choice he had the help and advice of his wife. Many another woman would have exploded with something like this: "James Smith, are you crazy, turning down a job that's worth twice what you're getting now? If that isn't just like a man, thinking about nobody but himself. I'll bet if you had to run this home on what I've had for the past twenty-five years, you wouldn't be so high and mighty thinking about the good you can do in that union of yours. Why, I'll tell you right now you're not half the big-shot you pretend to be . . ." And so on and on until, in the end, "James Smith" would have kept peace in the family by taking the job he didn't want, and neglecting to serve better the common good.

As you help keep your husband and your children ever conscious that they can be vital instruments in bringing God's love and truth into the market place, you will turn your home into a powerhouse for good. You will enrich their lives and the lives of all who cross their path—and you will enrich your own. You will help save them from the aimless search for empty pleasures that allure but never satisfy, the search which is startling evidence of a spiritual hunger that characterize those who have no purpose in their lives outside of themselves.

Into Writing

The fourth great field of influence where the Christopher ideal can be put to work is that of newspapers, periodicals, motion pictures, television and radio. All these spheres of influence need the fresh, wholesome, Christ-like approach of those who follow in the footsteps of Him Who is "the Way, the Truth, and the Life." Today, as never before, the world needs good writers and good technicians of the spoken and written word. Too much that is merely sordid, perverted, or subversive is offered to the public as information and entertainment.

Not only should your children be encouraged to go into this field, but you yourself can accomplish much individually and personally. An example of this is Mrs. Henry Mannix (mother of ten children), who did a magnificent job in bringing to the whole country, via radio, the safe and sane teaching that sex instruction belongs primarily in the home and not in the classroom. Over the "Town Hall of the Air" she brought this truly Christian concept to more than eleven million people who probably had never heard this important subject treated, certainly not by the godless, in such a simple, sensible and dignified manner.

Here are some of Mrs. Mannix's remarks:

"As a mother of a family, I have a natural interest in the preparation of youth for marriage and family relationship. As a citizen and a taxpayer, I also have a responsibility to know what may be included in such preparation if given in the classroom of the public school. If such preparation, given on a mass scale, would include sex instruction, my answer as a parent and as a citizen is emphatically, 'No.'

"As a parent, I know that the duty of giving sex instruction lies first of all with the mother and father. I cannot, in conscience, delegate this duty to the schools.

"Your common sense and mine, your personal experience and mine tell us clearly and sharply that mere knowledge of sex and sex relations is no guarantee of morality. In fact, sexual immorality among youth is often the result, not of ignorance about sex, but of too little will power.

"This much is certain: Information on sex should never get ahead of the boys' and girls' ability to understand at the same time their moral obligations toward the facts of life which they have learned.

"Instead of campaigning for sex education in the public

school, we should campaign for sex instruction in the home where it truly belongs."

Mrs. Mannix was not a professional radio commentator, but her common sense and Christian attitude on a vital topic of the day put to shame many tawdry attempts by professionally produced programs to distort the whole sex problem.

What son or daughter, with such a mother for a model, could fail to be inspired to use what talent God has given her or him to bring goodness and decency and the spirit of Christ's love into the professional preparation of all phases of public information and entertainment?

This much is certain. These spheres of influence desperately need good writers and good producers. You can supply that need by your influence and encouragement from the home.

To give another illustration of this Christopher objective in practice: One young woman in New York, the wife of a writer, was largely responsible for the Christ-like balance in a household threatened with being submerged in all the details and preoccupations of her husband's literary career. To his constant pursuit of carving a formidable niche in the writing field and his worrying that things might not go as he planned, she had one answer: to trust God and have confidence in that trust in the firm conviction that everything would turn out all right in the end. As the writer expressed it later, "Her goodness and love of me because she loves God so much is like a clean, refreshing breeze that sweeps the cobwebs of discouragement away whenever I get down in the mouth. That may sound poetic, but it happens to be the truth."

While these are isolated cases, they do show what can be done in encouraging children and grown-ups to go into and stay in the writing field. Yet parents—mothers *and* fathers—must also impress on grown-ups and youngsters alike that years of hard work are part and parcel of such "going." Too many parents expect their youngsters to start out as vice-presidents, so it is not surprising that their children too often feel the same way. The writing field is a profession and, like any profession, requires constant practice in perfecting skills. But, acknowledging this, the task still remains to get people into the field, no matter in how lowly a position. As the woman whose son toted wastebaskets around a government office pointed out, being on the spot is the first step up the ladder and the best guarantee of bringing Christ's love and truth where too often there have been only indifference and error.

In addition to the four main fields already mentioned, there are other important spheres of influence which should be considered as offering splendid opportunities for Christopher work. For instance, there are library and social service fields which are in serious need of representatives who have had deeply impressed upon them sound American principles. You can—and no doubt will—do much to answer that need as you grow in appreciation of the fact that there is little chance of Christ prevailing in the world until the homes which possess His peace share it with the world that does not.

"Every woman," to quote Pope Pius XII, "has then, mark it well, the obligation, the strict obligation in conscience, not to absent herself but to go into action in a manner and way suitable to the condition of each so as to hold back those currents which threaten the home, so as to oppose those doctrines which undermine its foundations, so as to prepare, organize and achieve its restoration."

"HE THAT IS NOT WITH ME IS AGAINST ME"

It is simply a choice of influencing or being influenced. And that last is the sad condition of 100,000,000 Americans, or seven out of every ten persons, who are not regularly reached by anyone in the name of Christ, leaving them openly susceptible to the half-truths and the deceiving glib come-on's of materialism. These people are living off the benefits of Christianity, but they are largely unaware of the major truths which are the basis of all their liberties and which constitute the very foundation of our country. These truths are the chief obstacles to every subversive attempt to enslave our nation. They have been stated earlier in this book, but fundamentals as important as these bear repeating so that your children may be enabled to know them. Briefly, they are: *belief* in a personal God; in Jesus Christ, true God and true man; in the Ten Commandments; in the sacred character of the individual; in the sanctity of marriage and the sanctity of the home as the basic unit of the human family; in the human rights of each person as coming from God, not from the State; in the right to private property with its consequent obligations; in due respect for domestic, civil, and religious authority.

Finally, as a summation of all these, there should be emphasized a belief in judgment after death, when each individual must render an account of his or her stewardship to determine an eternity of Heaven or of Hell.

It won't do much good merely to be against Communism and the many other forms of materialism, or to be afraid of them, or let chills run up and down your spine, to denounce them to the president of your sodality or hold club meetings for the purpose of simply condemning subversive infiltration. The newspapers are too full of such headlines as "Clubwomen Denounce Iron Curtain," "Clubwomen Urged to Work Against Communism," "Women Meet to Discuss Means to Fight Communist Aggression."

Too often all the countless discussions, all the club meetings, all the resolutions passed and sentiments expressed, unfortunately accomplish little. Too often do they add up to just one thing: "*talk*, but *no action*." And just as actions do speak louder than any volume of words, so is it vital for each of you as Christophers to work as hard for Christ as His enemies are working against Him. Many among the one hundred million Americans are waiting, uncertain as to what road to take. It is up to you to begin to train your children now, so that they may become the Christophers of the future and carry on where you leave off. All your other activities, interesting as they may be, might well subordinate themselves to this one goal, because all those other activities rolled together will advance the free, God-given way of life very little.

One illustration of this is that of an alumnae group of a well-known Eastern women's college. The ladies in the club, fine people in many respects, unfortunately restricted themselves as a group to just three functions: (1) bridge parties; (2) theater parties; and (3) a costume dance once a year. Typical of many others all over the country who underestimate their power for good, they had not caught the idea that only by integrating business with pleasure, by working constructively for the things that insure the democratic way of life and make their legitimate good times possible, could their future as free people be assured.

True, all work and no play may make Jack a dull young man and Jane a dull young woman. But *all play* and *no work* for that which is just and good will leave the field clear to those intent on undermining our very civilization.

THE PROBLEM OF IDLENESS

For those women who have not been blessed with families or whose children have reached maturity, idleness can be a heavy burden. In a recent magazine article the Bureau of

Labor Statistics is quoted as listing "twenty million women, nearly half of all adult female Americans, as essentially idle. They do not have children under 18, they are not members of the labor force, they do not work on farms, nor are they aged or infirm. With not nearly enough to do, many of them are bored stiff. . . . Many are over 40 and belong to a generation which frowned on work for any but poverty-stricken women. Their husbands have worked hard to give them an easeful life. Now that they have it, it is a burden. . . . As a result, many of these idle women fall back on numbing rounds of club meetings and card-playing. They read too much low-grade fiction and escape too readily into dream realms of movies and soap operas."

A terrible indictment, to be sure. Yet such an indictment is not applicable to all women, thank God. Good, God-fearing women have found that the one sure remedy for idleness is to concern themselves with trying to make the world a little better off because they are in it. They are a source of inspiration to their husbands and their children, and they are a power for all that is decent and fine in the community.

When they join clubs, it is not for purely social reasons. They have a purpose—a Christopher purpose—to help bring Christ back into even the most obscure part of people's lives. They realize it is not enough to foster goodness in the home. They know they must *release* that goodness wherever and whenever they possibly can. Their motto is simple, yet so true: *"Nothing ventured, nothing gained."*

They will not be like the two socially prominent ladies during World War II who complained bitterly about the horrors of war and the ones responsible for it, only to be brought up short by a remark from one of their friends.

"You and I are responsible for the present sad state of the world," this friend asserted. "We've wrapped bandages, made up kits, attended meetings, and thought we'd done our bit.

Well, let me tell you, we haven't! Right now, in Berlin, women like us are doing those things—have been doing them for years, in fact—and it didn't stop Hitler from taking over Germany. The trouble with us is we haven't tried to spread the good ideas that can influence the basic trends and help make our way of life possible."

DOING SOMETHING POSITIVE

No, you will not emulate these people. Instead, you will follow the example of the woman in a California city who made the whole community realize what it means to be a Christopher.

A young Negro, studying to be a teacher, had taken a part-time job as a filling station attendant to help support his wife and himself until he got his degree. Some of the station's customers objected to being serviced by a Negro and told the station owner they'd take their business elsewhere, unless the boy was fired. Rather than lose business, the owner was about to agree—until a woman neighbor of his heard the story and decided to do something about it!

"How many customers do you figure to lose?" she asked him.

"Oh, eighteen, maybe twenty," was the reply.

"If I get you twenty new customers, will you keep the boy on?" this woman shot back.

The man thought for a moment. "You bet I will," he said, finally.

Not only did this woman get the station owner twenty new customers, she actually got him five more for good measure! More important, she made it possible for the Negro student to keep his job and continue his schooling.

There is Christopher purpose in action—and thank God for it.

Then again, there is the case of a Christopher keeping a young Jewish couple together, when all signs pointed to a breakup in their marriage and to eventual divorce. A materialist would have shrugged her shoulders and muttered something about "not trying to tie people down." This Christopher talked the couple back to sanity and happiness.

What was it Christ said? . . . *"Blessed are the peacemakers: for they shall be called the children of God."* (*Matt.* 5:9)

TAKE THE INITIATIVE

It is easy to fall into the attitude that changing times make it more difficult for succeeding generations to guard the sanctity of the home and to build strong and resilient families. It is easy to blame wars, depressions, booms, industrial and scientific revolutions as making much of American home life a weird and confused kind of existence. (*According to 900 experts attending the recent National Conference on Family Life in Washington, D. C., among the harmful changes interfering with proper home life were listed: the sharp increase in divorce, more housewives—one fourth in all—working outside the home, changing standards of sexual behavior, decline of interest in religion, drastic altering of family relations, the reduction in size of the average U.S. family from 5.7 persons in 1790 to 3.6 today, an increasing number of families leaving the farm—83% now live in urban areas—and such other factors as economic insecurity and the increasing mobility of individuals and families.*)

It is our conviction, however, that this present dangerous trend can be reversed so that normal, healthy family life will once more take its place as the backbone of our civilization and bring an abundance of peace and happiness to all mankind. To accomplish this means that the home will have to take the initiative and influence the world—instead of allowing itself to be influenced. Once you are convinced that it is much more hopeful and constructive to use every means possible to bring the peace of Christ that is in your home out into the mainstream of life, than to withhold it from the great majority who want and need it so much, then you will enthusiastically initiate from the sanctuary of your home many Christopher practices which will have an ever-widening influence for good.

To make this a reality, we submit a few proposals which you may find helpful:

(1) *Think in terms of the world.* No matter how remote you may be from the market place, you can begin to reach out to all mankind. The very desire and attempt to do this will bring a blessing upon you, your home, and humanity. You will be imitating the world vision of Christ. Everything you do will take on new meaning, as it did for one housewife who caught this perspective: "Thank you for inspiring an 'ingrown' homemaker, whose life has previously been bounded on all sides by homely details of child care, family feeding, and furniture dusting. Now I can see how this little world can take on new light as a fertile field for planting and living Christ for the bigger world. And so on from there!"

(2) *Pray for the world as well as for your home.* The true Christopher will go far beyond the family circle with supplications to God. On the wings of prayer one can literally reach out over the globe itself. It is helpful to fix on particular intentions, a different one each day, each week, or each month if one chooses. Offering prayers for some specific purpose assures better continuity and greater sincerity. It isn't difficult to acquire the habit of offering a daily prayer for our President, for Congress, for the United Nations, for the

millions in Russia and in Soviet-dominated lands, for the Communists themselves, for all who suffer because of their race, color, or creed, for the billion and more men, women, and children over the earth who have not yet heard that Jesus Christ was born, lived, and died for each and every one of them.* One lady, who, in order to make ends meet, has to hire out as a laundress after finishing her household work, prays daily for one of America's top labor leaders for, as she says, "I don't know of anyone who needs prayers more."

In the midst of your work around the home you can say a passing prayer for all who died the day before. The obituary column in your morning paper can be your reminder for that. When you attend a movie, a football game, go to the beach or any other place where people congregate, take a moment to offer a prayer for all present. Eternity has begun for each of them, even though the majority never realize it. The more you pray for *everybody*—the poor, the rich, the strong, the weak, the friendly, the hostile, the wise, the stupid, the ugly, the fair—the more will you grow in love for them. You will experience a sense of participation with Christ

---

* No particular form is necessary. You can make up your own prayer or use the following Christopher prayer:

"Inspire us, O God, with such a deep love of our country that we will be actively concerned in its welfare as well as in that of all our fellow countrymen for time and for eternity. Teach us to show by word and deed the same zealous interest in protecting and furthering the Christian principles upon which our nation is founded that others display in belittling or eliminating them.

"Guide and strengthen the President, his Cabinet, the members of Congress, the delegates to the United Nations, the Governor of our State, the officials of our community, and all others, in high position or low, who are entrusted with the task of protecting for all citizens those rights which come from Thee and from Thee alone.

"Teach us likewise to be worthy instruments in extending to all men of all nations, Thy children and our brothers, the same peace, freedom and security with which Thou hast so abundantly blessed our land. Through Christ Our Lord. Amen."

in the salvation of the world that is possible in few other ways.

(3) *Dispose your children to lead lives of purpose.* A tremendous change for the better would take place if one-quarter of the 37,623,000 families in this country were to encourage at least one child in each family group to dedicate a life to some career through which the best values learned from parents could be channeled to the "big market." Unfortunately and without intending any harm, many parents prepare their children for life pursuits that are discouragingly negative and restrictive. They fence them in as far as anything creative is concerned. They train them to be aimless followers rather than leaders. In a hundred different ways they mold them to routine passiveness and to taking as much out of the world as possible; and, by implication at least, they give them to understand that they should not be overly concerned with putting anything in.

Even those parents with strong religious backgrounds are increasingly becoming entangled in the double game of trying "to serve God and mammon," with mammon slowly but surely winning out in their children, even more than in them. There is a tragic tendency to ignore the hidden power for good in each individual, and to deaden it if it does start to blossom forth. As a poor and harmful substitute, these same parents hold continually before their children's growing minds standards of worldly success—more money, better clothes, nicer homes, more expensive cars.

It would surprise these parents to know how often their offspring are disappointed in the lack of inspiration given them. Recently one young woman discovered a dangerous situation at a large teachers' college. This woman had the faith and ability to help remedy it. Yet, when asked why she didn't become a teacher herself, she replied, "I wanted to, but my mother and father told me to go and get a job where I could earn more money!" Many good German parents spoke the same way to their children and learned only too late that, by keeping them away from the vital fields, they probably did more than the Nazis themselves to pave the way for their nation's doom.

For the first fifteen or twenty years of their lives, your children look to you for guidance, not only in the small things, but in the big things, of life. You can train them to be Christ-minded or worldly minded—both possibilities are there. It is up to you to set the pace and to point the proper direction. You can start improving the world, once you see in your own flesh and blood the best personal representatives you could ever have as Christophers. They will be the hope of the world when they, and enough more like them, get into the thick of things. And as they become active Christbearers, they will bring into the market place the goodness you passed on to them from God. These children of yours may some day touch the lives of countless persons as teachers, as government workers, as writers, as experts in the labor field, as librarians, as social service workers—if you start right now to develop a missionary outlook within them.

(4) *Get into trends, national as well as local.* No matter how little time you have to spare from the duties of your home (which must always take precedence), try to use any spare moments on the bigger national projects as well as on those of your immediate environment. Don't, by any means, overlook local issues. They are important. But you will find that the more you interest yourself in the bigger problems, the more concerned you will be with the more important phases of local enterprises. Always remember that those who are against God are ever on the alert to poison the mainstream of life, knowing that the average person with religious con-

victions ordinarily moves in a very small sphere and shows little interest in bringing his principles to the market-place.

For you this is as ringing a challenge as it was to a lady in Detroit, one afternoon not long ago. About to mail her resignation to the Parent-Teachers Association (today the P-TA has an all-time high membership of 5,127,896), she happened to meet a friend who is a Christopher. After a brief conversation, the about-to-resign P-TA mother took the letter out of her purse and tore it up. "It never occurred to me that one person like myself mattered. But I see it now," she exclaimed. If you join an organization or a club, make it one where you can do a little missionary work. Some of you can be more than mere members. You can get on committees, take official posts, and assume leadership in a variety of ways—not, for personal advantage or privilege, of course, but with the distinct purpose of serving the general good.

One housewife, who brought the spirituality of her home out into the market place with a simple, forceful reminder to tens of millions, is Mrs. Herbert W. Hines, Mother-of-the-Year for 1948. Recently invited to be one of the eighteen participants in the *Life* Round Table held at Rye, N. Y., to discuss the third right enunciated in the Declaration of Independence, the "pursuit of happiness," Mrs. Hines stated clearly and convincingly, "I think happiness is primarily a spiritual matter. Religious faith has more to do with bringing happiness to an individual than anything else." This was in direct contrast to the statement made by Dr. Sidney Hook, chairman of the Department of Philosophy of New York University. Dr. Hook, according to the news report on the gathering, championed the growing secularist point of view, taking the stand that "moral rules for the guidance of life can be upheld without reference to religion." This materialistic concept by the educator might have had a widespread detrimental effect, had not an average housewife and mother made her voice heard on behalf of an elementary truth, understood by practically all but the tiny minority who are determined to eliminate all trace of God from American life.

Participate personally in all local, state, and national elections, not only by voting, but by getting others to vote as well, assisting them to reach a proper understanding of the issues at stake. Try to get full and authoritative information on candidates and all measures to be voted upon sufficiently in advance so as to be able to take steps to see that this information is passed on to as many as possible.

Check into the teaching in all schools—elementary and high schools, colleges and universities—for which you are paying taxes. See that all teachers and instructors are upholding the Constitution as they have sworn an oath of allegiance to do. Whenever you find any defects, go yourself—and take others with you—to the school in question and request fulfillment of its obligation. It is usually more effective to go directly to the institution involved rather than to a board of education. Remember, this is your right, whether or not you have children in the school. As a taxpayer, the school is your concern as much as it is anyone's, and you, therefore, have a responsibility to it.

(5) *Write letters.* This powerful means is at the disposal of every parent. (You will find suggestions about this in Chapter XII, Letter Writing—A Service to Society). A habit easily formed, it is an excellent means of keeping alive a sense of participation in, and responsibility to, the big world that lies beyond the home. One young mother, who does her bit by writing letters of approval or disapproval as part of her apostolate, told us, "I can't tell you how much I appreciate being a Christopher, even a silent one. Being the mother of two and expecting another, I'm tied to my home, but I'm still rarin' to do something concrete. I've had some interesting

experiences in letter writing, yet I never dreamed so much good could be accomplished with so little effort. I'm beginning to see more clearly than ever that all the household tasks in the world will matter little, if we bury whatever other talents we have."

(6) *Persuade others to be Christophers.* You will frequently find an opportunity to encourage at least one other person to be a doer, rather than a talker. It may be done by a word to your neighbor, your grocer, your hairdresser. It may be a note to your cousin in Wyoming, who hasn't decided what kind of a job to take after graduating from college. Or you may start things moving in the right direction simply by a conversation over the phone. One woman told how she made a passing remark about a year ago in just that way. When a friend began bemoaning the confusion of the times, she countered with "Well, I guess people like you and me can take our share of the blame. We want good government, good schools, good everything else, but we don't lift a finger to do anything about it. I can't think of one of our friends who is encouraging her kids to take any kind of a job except where they can feather their own nest." To this woman's amazement, six months later she learned that, as a result of that brief comment over the phone, her friend's son had taken a post on a board of education in Oregon and refused a tempting business offer which promised more money and a greater degree of financial security for the future.

(7) *Be selective and get others to be likewise.* The fields of education, government, labor-management, communications, and other allied spheres that influence the thoughts and actions of millions, in the correct order of things should be your servants, not your masters. It is up to you to see that this order is not reversed. The best way to accomplish this is to

see that these fields are staffed from top to bottom by normal, sensible Americans, rather than by those whose perverted reasoning is an ever-increasing threat to our democracy.

There is another means to achieve this purpose, however, and it is one that is not used often enough. It is your right to be selective, i.e., to *accept* what is good and *reject* what is evil. Most appreciate that they have a right of acceptance, but too often overlook their right of rejection. This distinction is most important. The apostles of atheism, subversion, perversion, viciousness, and rottenness of all types are forever abusing their God-given freedom to destroy freedom. Don't allow them to confuse you. Freedom must always be distinguished from license. One may be free to sell *good* oysters, but he has no right to sell bad ones.

From your home you have innumerable ways of exercising your right of acceptance and rejection. Do not worry about your sense of judgment. The average American mother and father are well blessed with common sense, fairness, and safe norms of decency.

As citizens and as taxpayers, you can make your voices heard by insisting on truth and integrity in education and government and by taking steps to eliminate all that is opposed to them. With regard to the objectionable in newspapers, magazines, books, movies, radio, and television, you can move mountains if you will but pass the word along and enlist, in every way you can, the cooperation of other parents. Censorship can be a dangerous means, but there is little chance of anything but good coming from the individual, personal judgment of people like you. By giving your patronage generously to what is good and withholding it from what you judge to be evil, you will be amazed at the vital power in your hands. The good you can do merely by not going to a movie that you think is below par, by turning off a radio program that borders on the vulgar or subversive, by not buying a magazine which makes a policy of introducing stories or pictures that are out of place in your home, will be a revelation to you. If enough of your kind of people do that consistently and phone around the neighborhood to get other parents, who think similarly, to do the same, you will be starting a ground swell that cannot fail to have telling effects.

In one of his recent columns, George E. Sokolsky touched on this point very penetratingly. "Each individual enjoys the privilege of rejecting what he believes to be untrue, harmful or malicious," he wrote. "He is lawfully entitled to express that rejection and to state the reason for his choice, either verbally or in writing or by such an act as withholding from purchasing a commodity or making a contribution. For instance, I never purchase a ticket for a motion picture written or produced by a Communist or a fellow-traveler or in which such a person performs no matter how small a part. That is my choice and I am fully within my right. I make no contribution to a philanthropic institution or to a public cause with which even one Communist is connected or the record of which indicates an acceptance of or an alliance with Communists. That is my right and privilege and no one can prevent me from pursuing my choice."

Yes, there are hundreds of ways in which you can start, as a committee of one, in being a Christopher in the sanctuary of your own home. You, and a million others like you, can develop together a force that nothing will be able to stop, that will sweep over the country and to the farthermost parts of the earth. You will have some inkling of the important role you are playing as a real partner of Christ in saving the world, a knowledge that will buoy you up in the midst of the difficulties that must be the lot of anyone who associates himself or herself in such an intimate relationship with the Crucified One. His lot was suffering from the crib to the cross, because He loved even the least of men so much. But you will never know, until you stand before the judgment seat of God, what your cooperation meant, how much you counted in bringing innumerable others to the heaven of happiness that Christ prepared for each and every human being. Then, in the perspective of eternity, you will see what a joy and a privilege it was to take things a bit hard on earth, in an attempt to make them a bit easier for those who have not been blessed as have you.

THINK BIG AND ACT BIG

But you will have to think and act in a big way—in terms of the world, not only of the neighborhood; of all men, not just a few. You will have to be daring and take literally the words of the Master when He said, "Launch out into the deep." In cautious, shallow water the returns are always small. Only far out in the deep, where the waves are rough and the chances great, is there much to be gained.

Rather than devote your time and energies to *theorizing* while the enemies of Christ are *doing*, rather than talk only to your own small circle while the godless talk to a hundred million others, rather than expend your lives in wishful thinking, in passing resolutions, or in complaining about conditions—with faith, with will, and with courage you can light your lantern and boldly carry it into the darkness of error and confusion and hate.

You women are far too important to preoccupy yourselves only with little things; too powerful a force for good to "fiddle while Rome burns." With God's help, you can bring the Christ-like qualities of the happy, Christian home back into a blind, unhappy world. Like Our Lady—the first Christ-bearer—literally and figuratively you can help renew the face of the earth.

For all of you there is a breath-taking opportunity, a tremendous challenge. There is no time to lose. Already too long on the march, the forces of evil have ravaged half the globe. With quick daring, however, and by acting at once, you can stop that march. You can be God's means—God's handmaidens—in restoring to a weary, heart-sick world the peace for which Christ suffered and died!

XII

LETTER WRITING

A Service to Society

"What is the common man thinking? The life history of democracy can be traced as an unceasing search for an answer to this vital question. . . . public opinion can only be of service to democracy if it can be heard."

The Pulse of Democracy
by GEORGE GALLUP AND S. F. RAE

LETTER WRITING—intelligent letter writing with a constructive message—is a very important service in preserving the God-given liberties of our free society. The letter you write *today* may do much to preserve tomorrow your own home and the homes of families a thousand miles away. Indeed, a letter is a form of life insurance for our nation.

If you will think back some three years, you may recall the attempt that was made by certain subversive elements to ease J. Edgar Hoover out of his job as head of the FBI. These elements, made up of some twenty different committees of three or four persons each, were continually at work—at dinners, receptions, in legislators' offices, at diplomatic functions, and so on. The tactics they used were shrewd and quietly destructive. On one hand, they set in motion all sorts of rumors aimed at destroying the effectiveness of the FBI. On the other hand, they let it be known—purely in the "public interest," of course—that Mr. Hoover deserved to be "promoted" to some higher spot in government service, thus paving the way for the elimination of a major obstacle in their plans to undermine America.

What you may not know, however, is that the actions of one woman in Washington, who was aware of what was going on and did something about it, prevented such deplorable tactics from meeting with success. This woman wrote a Christopher friend in New York, outlining the situation in detail. A day or so later she phoned this Christopher and told him, "Maybe you ought to try to do something from up there. Every bit will help—and Lord knows they deserve it!"

The latter's reaction was one of bewilderment at first. "If the FBI can't take care of itself," he asked, "what can a little fellow like me do about it?"

After giving the matter some thought, however, he decided he should at least make an effort. First he contacted ten close friends and suggested they write their Congressman about what was happening. The shock he received when almost all of them told him they didn't know who their Congressman was, spurred his determination instead of lessening it. Under his urging, the ten friends promised to get the necessary information and follow through with letters to their national legislators. Next, this Christopher, learning that his promptings were having some effect, extended his letter-writing suggestions to acquaintances all over the country. Soon letters began to pour into Washington from every part of the U. S.

The result? Mr. Hoover's assistant stated that this barrage

of letters "nipped in the bud" this particular attempt to sabotage the FBI. Had the woman in Washington never written that first letter, however, a whole chain of events leading to the protection of one of our most effective agencies for national security might never have been started on its way.

Persons in positions of responsibility—legislators, newspaper and magazine writers, motion picture producers and radio network directors—are much more susceptible to public opinion than is generally realized. One of the outstanding Hollywood motion picture reporters stated recently that the effect of constructive letters has been to change for the better much of the content of her movie gossip columns. Mothers and fathers all over the country, it appears, had written so many letters to her, protesting in a friendly but determined way about the strengthening of the trend towards divorce through constant references to Hollywood marital breakups, that she finally came to see the importance and reasonableness of their opinions.

In *The Reader's Digest,* George E. Outland, a Congressman from California, recently pointed out that every morning at ten o'clock in our nation's capital finds the four hundred and thirty-five Representatives and the ninety-six Senators doing the same thing: *reading their mail.* "Congressmen may miss committee meetings," he said, "absent themselves from the floor, fail to show up for roll calls and votes. But they always read their mail." Sixty thousand letters a day pour into Congress. One single district alone sends its national legislators one hundred and twenty-five letters each and every day.

From their mail, Congressman Outland continued, our Representatives in Washington know what the people "back home" want and expect. Yet it must not be thought that they simply take the total number of letters for an issue and the total against the same issue and decide which is the heavier pile. "One thoughtful letter will outweigh half a dozen which simply say 'vote for this' or 'vote for that.' One spontaneous outburst on your own stationery is worth a hundred mimeographed letters or newspaper clippings in some write-your-Congressman drive. . . . Multigraphed telegrams are a dime a dozen. . . . Don't waste your time signing canned letters, or copying letters someone has prepared. . . ."

One man who has been in Congress for ten years says that the letters which really count are those that show your legislative representatives three things: (1) that it is you yourself doing the writing, (2) that you know something about the subject, (3) that you have done some thinking. "If every voter wrote one letter like that once a year," says this legislator, "I believe we'd have a fifty percent better Congress."

The power of a good letter, therefore, should never be underestimated. A single letter—sometimes even a brief note—has been known to change the course of life for many a man and woman. A few good letters, timely and sincere, have been able to influence the thinking of millions.

MAKING YOUR OPINION HEARD

Many people fail to write letters because they have the attitude "What good will it do? What's done is done."

How faulty this reasoning is can best be illustrated by what one of the leading executives of a large radio corporation said in defending the type of programs his company aired to the radio public. "If you don't get all the educational programs you want," he said in effect, "if you don't get the kind of music you like, the kind of comedy, mystery story, soap opera, or whatever else you wish, it's your own fault. We listen to our listeners. They make our programs."

The power you can exert, not only in radio, but in all

spheres of influence once you become articulate was well illustrated not long ago by what happened to a chain of motion picture theaters in the Mid-west. This particular theater chain made no distinction in the sort of programs they showed on Friday evenings and the features they displayed on Saturday afternoons for children. One mother thought there should be a distinction. She thought weekend movies ought to be adapted to the needs of the children who attended in large numbers. "You ought to have pictures more suitable for youngsters," she wrote the head of the theater chain. "Instead of glamor and the gun-play of gangsters, why not substitute wholesome films—some of the better westerns, for example? Or travelogues or comedies? Youngsters oughtn't to be exposed to the atmosphere of the roadhouse, the police blotter, the divorce court. They shouldn't spend several hours of their time each week seeing pictures which instill in them unrealistic desires for slick limousines, penthouses and lives of ease and luxury, as so many current movies do. Such films only give them a false perspective of life. . . ."

The management brushed the letter aside, as the theater executive frankly admitted. "Just let her cool off," was his terse comment. "She'll forget the whole thing."

But the lady didn't forget. She wasn't a crank, and she wouldn't be ignored. Off she went to the two groups in her hometown to which she belonged—a Catholic society and a civic garden club. She tackled her friends in both organizations, urging them to write to the management. She recommended that their letters be brief, courteous, and *firm*.

The reaction to these public expressions of opinion was not long in coming. Such a volume of letters poured in that the management reluctantly decided to shift over temporarily to the kind of pictures requested, though they were "fully convinced" the proposition wouldn't work. Attendance would drop off, they said. They'd lose money and with it their reputation for being smart businessmen.

But things turned out quite differently from what they expected. "We not only make everybody happy," the head of the theater chain exclaimed afterwards, "but we make much more money under the new arrangement, as a matter of fact, than we did under the old."

In Rochester, N. Y., a young high school girl recently wrote the editor of that city's newspaper, the *Times-Union:*

"All of us have been reading lately of the shocking rise in the divorce rate. Too little is being done to correct the situation. Novels and the motion pictures furnish us with escapist literature, when what is needed is something to bring us sharply to our senses, and help keep a sacred ceremony from becoming a pitiful farce."

This girl went on to advocate the use of all means possible to emphasize and make Americans aware of the sacredness and dignity of marriage and the vows they had sworn to keep.

The letter so impressed the editor of the *Times-Union* that he declared in an editorial:

"A contributor to our Readers' Forum today has a suggestion that should not be allowed to go the way of yesterday's newspaper. It cries for action. Divorce and tandem marriages are glamorized on every hand. A few weeks ago the idols of American Youth in two of their top interests ran off with other men's wives and, after hasty divorces, married them. Society must do something to make youths believe in marriage.

"Our correspondent may not have the whole answer. But it is an idea that should be kicked around and looked at from all angles until a scheme that can be realized comes out of it."

An occasional letter sometimes demands more forceful

language than normally is used. The written reply, appearing in *Time* magazine, of one labor leader to the appeal of William Z. Foster, chairman of the Communist Party, for funds to fight the Mundt-Nixon Bill is one such letter. It met with such a storm of enthusiastic approval that its good effects will continue for some time to come. The labor leader, Harry Lundeberg, boss of the West Coast AFL Sailors Union of the Pacific, wrote Foster the penetrating reply that he (Foster) had "a nerve appealing to a bonafide American trade union for help in view of the scabby disruptive tactics employed by your so-called political party against the American trade union movement and against the United States as a whole.

"All through your letters," Lundeberg went on, "you refer to Fascism, stating that your party is anti-Fascist. Who are you kidding? There are no bigger Fascists than the Communists. The only difference between Stalin and Hitler is that Stalin went Hitler one better. It was the Communist Party that joined hands with the Nazis to break up the Socialist Party and the trade-union movement in Germany. . . . Don't try to propagandize people who know the score.

"As a matter of fact our organization classes the Communist Party as an enemy of the working class. As far as we are concerned, they can take the whole scabby, stinking Communist Party and kick it in the middle of Siberia and let it have a taste of Uncle Joe Stalin's slave camps. . . . It is our considerate opinion that this is a fit place for the American Communist Party, its stooges, its fellow-travelers—long-haired ones, short-haired ones—and what have you. . . ."

The letter of a woman office worker from Buffalo, N. Y., on a particularly necessary piece of legislation up for Congressional consideration won a public tribute from Senator Ives of the Empire State for the worker's interest. Not only that, this woman was instrumental in prodding thousands of her fellow citizens to make their voices heard in favor of the measure. This is how it happened:

Certain anti-American elements who were working hard to defeat the Bill had flooded both the House of Representatives and the Senate with letters and telegrams of vilification and protest. Senator Ives, speaking of this situation, indicated many letters in opposition to the proposed legislation had been received—and he referred to the city of Buffalo as one point of origin for a goodly portion of them. *One* person, however, an office worker named Betty Baldwin, by a simple, sincere letter, set in motion a whole series of events that did much to dispel the bad impression left by the actions of the subversives. One man, prominent in Buffalo's civic affairs, immediately upon learning of this sent six telegrams to important members of Congress in Washington, and countless other public-spirited citizens followed suit. When questioned as to why she had written her letter in the first place, Miss Baldwin replied: *"I'm a Christopher."*

Last spring in New York City when the Actors' Equity Association (representing the acting profession in the legitimate theatre) met to elect a new slate of officers, a few typewritten words on a yellow piece of paper helped prevent the left-wingers in the Association from gaining control. These leftists, numbering about sixty percent of the total membership of two thousand, were apparently dissatisfied with the regular ticket selected by the nominating committee which, in turn, had been chosen by the general membership. They nominated an independent ticket—a permissable procedure.

At the meeting discussing the candidates, for and against, Broadway star Bert Lytell got up and made a speech in favor of those of the regular slate. The leftists countered with a barrage of telegrams and letters favoring their candidates and aimed especially at influencing the younger members of the Association. At the height of the excitement, Lytell got the floor again and pulled just *one* telegram out of his pocket. He proceeded to read it aloud. It was an enthusiastic endorsement of the regular ticket—signed by Katherine Cornell.

A hush fell over the audience. The younger members, previously extremely vocal in their opinions, were the most silent of all. Much as they might have wished to, they could not dispute this telegram from the First Lady of the American stage.

In the election which followed, seven out of ten of the regular ticket were elected. That one "voice" in the form of a telegram made the difference!

A parent, writing to the New York *World-Telegram*, a few months ago, crystallized for thousands of people their appreciation of the protection given them by their Board of Education in the matter of safeguarding a fundamental principle of the American educational system: respect for the religious convictions of all our citizens. The correspondent, Mrs. M. N. Bonbrake, wrote:

"I think it is time a 'parent,' speaking for many parents, came to the defense of our Superintendent of Schools, Dr. Jansen, and our Board of Education, regarding this much-discussed ban on the *Nation* magazine.

"Not long ago Dr. Jansen and the Board of Education decided to ban the *Nation* magazine from public school libraries, after it had published a series of six strongly anti-Catholic articles. At that time, Dr. Jansen gave to the press this reason for the ban:

> 'A child's religion is a sacred thing between himself and his parents and we have no right to put into the hands of one pupil a magazine article attacking the religion of his classmate. The fundamental principle of the educational system of our great city is respect for the faiths of all our children.'

"I would like to congratulate Dr. Jansen and the Board of Education for defining tolerance in the wisest and most understanding words I have ever heard from a public official. Had these articles been anti-Semitic, anti-Protestant, or anti-Negro, Dr. Jansen and the Board of Education would have acted in the same manner. They have done so in the past.

"It is a great comfort to all parents in New York City to know that the faith of every child in the city schools, whether he be a Catholic, a Protestant, or a Jew, is being protected at all times with complete impartiality. Dr. Jansen is not himself a Catholic; his action was based on the highest motives and with the general welfare of the school children of New York City in mind."

The clean-up drive started by comic book publishers over the country is definitely attributable to the weight of public opinion brought to bear by educators and parents' groups. Through direct contact and on an even wider scale through the medium of letter writing, many of these publishers were persuaded to approve a code of moral standards which will apply to over fifteen million of the fifty million comic books sold every month. The balance of the major comic books publishers are expected to accept this code shortly.

From these—and literally thousands of other letters which could be listed—it should be evident that a letter with a constructive message can be a great force for good. And it can be an even greater force for determining public policies than are those letters whose only purpose is to confuse, to intimidate, to vilify.

PRELIMINARY PREPARATION FOR GOOD LETTER WRITING

In letter writing, as in any other kind of writing, there are certain preliminary rules, which anyone who hopes to persuade others to see the point he or she is trying to make would do well to follow.

First of all, there is the *remote preparation*. This consists of (1) observation, (2) reading, and (3) reflection.

Anyone can train his or her powers of *observation* and learn to see accurately and to retain what he or she sees. The importance of *reading* what goes on in the world in newspapers, in magazines, and in books hardly needs any emphasis. In addition to being a valuable aid in letter writing, it is one of the contributing factors to a well-rounded education. Observation and reading are of little use, however, unless people acquire the habit of *reflection* on what has been observed and read. The man who does not reflect, as Cardinal Newman said, sees "the tapestry of human life as it were on the wrong side, and it tells no story."

Though not a technical rule like those of observation, reading and reflection, being sincere is just as important to good letter writing as any other quality which covers mere mechanical proficiency. We will never succeed in influencing others through our letters if, in order to make an impression, we pretend to possess what we do not actually have. It is much better to utilize, as best we can, what we do know. We should stick to the facts and express our own honest feelings. To do otherwise, to give expression to thoughts that are not our own, is to court difficulties

SPECIFIC LAWS TO FOLLOW

All writing—letter writing, essay writing, book writing, short story or novel writing is based on four fundamental laws: (1) unity, (2) coherence, (3) emphasis, (4) interest.

Unity means that the letter must be about one thing, just as good business practice insists that commercial correspondence limit itself to one topic in each exchange of notes. Unity is achieved without too much effort simply by asking oneself the question, "What do I want to say?" before taking pen in hand or sitting down at the typewriter. Failure to ask this question is responsible for the greatest number of mistakes in any sort of writing.

For your letter to have *coherence,* one part should follow after another, logically and naturally. Material should be arranged so that its order of importance is apparent to the reader. Some parts of your letter, of course, will be more important than others and so you will want to make certain things stand out.

This involves what is known as positioning of ideas which, properly done, makes for *emphasis.* People tend to remember most what comes at the beginning and what comes at the end of any piece of writing. If anything, the last thought expressed is remembered best of all (but an effort should be made to have letters so interesting that readers will read to the end). The *proportion* of space you devote to any one idea is quite likely to be the measure of how much you want to impress that idea on those who read your letter.

The most effective way to capture the readers' *interest* is to use concrete matter freely. Examples, illustrations, comparisons, stories, descriptions, factual reference from newspapers, magazines, etc., will aid in this. They will help to rivet the attention of the reader to the ideas you wish to put across. The dull letter seldom succeeds in impressing anyone.

Give yourself to your letters. Understand what you are writing about. Gather sufficient evidence to support the point you are trying to make. Present your ideas attractively.

Be brief, but not curt. Use a moderate tone in all your letters. Friendly, constructive criticism (if that is your intention) will accomplish far more than angry outbursts. It is the old story—mentioned elsewhere in this book—of "disagreeing without being disagreeable." The head of an eastern manufacturing concern who wrote to one of the movie studios regarding a picture he felt put crime in a too-favorable light, illustrates the point very well. After commending the studio for its efforts in the past to keep its entertainment standards high, he stated in detail his objection to the film in question. And he concluded with these well-chosen words:

"If I am wrong, please overlook this letter; if I am right, I am happy to be able to call your attention to what must be an oversight of your splendid organization."

Regarding the technical construction of your letter, it is suggested that you make an outline if it is at all possible. It will help you follow the laws of good letter writing.

Keep your paragraphs short, three to five sentences, and your sentences correspondingly brief, fifteen to twenty-five words. Use language with which your reader will be familiar. Avoid slang or trite, hackneyed phrases. Whenever possible, begin with an anecdote, a case history, or by posing a problem. End with a summary and make your last sentence one that will linger in your reader's mind. One authority sums this all up in these words: "Logical organization, avoidance of clichés and jargon, adequate transitional aids, and other such rhetorical maneuvers will help marvelously in sustaining reader interest. But in my opinion the two stylistic devices which most contemporary editors are seeking are *conversational quality* and *concreteness.*"

You may not always be writing to an editor, of course, but these rules apply whether you are writing to a publication, to your Congressman, to your local legislative representative, to a radio station or motion picture studio, or to some organization or society. These rules are not arbitrary enactments of grammarians. They are based upon sound psychology —upon an insight into human nature. And, in writing letters, it is human nature with which you have to deal. As for style, fundamentally any particular approach to writing is but a thinking-out put into language. Providing you mean what you say and say what you mean, there will not be any need for striving after an effect. Pretentiousness here, as anywhere else in life, may antagonize rather than persuade.

AN EXAMPLE OF GOOD LETTER WRITING

The following letter to *Life* magazine is illustrative of what we mean. Its friendly tone, its objectiveness, its stress on decency in the presentation of printed and pictorial material, and its sincere belief that the editors of the publication to which it was sent would give it their earnest consideration, could not fail to have made a favorable impression.

The letter reads:

"Gentlemen:

"Like millions of other housewives I have been a reader of *Life* magazine for several years. In fact, I never miss an issue. I find each and every issue crammed with interest. I should not like to have to do without it.

"But I am beginning to wonder if I ought to keep on taking *Life* into my home. As a mother of two children, I am keenly aware of the problem of juvenile delinquency. Fortunately, so far I have had no personal contact with the problem. But I am not so naïve as to suppose that it can't happen here—in my own home.

"We all know that impressions received through the eye are by far the most powerful. And it is also well-known that juvenile delinquents admit under questioning that many of their criminal activities are induced, fed, and fostered by the kind of reading matter—usually pictorial—with which they come in contact.

"On these grounds, it seems to me that many of the pictures and advertisements in *Life* are questionable. In fact, it seems as though every issue carries a large number of pictures of 'bathing beauties' dressed so scantily as easily to incite young people to seek 'excitement' and 'adventure.' J. Edgar Hoover has repeatedly pointed out the unfortunate effect of this search for thrills and has blamed 'poisonous reading matter.' Therefore, my problem amounts to this: with a growing boy and a growing girl in the house, ought I to buy *Life*?

"Some people take the unrealistic attitude that all is needed is sound home training—and then there need be no fear at all about exposing youngsters to any sort of incitement to evil. That this is not true can easily be shown by an examination of the records of Child Guidance Clinics over the country. The best home training is no insurance against delinquency. Mothers must make every effort to prevent the malleable characters of their children from being molded into the curious shapes of evil one finds everywhere today.

"So—there it is: my dilemma. I want to keep on getting *Life* magazine because it affords me pleasure. But I must safeguard the mental health and emotional stability of my children. Maybe the solution to my problem is in your hands. *Life* could go on being beautiful without the bathing beauties. In fact, it would be in better taste. Knowing that you are always open to suggestions, I feel sure you will take this in the spirit in which it is offered.

Sincerely yours, . . ."

WRITE A NOTE OF APPRECIATION

In all this discussion on good letter writing with a constructive message, there should be mentioned an additional type of correspondence which is almost equally important, namely, the note of appreciation.

People and organizations welcome constructive criticism and suggestions. A letter of praise for a job well done is a powerful stimulant for persevering effort along the same lines.

Even a brief note of encouragement often has far-reaching results. Among the thousands of letters, telegrams, and telephone calls of appreciation which poured into the *American Broadcasting Company* not long ago, praising the network's documentary broadcast, "COMMUNISM–U. S. BRAND," was this note of appreciation from a listener: ". . . [this program] was brilliantly written and produced and a special tribute to your courage and vision. As a sincerely appreciative American, may I earnestly hope that this is only the beginning of many many more of this same type program under your completely able guidance. May God bless you in all your undertakings."

Letters like this are incentives to continue the good work in the future. Here are six reactions to such notes sent by Christophers. All are in similar vein. Yet even in the slight variation of the wording all show a profound sense of gratitude that people have taken the time to inform them of their interest.

". . . *Greatly appreciated your letter,*" wrote one outstanding columnist to a reader. "*I get my share of unfavorable mail, so letters like yours are doubly welcome.*"

"*I appreciate the encouragement we received in letters like yours,*" was the grateful acknowledgment of a school superintendent to a public-spirited correspondent.

From *Time* magazine to a letter writer who praised the publication for a splendid article: "*Thank you very much for your warming note. . . . Showed it to all hands concerned . . . and they were naturally much pleased.*"

Answered *Newsweek* to another writer: "*Thank you very much for taking the time to let us know you liked the story.*"

Wrote Julius Ochs Adler, general manager of the *New*

York Times, to another reader: "*Thank you for your generous commendation upon my recent talk before the Chaplains Association regarding the outlawing of Communism which I highly appreciate.*"

"*It is most heartening to know,*" replied one prominent official in the State Department to a correspondent, "*that I have your support in undertaking what promises to be a difficult although interesting assignment. . . .*"

Of course, it is quite possible that you may not receive any reply to the letters you have sent to editors, government officials, civic leaders, and others. Don't be surprised at this. Persons in such positions are usually so deluged with work that no matter how impressed they may be with what you have to say, they often have neither the time nor the facilities to tell you so. However, your letter *registers,* even if they cannot thank you for it.

One of America's foremost magazines, with a tremendous circulation, passes through thirty-five different hands every constructive letter received. Even if a letter is utterly opposed to their editorial policy, it receives the same attention they give to pleasant notes of commendation.

So whether you do or do not receive an answer matters little. What does matter is that you are on the alert, reaching others with sound, healthy ideas. Your letters, you may be sure, are read. And they do have their effect.

ONE LETTER A WEEK

You could easily write one letter a week, whether it be of praise or of constructive criticism. In some instances, you might even be able to write one good letter a day. All it takes is a few minutes of your time and a three-cent stamp. And all you have to do to make sure your letter is a *good* letter is to remember these principles: (1) write as you would to a friend—be personal, not impersonal; (2) be constructive, not destructive; (3) be specific, not vague; (4) make your point but don't keep repeating it; (5) be brief, but not curt; (6) be yourself, think for yourself, write for yourself; (7) write as you would talk; (8) offer a positive suggestion, don't just complain; (9) inject a friendly feeling along with the facts; (10) be neat and be sure to sign your name and address clearly. Letters without addresses are disregarded.

Like the young woman in Buffalo who, when asked why she wrote to Senator Ives, replied, "I'm a Christopher," you can make the thoughts you put down on paper perform a real service to society. As a Christopher, you have the responsibility to express your opinion on every subject which affects you and your neighbors. By the few lines you may send to some newspaper, some movie studio or radio station, to some local or national legislator, you may be the means of bringing untold numbers that much nearer to the God-given principles on which our republic is founded. And you may likewise bring untold numbers to a better appreciation of the Truth for which Christ suffered and died.

XIII

TO BUSINESSMEN—A CHALLENGE

THE TREMENDOUS IMPACT for good one businessman made on the lives of thousands was well illustrated recently in the farewell tribute paid him following his untimely death. In the June 28, 1948, issue of the *Labor Leader* are found these eloquent words:

"The death of Basil Harris, president of the U.S. Lines, removes a Catholic landmark from the New York waterfront. He knew the shipping business and made it a profitable enterprise. For this his associates honored him and sought his counsel.

"But the men who went down to the sea in his ships, the men and women working in his offices, the longshoremen and the union officials, all these respected and honored him for much better reasons. 'He was a man of his word,' they said—fair and square, a man who never belittled any man by his wealth or power.

"The inspiration of his life was Christ and he served Him well. All the titles and dignities that honored him meant little to him; indeed, it was he who distinguished them. He would have rejoiced with a great-hearted laugh at the way the announcement of his death was received in a waterfront bar. The Tussler pushed his cap back, drenched the news with his beer. 'God, that was a good guy!' The gang's 'Yep' would have sounded better to Basil Harris than any choir's amen."

The 1,500 persons who attended Mr. Harris' funeral at Rye, N. Y., on June 21, 1948, included very many business leaders, to be sure. But a far greater number of stevedores, dockmen, teachers, caddies, grocers, taxi drivers, gardeners, policemen, office help and others came to bear witness to their love and affection for one who had, at all times, given those very things to each of them.

In many ways Mr. Harris was a Christopher. Love of *all* people, the distinguishing mark of the true Christ-bearer, was certainly a part of him. Many know of the generosity he displayed in sharing his material possessions, but only a few are aware of his countless daily acts of kindness to those who needed and wanted more than money. He was motivated from within by some greater power than mere human philanthropy, an activity all too seldom accompanied by personal solicitude. The most significant tribute, perhaps, that could be paid him was the quiet service he rendered during the depression of the '30's. Countless unemployed men and women who sought desperately for jobs found, when they approached Harris, the helping hand they needed. "I don't know of anyone who has gone to him in search of a job that he hasn't helped get one," an associate of his commented at the time. "I take off my hat to him. Most of us give money, but Basil does that and more. He gives his time. He gives himself!"

The driving force back of all this was a deep spiritual sense which had been stimulated while Harris was a student at Princeton University. One evening near the end of the school term he visited three classmates who roomed together, in order to go over some examination material with them. After a couple of hours of study one of them decided to go to bed earlier than the others. He said good night, and then went off to his corner of the room. Once into his pajamas, he knelt down and, for about ten minutes, recited the Rosary.

This simple expression of faith made a lasting impression on Harris, and during his lifetime he referred back to it continually. As for the student, little did he realize that what he had done was to be the turning point in the life of one of his companions. Years later Basil Harris became a Catholic and from then on his entire outlook was dominated by a devotion to God that was strong, resourceful, deep, and constant.

Unlike many other successful businessmen whose very expressions betray preoccupation with power and wealth, Harris displayed a wonderful sense of humor and gaiety. He took pleasure in giving others pleasure. He was particularly kind and cheering to the poor who often get the least personal attention.

Wealth, as such, meant little to him, and his feeling in this regard was well expressed in a remark he made one day while en route from Washington to New York. Reading in the paper about a millionaire who had just died as he was in the process of building a large new estate, he exclaimed:

"That sounds like the fellow in the Gospel—the one who pulled down his barns to build bigger ones and forgot he was to appear before God that very night for the final payoff."

At the other end of the economic ladder, a *small* businessman, a tinsmith in New York, saw his goal in life with the same clear vision as did Basil Harris. The purpose of this tinsmith, one Paul Antonio, was to make the world a little better than he found it. Because he tried to think and act in terms beyond the confines of his own small shop, one thing in particular that he did bears mentioning now.

Some time back he was hired to build and install the black steel ballot box which is now used by members of the Security Council of the United Nations at Lake Success when they cast their votes on world issues. When the box was opened just before the first Security Council session, there at the bottom was a brief message written in clear handwriting on a cheap piece of notepaper. The message read:

> "May I, who have had the privilege of constructing this ballot box, cast the first vote? May God be with every member of the United Nations Organization, and through your noble efforts bring lasting peace to us all—all over the world.
>
> (signed) "Paul Antonio, mechanic."

By this one simple act did Antonio give the Council members a reminder of the importance of the supernatural. At the same time (because the incident was widely publicized for its human interest angle) he got the same lesson over to millions in our land and over the world.

THE PROPER APPROACH

There are many businessmen who feel and act as did Paul Antonio and Basil Harris. But there are many, many more —and these constitute the majority—on whom a God-given concept of human existence has not made a sufficient impression. These men are good, solid citizens, however. They stand for law and order. They are a credit to their community. But, unfortunately, they often *underestimate the power for good* which they could exert on a large scale. They restrict themselves, in so many ways, to spheres that are local and small. They do not participate actively and in great numbers to influence for the better, as surely as they could, the trends that convulse mankind today. Theirs is the lack of recognition of the "truths that make men free."

They may acknowledge that the world is sick, yet too often they neglect to do what is only ordinary common sense to cure its ills. And by their neglect they leave the field to those who have a well-calculated, carefully prepared plan to revolutionize the earth and reshape it in the form of a totalitarian, godless global state.

A French businessman who visited this country not long ago made a statement which illustrates this situation in all its stark reality.

"My interests were limited to my business, my house, my weekends," this Frenchman said. "I paid no attention to our government, our schools, our labor movements. I found out rather late that those who were very much interested in every phase of France's public life were men whose one evil objective was to wreck our country. That they have nearly succeeded is due to the neglect of men like myself to give time and intelligent effort to what concerns the common interests of all. It was my mistake as a businessman. I hope American businessmen do not make the same mistake."

American businessmen *have been* making that mistake, unfortunately. Their handicap has been that too often they have identified themselves with things, rather than with *ideas.* They do everything possible for the comfort and convenience of the body, forgetting that the totalitarians hit first, last, and always for the intellect and soul of each and every man, woman, and child. The godless know that whoever controls the thoughts of man, controls all else. They know they can regiment whole peoples, depriving them of their God-given liberties. In Russia where an organized minority of the godless hold complete sway, they have done exactly that. Robert Ripley in his feature, "Believe It or Not," points out that a Soviet citizen

May NOT own land	May NOT be tried by a jury
May NOT choose his own job	May NOT absent himself from work
May NOT strike	May NOT picket
May NOT employ labor	May NOT travel
May NOT own jewelry	May NOT ring a church bell

May NOT be friends with a foreigner

And is FORBIDDEN

Freedom of SPEECH	Freedom of ASSEMBLY
Freedom of RELIGION	Freedom of SOUL

For a businessman reading this to reply with the somewhat hackneyed "It can't happen here," is to ignore facts without even realizing he is doing so.

By the very nature of his calling, a businessman should be a force for good in and far beyond his community. Yet, of all groups of people, as one business firm itself pointed out, "businessmen are most laggard in their interest . . . in the exchange of ideas."

People feel this lack of interest. You have only to recall what happened at the political rallies of the Wallace party in Philadelphia last July. Not all of the convention delegates were totalitarian-minded. Many were confused individuals who were not being reached by anybody. Still, to quote

Joseph and Stewart Alsop in the New York *Herald-Tribune*, ". . . . The great majority of the people here are being used, carefully and astutely by the Communists."

There lies the great peril to this country—the failure to show concern for those of our population who need concern the most. Anne O'Hare McCormick, writing in the New York *Times*, was even more specific in this regard. "The danger in all this does not arise from the power of Mr. Wallace," Miss McCormick stated. "It arises from the babes in the wood that constitute a large part of his followers. If this convention represents a cross section of the United States, the woods are full of peace-seekers, panacea-seekers, instinctive isolationists, thwarted people of good will who are ready to listen to demagogues. . . ."

GOOD DEEDS WASTED

Often a businessman will give a new wing to a college or university and yet have little or no idea what will be taught in the building he donated. Not infrequently, the very principles for which he stands will be undermined in the classrooms he built.

Again, with but few exceptions, the huge foundations created by prominent businessmen are confined to the physical and material, seldom to the development and furtherance of the basic principles on which our country, *as a free democracy*, exists. For example, only recently it was discovered that a Communist had gained an important post on a large foundation established by a well-known industrialist. And this subversive took every advantage of his position to sabotage with a few well-chosen, dishonest ideas the noble purpose for which the foundation was built.

From one end of this country to the other, tens of thousands of our finest citizens are engaged in various forms of small business. These people constitute part of the backbone of our nation, but their primary preoccupation is with the *small* problems in their midst. Meanwhile they are being saturated with poisonous ideas by other men who, daringly bold, are gambling for big stakes and are "playing for keeps."

These doers of evil are not "outsiders." They are part of our American society. With amazing prophetic accuracy, in the nineteenth century the great British historian and statesman, Lord Macauley, pointed that out.

"Your republic," he said, "will be pillaged and ravaged in the twentieth century, just as the Roman Empire was by the barbarians of the fifth century, with this difference: the devastators of the Roman Empire came from abroad, while your barbarians will be the people of your own country and the products of your own institutions."

CONCEPT OF GOD IGNORED

Most thinking people are aware that some sort of a breakdown along these lines is going on in America. What they don't seem to realize, however, is that probably the greatest single factor in the rise of the godless philosophy of totalitarianism comes from allowing the concept of God to fall into disuse. Some businessmen have lost all sense of the Brotherhood of Man under the Fatherhood of God. They have lost the realization that every human being is a child of God, made in His own image and likeness. One British colonial industrialist not long ago expressed the tragedy of this attitude when he said:

"There was a time when I might have been interested in helping poor devils in need. Once I even thought of building a hospital out here for the study of tropical diseases. But I kept putting it off until I had more time and money. When I began in this hole, I was going to quit as soon as I had ten thousand pounds. When I got that, I decided to make it twenty. Then I went on piling up money until it was too late; the stuff has buried me!"

This man had lost contact with human kind. In the tired, slow shake of his head as he spoke, it was obvious that he was alone, and fated forever to remain so unless he made a sincere effort to regain his sense of perspective, to regain the true belief that fame and fortune in this life are fleeting and the things of Heaven are not.

THE SITUATION IS NOT HOPELESS

This man's case—and thousands like his—are not hopeless, however. There is still time (though the hour is growing late) to get "back on God's side." But men of good will must be more than just against past personal evils and present public ones, such as Communism, or Nazism, or Fascism. All these evils spring out of warped attempts to correct abuses and right wrongs. And even if all these philosophies were suddenly eliminated, the principal problem would still remain, that of the godless materialism which is the cancer in the life of America. Just as disease strikes, not because of the power of the germ but because of the lowered resistance of the body, so a great many otherwise good people who have scarcely a speaking acquaintance with first principles are becoming easy targets for many popular errors.

Sound-thinking, God-fearing people must be for something; they must be for the daily application of all the God-given principles upon which this country is founded.

Businessmen could be the shock troops of these good ideas once they see that it is from ideas alone that the great forces in the world, good as well as evil, proceed. If they will apply the same ingenuity and devotion to the spreading of good, sound American ideas that they apply to their own private pursuits, they can arrest and change for the better–more effectively, perhaps, than any other group–the disintegrating process that is menacing more and more the best interests of our country and our civilization. Businessmen striving personally and individually, however, can easily bring about a change for the better if they will devote a comparatively small part of their time and effort, and perhaps no more than one-tenth of the money now being expended on their present charities, to preserve and spread the fundamental American principles which make their business, their private pursuits, the very life of their nation, possible.

To their credit, more and more business and professional men are beginning to realize their responsibilities and, more significantly, are beginning to do something about it. One zealous Christopher, an Indiana lawyer, drew up with a group of friends an advertisement and arranged for it to be given eye-catching space in several daily newspapers in the Middle West. The cost in one case was borne by a chamber of commerce, in another by an insurance company. One daily, the Cleveland *Press,* even ran an editorial on it. Though it appeared only once, it brought home to countless readers a positive fact of which many of them are losing sight and of which they need to be reminded. The advertisement read:

DO YOU BELIEVE IN AMERICANISM?
–Then–
HOLD THESE TRUTHS

One hundred and seventy years ago today, our Founding Fathers, in the Declaration of Independence, expressed THE BASIC PRINCIPLES OF AMERICANISM in these words:

"We hold these TRUTHS TO BE SELF-EVIDENT:– That ALL MEN ARE CREATED EQUAL: that they are ENDOWED BY THEIR CREATOR WITH CERTAIN UNALIENABLE RIGHTS: that among these are life, liberty and the pursuit of happiness. That, to SECURE THESE RIGHTS, GOVERNMENTS ARE INSTITUTED among men, deriving their just powers from the consent of the governed;—"

Thus, as a good American, you must believe that:

1. *God is the Creator of all men.*
2. *Your rights and the rights of your fellowmen are God-given,* and for that reason alone *no power on earth can take these rights away.*
3. *As a personal creature of God, each of us is equal in the sight of God to every other person,* and for that reason *each of us is entitled to the equal protection of all the laws of the land.*
4. *Government is not man's master: on the contrary, government is man's servant, chosen by man to protect the God-given rights of mankind.*

Upon the firm foundation of these truths the glory and prosperity of our beloved country has risen steadily through the years to be the crowning wonder of the world. These truths have made America great. Only these truths can keep America great. If you want to be a good American and preserve the blessings of liberty for yourself and your posterity —then—

HOLD THESE TRUTHS

Emulating the examples of the Indiana lawyer and his associates, a group of businessmen and newspaper officials in the Mid-west have embarked upon a campaign to get service clubs and parent-teachers organizations in states not requiring the study of the Declaration of Independence to correct this condition at once. Further, several of these same men have set up a program urging that the head of the household read the Declaration and the Preamble to the Constitution to the entire family on the Fourth of July.

In similar vein, just a few months ago the Beveridge Paper Company of Indianapolis announced its determination to work for a wider recognition of the basic American doctrine which is the heritage of free men in a free society. "We hear a great deal these days about various 'plans'—the 'Five Year Plan,' the 'Marshall Plan,' and many others," this company wrote. "We think it is well for us to give heed to another 'plan' adopted July 4, 1776—the Declaration of Independence. We have had copies of this prepared and are enclosing one herewith."

In addition to these methods of bringing to public consciousness our priceless, God-given heritage, many businessmen have also found other means of getting into the mainstream of life the sound ideas whose widespread distribution will do much to preserve our free way of life. In some cases they have done this personally. In other cases where they have been unable to get into the thick of things themselves, they have encouraged and actively assisted others to go into the market place. Some of these enterprising businessmen hold prominent positions in industrial and financial life. Others are less in the public spotlight.

A stockbroker in upper New York State has encouraged his two daughters to become teachers and his son to go into government service—with a Christopher purpose.

A forty-six-year-old Cincinnati businessman gave up a $30,000-a-year manufacturing position to prepare to join a college faculty where he can teach American government. He claims as the motivating reason for this step the deep impression made upon him by many young people "who want to participate in politics but don't know what to do." And he continued, "When I decided to go back to school after being away for twenty-six years, I was afraid my friends and business colleagues would think I was crazy or something. I was astonished to discover that ninety percent of them—many of whom I thought were only interested in making an honest buck—considered it a wonderful idea and wished they could do the same."

A businessman in Boston is currently helping his son in all the necessary preparation required prior to his entering the labor relations field.

A public accountant who assisted his son to follow a career as a film scenario writer has seen his interest pay dividends a thousand times over in several outstanding motion pictures this young man has already helped prepare.

An insurance man in a firm which employs some one thousand persons, is acting as a committee of one to step up interest among the workers about getting better-quality Americans into the four spheres which mainly influence our lives today—education, government, labor-management, and communications.

A lawyer who found himself, in his own words, "getting so wrapped up in law practice I've been overlooking the more important things of life," has completed plans to go into government service with a Christopher motive in mind.

An official in a large New York publishing concern goes on record with the following: ". . . Last year I was asked to consider running for the School Board in —— but I decided against it. Later, when I mentioned my refusal to a Christopher friend of mine, he told me it was my duty to run. So this year when a similar request was made of me, recalling his advice, I did run and was elected. Now that I'm on the Board I can tell you I never realized there could be so many wonderful opportunities to further fundamental American principles. My only regret is that I didn't realize it sooner . . ."

As soon as there are more people like these "turning on lights" in our country than there are enemies "turning them off," then and then only will the "darkness" begin to vanish.

SAME METHODS—A DIFFERENT GOAL

In a specific way, businessmen can learn from the godless how they carry their ideas into every field in which they can reach the most people; how they put thousands of their *missioners* into all fields that sway men's thoughts and actions.

And as businessmen pattern their *procedure* after the godless—but with a different goal and a different motive—as they inspire tens of thousands of Americans to dedicate themselves to the task of bringing into every phase of public and private life the idea that there is a personal God, that man is more than an animal, and that all the rights he has have their origin in, and depend upon, the Almighty, they will restore a sense of personal responsibility and individual accountability as an integral part of American life.

The sobering effects of such a task are well emphasized in a passage from a recent motion picture where a father, speaking to his son, said:

"In a sense we are all servants, placed here on earth to serve. Some of us, by the will and omniscience of the Divinity, have been given a greater task than others; I count myself, somewhat to my sorrow, as a member of that group. It is a very grave thought to me to think that I may soon have to render an account of my stewardship to my Maker. I have held control of some large industries in this country and through them I have controlled the lives of many people. This is a solemn thought and someday it will be a solemn thought for you. There are certain definite obligations for one

in my position and one in yours—and one of them is to try and make your life worth while with the advantages God has given you."

Such realization, belated as this man's was, is a wonderful thing. But similar realization in all spheres of our national life must come, and come quickly, if we are to avoid disaster. Make no mistake about it. The twentieth century has brought into being for the first time in all history a vigorous, aggressive, ruthless crusade to spread evil from one end of the earth to the other. It is global in scope, and it is here to stay. It is spreading with astonishing speed; it is ever on the march. By its deceptive and destructive allurements, it has already blighted, poisoned, and enslaved hundreds of millions of people.

Businessmen can do much to change this trend. And it will be a glorious thing if the businessmen of America who accomplished so much to win the recent war will go one step further and help win the peace for which the world still longs. Julius Ochs Adler, vice-president and general manager of the New York *Times,* speaking recently on the subject "Preparedness by a Free People" before the seventeenth annual four-day conference of the Chaplains' Association of the Army and Navy of the United States, at the Hotel New Yorker, keynoted that same idea.

"None of our freedom is absolute," he said, "nor could it be and long survive. Freedom of the press does not include the right to print the libelous or obscene. All of our freedoms are restricted at the point where their abuse might imperil the rights, comfort, or safety of the community as a whole. Why then should we absolve from restrictions a group [the Communist party] whose loyalty is not to this nation or its flag, whose demonstrated creed is the extinction of freedom wherever they get power."

Mr. Adler then went on to describe the Communist creed as lacking in the spirit of give and take, and as narrow and intolerant. "Infiltration, conspiracy, sabotage, organized turmoil and agitation," he added, "all masked under a hundred innocent-sounding names behind a thousand unsuspected fronts . . . the origin, orientation, and direction of Communist policy is not American. Its membership is not public. . . . Communism does not believe in the basic freedoms nor does it grant them where it is in power. However, to accomplish its destructive purposes, it vehemently insists on those freedoms whenever they are available." Urging preparedness on a wide front, Mr. Adler concluded, "We can drift toward war if we are apathetic, disinterested, careless, or ill-informed."

Carrying that last thought still further, peace will come only when the basic idea on which our country was founded—that man gets his rights, not from the State, but from God—becomes a world reality. The problem of bringing this about is largely one of *distributing* or merchandising the basic idea.

Since, by the very nature of their work, businessmen must be specialists in distribution and experts in merchandising, they should inevitably succeed in seeing that this fundamental idea is given wide circulation and thorough integration into every phase of American life. It should be an easy matter for them to out-distance the forces that are now working feverishly to infiltrate and to spread their stupidly false idea that man is nothing but a creature of the State.

Considerable experimentation has proved this can be done with relative ease. All over the country thousands of Christophers—Christ-bearers—have been encouraged to go into the four important phases of public life and have been encouraged to show the same determination in restoring basic *Christian* ideas as others are displaying in throwing them out. The success of these businessmen-Christophers in every field is living proof of what can be done. All that remains is to increase the number of distributors of good ideas. Businessmen can certainly be effective Christophers themselves; and, by the same token, they can and must get others, *many others,* to be Christ-bearers.

There is no time to lose. Things are moving fast. It is either lead or be led, influence or be influenced. To survive individually, one must strive persistently in helping all to survive. Now, as never before, it is "one for all and all for one."

As businessmen rise to this glorious challenge of spreading ideas, as we know they can, the prospects for peace will begin to glow ever brighter. But nothing—nothing—must be taken for granted. Success will be directly proportionate to their thinking in terms of *all* people, not merely a few; in *ideas,* not merely things; as they give *themselves,* not merely their money; as they take the effective measures to circulate *good* ideas, not merely watch passively from the sidelines.

As businessmen—as Christophers—do all these things, it will be living, inspiring proof that they need not *"be overcome by evil, but overcome evil by good."* (*Romans* 12:21)

XIV

STUDENTS

A Big Job Ahead

ONE HOT EARLY SUMMER AFTERNOON seventeen years ago on a high school baseball diamond in a New England town, Bill Daley, a wiry, laughing youngster of fifteen, stood on the sidelines squinting into the sun, watching his teammates stepping up to the plate to take their "cut" in pre-game batting practice.

His eyes were shining, his lips drawn slightly apart with excitement, his body tensed as he took in every move his companions made. For baseball was his love, his whole life. Had you asked, at the drop of a hat he could have given you the batting and fielding averages of every well-known big leaguer. And had you asked, also, what was his ambition in life, he'd have told you simply: "To play baseball as a 'pro'! You know, in the 'big time'!"

Bill Daley never realized his ambition. After that particular day he was never to play another game of any kind in his life. Before the afternoon was half over he was lying in a hospital, victim of an accident on the field about which he has only the haziest recollection beyond the fact that somehow during the game he fell and landed heavily on his back. When he tried to rise, he found he couldn't move. There was a strange numbness in his legs and a tightness in his back that sent cold sweat pouring down his face, smarting his eyes, salting his mouth as he bit his lip to keep from crying out in panic.

At the hospital the doctors were friendly and very kind. He'd suffered a spinal injury, they told him, but added that he wasn't to worry. They'd do everything in their power to help him.

But as the weeks went by and became months and, finally, years, and their efforts proved to be in vain, Bill had to acknowledge to himself what was to be his lot in life—that of a hopeless, bed-ridden cripple!

Many a boy would have been tempted to turn against the world for the way it had cheated him out of all the normal, good things to which a lad of his age had a right to look forward—the ball games, the hikes, the swimming and campings-out during the summer vacations, the weekly trips to the local movie house, all the hundred and one things a healthy, active youngster usually does.

HIGH PURPOSE IN A CRIPPLED BODY

It is to Bill's credit that after the first terrible shock had passed, he made himself accept his fate, refusing to feel sorry for himself. If things were to be this way, well, okay, he'd make the best of them. He wasn't the first boy to be a cripple, and he would not be the last. After all, he'd had fifteen years in which to race around. Some kids he'd read about never even had that long.

That was seventeen years ago. From that day to this, Bill Daley has never been able to move off his back. For a long time now he hasn't even been able to turn over and lie on his side because of the pain from rheumatoid arthritis which has developed. "I don't mind," Bill will tell you. "I decided long ago after . . . this . . . happened, to stop thinking of myself and devote the rest of my life to making the world a better place than I found it."

A cynic might have laughed at that, though not to Bill's face, of course. After all, what *could* a cripple do? Why, he couldn't even take care of himself, let alone do anything for anyone else. But, like the bird whose wingspread is such as to defy the laws of aerial motion (according to scientists), yet being unaware of the fact, *flies,* Bill never has recognized his handicap as an obstacle to completing what he set out to do.

To keep his mind occupied, he studied short-wave radio and in 1935 received an amateur radio operator's license. Using his own equipment, he kept in touch with "ham" operators all over the world, listening to their chatter, sometimes to their personal troubles, giving his advice, yet never once mentioning his own affliction. When the war came along, he volunteered his services as a radio operator and was accepted by the Coast Guard to monitor and intercept, from his home, any enemy signals he could pick up from Nazi submarines or surface craft which might approach the American coast, with instructions to relay such signals to Coast Guard headquarters. Exact details are still to be revealed, but Bill did do a tremendous job, as those familiar with the case have stated many times.

When the war ended, he found his real vocation in life. In February, 1946, after learning about the plans of the Christophers soon to get under way, he set about spreading their idea by mail. Together with this he became active in everything aimed at the good of others. From his bedside in a small, unpretentious flat where he lives with his mother, sister, and blind father, there have poured out hundreds and thousands (the actual count at last report being some 3,471) of pamphlets, booklets, clippings, and news notes which he had asked to be sent in bulk to his home. And from all over the country and even from overseas, came messages from people in all walks of life, telling him how much what he was doing meant to them, never suspecting for a moment that this human dynamo correspondent of theirs was paralyzed.

When you ask Bill his plans for the future, with typical Daley good humor he comes back with a crisp "to keep on with what I'm doing—only to do it bigger and better.

"Y'see, a few years back one of the leftist boys canvassed our neighborhood and left some literature. The literature didn't interest me, but the man's misguided enthusiasm did. This is my country, too, and I don't want to have it taken over by a crowd which has no time for all the things America stands for. I decided right then and there to outdo, as far as I was physically able, any Communist who ever lived. After all, what have they got besides Karl Marx and his gospel of hate? Me, I've got the love of Jesus Christ! And who knows?—maybe through me a little of it may reach some of them."

THE OPPORTUNITY IS YOURS

Bill Daley's is admittedly a most unusual case. Not one young person in a thousand starts life with such a terrible handicap. But the fact that one person has been able to do what Bill Daley did should be a source of inspiration to everyone. If a crippled boy of fifteen could start making plans for the future to reach as far as he could with that message of love and hope, no excuse can possibly be made for the vast majority of you healthy young people to avoid your responsibility to all mankind.

"Go you into the whole world," Christ Himself said. He meant that for every generation. He meant that you also should have a part in carrying His truth and love into the market-place.

Within each of you there is one thing you possess in common with Bill Daley: love of God and of your neighbor because in each and every human being is the Divine Image. Within each of you, were you to release it, is the capacity to make the whole world a better place than you found it.

There is a big job ahead of you. In the newspapers, in your books and magazines, over the radio and in the movies, you have seen and heard how those who deny God are battling to win the world away from Him Who created it. Still, reading and hearing and seeing all this, perhaps you have told yourself: "This doesn't concern me now. When I'm older and out of school or college will be time enough to think about it."

If you have ever thought this, or are thinking it at this moment, you have made or will be making the greatest mistake of your life. You will be leaving the future of your own country in the hands of those who, even now, are being trained to take over your democracy—and the world!—once the opportune moment arrives.

And don't be deceived. These people, many of them students like yourselves, are not merely waiting and hoping for that time to come. They are planning for it now, working toward it now, sacrificing personal pleasure and gain for it now. Witness the twenty-five Communist schools over the country where tens of thousands of the godless are being fed into the mainstream of American life with each passing year.

In a very real sense, they are missioners, missioners with an *evil* purpose. They swarm into every phase of national life, particularly into the four great spheres of influence—education, government, labor-management, and the writing of newspapers, magazines, books, radio, television and motion pictures—in the certainty that once they control the thoughts of your nation, they control its destiny.

The Nazis before, like the Communists now, were shrewd enough to see this. That was why they put every subversive they could find into teaching, for example. Their one fixed objective was to train German youth in the idea they were *animals,* nothing more.

And the tragic results speak for themselves. After twelve years of this schooling, six million young Germans, of themselves fundamentally no different from yourselves, actually began to think and act like animals. *"But that can't happen here,"* you may start to say, *"this is America!"* Yes, this is America and it is happening right here. A whole host of young people are growing up with little or no idea of God, and the number is expected to increase with each passing year.

Emphasizing this, the executive secretary of the Presbyterian Board of Christian Education in Philadelphia told the general assembly of his church in Seattle recently, according to the New York *Times,* that 27,000,000 children were not receiving religious instruction in this country and that, if the trend continued, "a pagan nation will result."

While figures from authorities of other faiths and government agencies vary slightly, the general picture in all respects is the same. A pagan nation means a godless nation, and a godless nation means a place where you young people will be nothing more than brute animals with your heads pressed down to the earth, never being allowed to look up and see the wonder and beauty of God's blue heavens. This very situation was of such concern to one student in New York not long ago that he wrote a letter of protest to the newspapers. Published in one of the largest dailies, it read:

"I am a student at ---- High School, and if anybody asked what I learn there I would tell them Communism. Many of the teachers are Communists through and through. We were told to bring in a Communist paper for English. We were also told to write a composition on why we like Russia and its ideas. What has this got to do with English? I appeal to you people who pay taxes so that we may get decent educations, to protest this farce and stop it."

THE HOPEFUL SIDE

It's a disturbing situation, yet by no means is it hopeless—far from it. American young people are not anti-religious. Their present-day mistakes come from lack of knowledge, rather than from malice or indifference. Indeed, they possess an unusual sense of decency and fair play, not only for all in this country, but for men of all nations. They are more Christian than even they suspect. They are not opposed to Christ. On the contrary, they are actually hungering for His truth. They are waiting for you, their fellow students, to bring Christ to them. But they will not come to you, for they do not know how or why they should do so. You will have to go to them, as Christ commanded you to do.

On the other hand, if you neglect to go and continue going to all people, you will be helping to plunge the world into a nightmare of misery and despair far worse than anything that has ever been witnessed before in history.

God's truth, the very foundation upon which the United States was built, does not belong to you good young people alone. It belongs to *everyone*. If others have not got it, it is up to you to share your "pearl of great price" with them. A good doctor does not sit in his office during an epidemic, complaining about the state of a community's health, yet doing nothing to relieve the situation. To go back a couple of thousand years, the early Christians did not sit in the catacombs, shaking their heads over the pagan cruelty of the Romans.

Neither should you keep Christ's love and Truth to yourselves. To your fellow students who do not have them, you owe the opportunity of possessing them, also.

THAT IS THE ONE THING WHICH TERRIFIES THE GODLESS THE WORLD OVER: *the fear that some day all those who believe in Christ will wake up and start acting their beliefs.* Once that happens, most of the great problems which plague mankind will disappear overnight.

LIVING PROOF IT CAN BE DONE

There is a saying that imitation is the sincerest form of flattery, and in many respects this is true. Moreover, when such imitation on your part follows the Christopher example of other young people like yourselves who even now are carrying Christ into the market-place, then it is surely the finest compliment human beings can pay to Him who made the whole universe and every living creature in it.

More than mere lip service to Truth is needed, however. One young man, whose father is president of one of New York's leading banks, showed what can be done. As a reward for graduating from high school, this youngster was told he could spend the summer vacationing at a Long Island beach. Instead, this student, who has picked up a little apostolic spirit all by himself and is an exemplary Christopher, quietly passed up the beach. Unknown to any but a few intimates, he spent each day during the summer in Harlem, caring for thirty-five or forty Negro youngsters. Of course, he could have given his allowance, but that would have been giving away only money. By giving his time, his thoughts, his solicitude, he gave *himself*. . . . What a change for the better will take place over the world when in small ways and large that one example is multiplied *one million times*! We believe it can be done!

Then there is the story of the young lady who recently graduated from college and set out to get a job. Any kind would suit her, she said, so long as it paid well, didn't require much work, and included a long vacation. On getting what she felt was the ideal position, she wrote us telling how well off she was. Our reply, sent immediately, was to remind her in a friendly way that she was not only well off but *far off* also. It was a pity, we wrote, that so many wonderful people like her, who could do so much to bring the peace of Christ into the mainstream of American life, were so quickly and inevitably winding up in dead-end streets because they had no thought outside of themselves. And we added that nearly everyone with a crackpot idea was making it his or her business to get into some key spot where they could make everyone else as crazy as themselves.

A few weeks later this same girl wrote us a second letter and in it was a most pleasant surprise! The advice had taken hold and she had just secured another job as assistant to the head of an important department in one of the nation's largest universities. This sudden shift from just a job to a job with a purpose where she was able to exert a far-reaching influence for good among thousands of students was due, as she put it, to the fact that for the first time in her twenty-two years she realized all she had been doing was taking care of herself. Discovering at last that she had an individual, personal responsibility to the rest of mankind, she wasted no time in doing something about it.

After a considerable amount of effort, she surprised herself and everybody else by landing a post at this university.

And while she gets less money, works harder, and will have fewer holidays than were in prospect before, yet it is source of real and deep satisfaction to her to have endless opportunities to be a Christopher—a Christ-bearer—to make the world a bit the better because she is in it.

EACH IN HIS OWN WAY

Another example is that of a young man now completing his graduate work in dramatics at Yale, who came to our office recently to learn about the Christopher idea. His hope, he said, is to establish, or least help to start, a theater movement in this country along the lines of the Abbey Theater in Ireland. Already he has begun to organize a company which will tour the country and give countless audiences the opportunity of seeing plays truly representative of the best in Christian tradition.

In radio a young lady Christopher, a Catholic college graduate, who works for the National Broadcasting Company told us in a letter: "The idea of being a Christ-bearer is a very appealing one to me. A number of friends here have expressed keen interest in the work of the Christophers. They are in constant contact with the public through writing and broadcasting and therefore can do much good. To discover there are so many people striving for the same goal that I am, of sharing with the general public the truths of Christ, is a comforting and stimulating thought. . . . In my own humble way I am trying to bring Christ to the radio field where He is sorely needed."

One young man, who began his career as an errand boy in the office of an outstanding magazine, is today an important producer in that field of the future, television. On his own admission, the thing that spurred him on was the Christopher purpose. Because of that purpose he has reached a position where he is influencing and will continue to influence to an ever greater extent, countless thousands all over the country.

A senior at the University of California, a girl with tremendous spirit and initiative, has gone on record with us as pledging herself, upon graduation, to get into some field where she can work just as hard to "save my country and my world as others are in trying to wreck them." And she concludes with: "No matter where or in what capacity I have to begin this job, I'll see it through to the finish."

An author who had several books, including *The Man, Charles Dickens,* published before he was thirty, states that he is a writer today because as a youngster in the fourth grade of a Chicago public school there had been impressed on his young mind the great good he could do as a writer. "When your first book is published, Eddie," his teacher told him one day after class, "I want you to be sure and send me a copy." The pupil, Edward Wagenknecht, was only ten years old at the time, yet she pictured his first book as a reality. Twenty years later, it was a reality and the teacher, Mary Dwyer, lived to have a copy placed in her hands by Wagenknecht himself!

At one leading university a group of young men and women have made it their business to get positions on university publications, student councils, and clubs with the view to spreading the Christopher idea and weaving it into every phase of student life. More than this, however, in many cases these self-same young men and women, mindful of the necessity of training others, have sacrificed the honor of actually holding various student posts in order to support and train lower classmen on the way up.

In your own country, strangely enough, less than one percent of the people are trying to destroy everything America stands for, including the basic truth upon which this nation was founded: that man is a child of God, that he gets his rights from God, and that the purpose of government above all else is to protect for each individual his God-given rights.

But while less than one percent aim at destroying your democracy, the job of preserving freedom is your job, is everybody's job. With faith and love, you can make noble even the lowliest and most hateful. Yet expect ridicule, opposition, and even persecution. But do not cease to try and reach all men, even the most godless and oppressive. After all, it was Christ Himself who said *"Love your enemies: do good to them that hate you: and pray for them that persecute and calumniate you."* (*Matt.* 5:44)

THE TIME IS NOW!

Right now, as students, you can begin to bring Christ to the world in a hundred different ways. Right now, too, you can prepare for the time when you are no longer in school by choosing a career that will enable you to play a vital, personal rôle in the big job ahead.

Start thinking of your life's work even as you read this. Don't drift into just any job. The godless never make that error. They always get into a position where they can spread their poisonous ideas. Don't take a job, either, just for the salary it pays. Don't be like the West Coast student who, when urged to tell what he planned to do when he finished college, replied "Gosh, I don't know. Try and get a job and really make some money, I guess. After all, that's what I'm being trained for."

You are not and should not be trained merely to fatten a bank account. You are being trained, or should be trained, to pass along your sound ideas to thousands of other students who will come after you. You may not make your fortune, but you will have the deep satisfaction, for time and for eternity, of knowing that the world, as Bill Daley said, will have been made a little better because you've been in it. All around you, if you look and listen, you will hear talk . . . talk . . . talk, and see not enough action. You will hear totalitarianism roundly and justly condemned by good people in all walks of life, yet their condemnation too often is just talk and nothing more.

These people do not yet realize that even if Communism were to vanish overnight—as, of course, it won't—the problem would still remain of bringing Christ back into the everyday life of your nation and of your world. For Communism is merely a disease that feeds on weakness. Correct the cause of the sickness and Communism, with all the other forms of totalitarianism, will disappear even more quickly than they came.

People are sick of talk about more housing plans, they want houses; they want an end of mere talk about food scarcities, they want food. You who know the Truth and are being trained to be the teachers, the government workers, the backbone of labor, the writers in the communications field, will have to integrate justice into these spheres of influence, so it may go hand-in-hand with charity.

On every side you will find distractions. If a boy or young man, you will be beset by the newspaper ads that ask so winningly "Do you want a better job—a promotion—quicker than you expect it?" as if getting ahead and making money were all of your existence. Or you will be bludgeoned by the business reports that state "Profit Motive Is Spark Plug of Progress"—with no word about your eternal destiny.

If you are a girl or young woman, you may be beguiled by the beauty offers that triumphantly announce "You Can Make Yourself Over in Just 5 Days!"—as if self-indulgence were your constant, all-consuming goal.

In books, magazines, newspapers, and motion pictures, you

will be bombarded with the same ideas. Over the radio, your material needs will be catered to with generosity bordering on the ridiculous. On some audience-participation shows, for example, you will identify a song or answer a question and the next day, to quote a recent radio column in a large metropolitan daily, "a van rolls up with a new piano, new car, fur coat, air-conditioning units, washing machine, furniture, motor-driven lawnmowers and, I suppose, funny hats and tin horns for everybody."

Stated simply, these ads and inducements and prizes total up to this: be selfish, not selfless. Take as much *out* of life and put *in* as little as you possibly can.

YOUR GOAL: TO PUT IN MUCH

These are not the reasons for which God made you in His Own Image. These are not and should not be the purpose of *all* your training. God wants each of you to love your neighbor as yourself for love of Him. He does not want your attitude to be that of the Gestapo: "Is my neighbor a Communist?" But rather, in the spirit of the parable: "Is a Communist my neighbor?" Reflecting on this, then, you realize you are your brothers' keeper. What concerns them concerns you. And concerning yourself about all men, you will start to lead a *selfless* existence. You will start to put into life as much as you humanly can—and take out as little as is necessary. Then will you be like the young lady, a sophomore in a Pennsylvania college who, dedicating herself to the distribution of the Christopher idea, wrote:

". . . I can do you a service and myself likewise by spreading Christian principles and learning to live them myself, thereby becoming a *whole* person, instead of the *half* person that I am."

You will be seeking first things first, and the incidental

things second. You will be living, "not by bread alone," but *in the Love of Christ* which is meant for all mankind. One tremendously inspiring example of man's faith, with the above thought in mind, is contained in the story of Captain Eddie Rickenbacker during the early days of World War II.

In 1942 a small group of men, headed by Rickenbacker, were flying across the Pacific when their plane was forced down at sea. For twenty-three days, from October 21 until their rescue on November 13, they were adrift on life rafts. Hungry, thirsty, exhausted from exposure, and despairing, their hopes and their courage were kept alive—by food and water?—no! They were sustained by these words of the Man of Galilee, read by Captain Rickenbacker from Private John F. Bartek's GI Bible:

"*Therefore take no thought, saying What shall we eat? or, What shall we drink? or, Wherewithal shall we be clothed? . . . for your heavenly Father knoweth that ye have need of all these things.*

"*But seek ye first the kingdom of God, and his righteousness: and all these things shall be added unto you. . . .*"

To seven men faced with death, these words from the Gospel according to Matthew, were a message of hope, bringing spiritual and mental life-sustaining food.

"Seek ye first the kingdom of God. . . ." For each of you students these words have a special significance. In planning your careers, they are the rule by which all your actions have to be governed. Anything less will lead you to exist as only half persons instead of the whole persons God intended you to be.

Your answer to the question, "What was the most important happening in history?" asked not long ago in the New York *Daily News,* will have to be that of fourteen-year-old Brooklyn-born Eddie Kelley. Five other people, all grownups, were asked the question before it came Eddie's turn to speak up. A businessman said the most important happening was "the settlement of Jamestown by the English." Another replied, "the defeat of the Saracens at Tours." Three women gave other answers: one said, "the splitting of the atom;" another, "the defeat of the Japanese;" a third, "the invention of the wheel." Eddie's reply put all five to shame.

"It was the birth of Jesus Christ," he declared, enthusiastically. "Christianity is the religion of the countries that rule the world. And Christianity, if we follow its teachings, makes all of us better people. And the world would be ever so much better if all of us would follow the teachings of Christ."

For Eddie there were no doubts, no false illusions about wealth or fame or the thousand and one things which loom on the horizon to distort your mind's vision. He wanted to tell the whole world the most wonderful Truth he possessed. And he succeeded. By a conservative estimate, his words reached at least one million readers of the newspaper (its circulation is almost three times that figure) in which his statement appeared. At fourteen, Eddie was a practicing Christopher!

YOU HAVE THE ANSWERS

The spirit which prompted as fine an answer as Eddie's is deep down inside each and every one of you. Sheila Kaye-Smith, one of the outstanding novelists of our times, told an audience in London not long ago that from earliest childhood she was interested in the idea of God and religion. Children, she emphasized, are naturally religious, and have the best religious approach—an entirely realistic one. To them, science may answer the question *"How."* But religion answers both the questions *"What"* and *"Why."*

In all generations and in all ages, this has been true. Likewise it has been true that many men and women have become so interested in proving the existence of God, that they have come to care nothing for God Himself.

For the Christopher who would really "bear" Christ, however, both knowledge of the Truth and constant reflection on Him Who gave it to the world go hand-in-hand. One cannot be divorced from the other. They are inseparable.

WHERE AND WHEN TO BEGIN

Whether you are in grade school, high school, or college, you can start right now to be a Christopher:

(1) Aim to play an active Christopher part in the "big show" upon finishing your education when you, as a mature person, will be mentally, spiritually, and physically equipped to tackle a lifetime job.

(2) Meanwhile, start aiming for a definite goal in life, for a pursuit where you will do more than merely earn money. Doing this right away will give you something to live for, something to work toward; in short, you will be going some place!

(3) While in school, you can start building for your future usefulness—and for your useful future—by

  (a) Praying for the great needs of the world and getting others to pray also.

  (b) Developing your writing skill in compositions, letters, articles, and the like.

  (c) Getting on debating teams, taking an active part in youth meetings, becoming members of school societies—all in themselves excellent training for the future.

  (d) Persuading your family, relatives, and friends to *vote* and *be informed* on *how* to vote and *why* to vote and *what* to vote for.

(e) Suggesting they take jobs that count. One girl, for example, wrote a friend in another part of the country with this idea in mind. The friend, in turn, got a job with a local radio station and later became its assistant manager!

(4) Think frequently and earnestly of the four important fields of

Education—with a teaching career in mind.

Government—not only local and state but national administration as well. If you want good government, you will have to take an active, positive part in conducting its affairs.

Labor—including union activities and management-labor problems as well.

Writing—covering the specialized branches of newspapers, books, magazines, motion pictures, radio, and television.

Think, also, of the fields of *social service work* and *libraries*. And some of you think seriously, too, of *religious vocations*.

In *all* these fields, the world is won or lost!

NOTE: See the chapters on education, government, labor, writing, social service and library work for detailed information.

(5) Avoid the tendency to indulge in flag waving. Don't belong to a group, project, or society merely to get your name in print or to feel you've done your patriotic best by attending a few meetings. Just as still waters run deep and yeast works quietly in leavening the bread, so what you actually *do*, not *how* you do it, is the thing that counts.

(6) Write letters to legislators, newspapers, magazines, radio stations, motion picture concerns, and columnists. One high school student in Rochester recently made her voice heard in just this way. She wrote her Congressman requesting him to protest against limiting American newspapermen in Russia to a mere handful while Soviet newsmen were free to enter the United States in droves. Friends said it was a waste of time, but this student knew Christ wanted everyone to keep trying at all costs. The result? Faith and courage were rewarded in a big way. Not only did the Congressman urge action by our State Department but, under unanimous consent of Congress, the letter was included in the Congressional Record.

Not a bad return for a couple of sheets of paper, a little ink and a bit of effort!

By adapting these few suggestions to your individual talents, you will avoid the "fringes" of everyday living. You will be heading instead for the *heart* of the great spheres which influence for better or worse the destiny, not only of your nation, but of your world. And you will be adding to, not subtracting from, the sum total of fine, decent, Christian living.

TAKE PEOPLE AS THEY ARE

If you would be a good Christopher, however, there are a few additional tips which you would do well to bear in mind.

One of these concerns your approach to young people like yourselves and, later on, to adult men and women with whom you come in contact. To be truly a Christ-bearer, you will always have to accept people, not as they ought to be, but as they are. Christ Himself did just that, for He found His followers among folks in all walks of life, in high places and in low. He accepted them all and asked only one thing in return: that they strive to do God's Will.

No matter what the difficulties, get in a spot in life where your influence for good can actually be felt. There is an old saying that "the absent are always wrong." If you are not there, others who would destroy your nation and your world will have that much smoother sailing. The absent never have an opportunity to speak. But by your *living presence* you can bear witness to the Truth.

Have patience. Success as a Christ-bearer is not won overnight. Don't be afraid to *burn* with the zeal for spreading Christ's love. The godless are far from being timid in expressing devotion to their "cause." As proof, sit in on an eye-witnessed account of one of their gatherings right inside Russia itself! Mrs. Cecil Chesteron, in *MY RUSSIAN ADVENTURE,* published a few years back, relates:

> "It was a meeting of the Young Communist Party, and a more powerful outpouring of the spirit I have never witnessed. The first speaker, a closely shingled girl with dark, passionate eyes, spoke for a quarter of an hour. She was, we gathered, calling on her comrades to testify their loyalty to the Soviet by offerings of labor and money. She was an ecstatic working, I should say, twenty hours out of the twenty-four under the stimulant of sacrifice.
>
> "The effect created was electric. The whole crowd was moved by a fervor that communicated itself like a magnetic thrill. The melancholy faces, the dull skins, the unstirred eyes, were lit by an inner flame. As one man they leapt to their feet, breaking into salvos of applause. The bands crashed out some chords, the children sang, a thin-faced boy took the floor. In a low, quiet voice, he told the tale, gradually working up the tension. They were typical,

these missioners belonging to the people: believing in the Soviet way of salvation, they were prepared to hunger and thirst, to go barefoot, to offer their flesh on a cross of nails in the Great Cause."

You who bear Christ should be no less loyal, no less enthusiastic. And, like fire from a furnace, you will warm the hearts of even those who seem to be farthest away from the Truth. The story of a lady in Baltimore bears this fact out. Very much opposed to anything Christian, she found herself strangely moved by the fervor of a young Christopher who made it her business to interest herself in her. "But why . . . why trouble yourself about me?" was her question. And the quiet reply came back: "Two thousand years ago Christ died for all of us. The least I can do is to work and love for Him as long as I'm able!"

KEEP PLUGGING AWAY

Be persevering in everything you do. Take to heart the example of the young man with genuine writing ability who kept plugging away at trying to place his material in the secular periodicals. Seventeen times he received rejection slips. On the eighteenth try, *Coronet Magazine* bought one of his stories for three hundred dollars!

Retelling this story calls to mind what Stephen Leacock, the eminent Canadian humorist, in his book *How to Write* pointed out. He said that he never succeeded as a writer until he was forty years old, simply because he was afraid of rejection slips. Fear of failure prevented him from making the effort required for success, and his one regret was the number of years he wasted when success might have been his twenty years earlier.

Pray always. For a Christopher to do effective work, prayer is absolutely essential. As a lay apostle you won't get far without it, for you won't be able to give what you don't possess. Without a strong spiritual life of your own, one that is rooted in eternal truths, you will accomplish little for yourself and little for others. There will be an emptiness and shallowness in everything you do without prayer. It is surprising, on the other hand, how your whole activity will be sparked with an ever-deepening faith if only a few minutes are set aside regularly each day for meditation and prayer. Then you will find yourself growing closer and closer to Christ. For you there will be an increasing thrill in the privilege of being a Christopher—a Christ-bearer—of bringing the Prince of Peace into the market-place.

Pray also, not alone for yourself, your family, and your friends, but for the President of the United States, the Congress, the Secretary of State, the United Nations, and for other intentions as suggested in Chapter XI, "Influencing the World from the Home." The test of your sincerity is in what you do for others. The people you do things for are the people you really love. If you say you have love for all men, yet do not reach out to all men, you probably do not have a real, genuine love for them.

Be *missioners* in the true sense of the word. Only in this way will you win the hearts and confidence of everyone.

"The prime requisite of a missioner," a priest writes from Latin America, "is to love his people. That's easier said than done. But there is no getting around it. If the Indians see that we like them, no matter what their faults are, they will gradually open their hearts to us. Once they realize we really want them to come into our homes, and act as they would in their homes, they soon accept us as one of their very own. But that means they must be absolutely free to come at any hour, day or night, often in crowds of twenty or thirty, abounding in all the fragrant odors of an unwashed people.

"Likewise, they must feel free to smoke their tobacco that

is sweet to them, but foul to us; spit on our floors just as freely as they would spit on their floor at home; bring in their mangy, half-starved dogs that are just as dear to them as the best fox terrior that any of our families had at home in the States.

"It gets right down to a literal interpretation of St. Paul's very sound advice of 'becoming all things to all men.' No better formula has ever been found for bringing Christ to men and men to Christ. Every day we see more clearly that our success with the Indians will be in proportion as we do just that."

Your biggest temptation will be to think in terms of "God and myself," to be absorbed in your selfish little world and to leave the running of the big world to those who either hate Christ or know Him not. Even when praying, it is easy to say "*our* Father" and yet mean "*my* Father"; to say "*give us our daily bread,*" yet mean "give *me my* daily bread"; to ask God to "forgive *us our* trespasses," and yet mean nothing more than "forgive *me my* trespasses."

All the talk about the brotherhood of man will mean little unless—unlike the solicitous subversives—you acknowledge that brotherhood *under the fatherhood of God.* Even from your kindergarten days, always keep that thought uppermost in mind.

So much depends on you young people, you students. Now and for another decade or so, your country carries the great and fearful responsibility of leading the world. On what you do now for Christ, by prayer, by getting others to become Christ-bearers, by going in all the many ways open to you in these years of preparation, and on what you will be doing in the future, hangs a large share of the fate of the world.

Realize and remember that the world is really depending upon *you* far more than you know!

XV

FIRST-LINE CHRISTOPHERS

One of the greatest forces for good in Hollywood today—a top-ranking executive of a major film corporation—once studied for the priesthood. After several years training over a quarter of a century ago, however, he realized that God meant his career to be in the world.

Leaving the seminary, he took a job as a bus boy in a restaurant in order to earn a living. But he didn't stay a bus boy very long. His religious training, curtailed as it was, had aroused in him a longing to reach as many people as he could during his lifetime with the faith and love of Christ that his parents had cultivated within him.

The motion picture field, then in its infancy, struck him as a particularly fertile sphere since it was already beginning to touch and influence the lives of millions who went to the movies week after week. He didn't stop to ask, "What can I do?" Insignificant as he was then, he was still convinced that by God's grace and his own hard work his power for good could somehow be felt. He began his career at the "bottom of the ladder" with a small motion picture theater. But menial as the work was, to him it was more than just a job. Into it he carried the high purpose that had motivated his studies for the priesthood.

His strong spiritual values imparted a meaning and a direction to everything he did. His sincere love of God was best reflected in his concern for *everyone* with whom he had contact—even remotely. As anyone with a fixed, broad-visioned goal (whether in itself good or evil) is most likely to forge ahead of those who drift aimlessly without any objective outside of themselves, so he advanced, slowly but surely over the years, from one position to another of still greater influence. Today he is a vital factor in bringing—with but few exceptions—to moviegoers the world over the best in quality screen fare.

In the headquarters office of one of the largest labor unions in the United States there is a young man of the Jewish faith who has devoted the last twelve years of his life to hammering away at the fundamental doctrines of the workingman's God-given rights and obligations. In his late thirties now, this man had the desire, as a boy, to be a rabbi. But much thought finally brought him to the realization that such a vocation was not his.

This early consideration of consecrating his life to religion made a lasting impression on him, however. Still imbued with the idea of serving his "neighbor" on more than a material basis, he got a job with a manufacturing concern, joined his local labor union, and set about trying to bring into the union's affairs some concept of spiritual values regarding the dignity of man. Since he first started his work of self-dedication, he has risen to an executive post in this union which represents hundreds of thousands of workers all over the country. Because of his fixed determination to push the truth, this Jewish worker has aided greatly in keeping control of his organization in the hands of those who acknowledge the basic relationship of man to God.

INTO THE MAGAZINE FIELD

A writer for many nationally known magazines and a contributing editor of one of the most widely circulated monthly periodicals, a man who has won almost unanimous praise for the high quality of his writings, has given as his reason for such quality the time, early in his life, when he actually studied for the Presbyterian ministry. In print (and when he speaks over the radio as well), his whole approach to the problem of everyday living has been in keeping with the purpose which first caused him to begin preparation for the religious life.

At every opportunity he has publicly demonstrated a sound sense of values and high ideals which are even more noticeable in the midst of so much that is cheap and tawdry in the writing profession. What prompted him to discontinue his religious studies is a matter that concerns him alone. Yet in the past twenty-five years he has consciously and actively carried over his "vocation" into the literary field. And rarely has he failed to impress both readers and listeners alike with his strong conviction of spiritual principles.

AS SECRETARY TO AN EDITOR

A young lady who thought of becoming a nun finally came to the conclusion that it was not God's Will for her to follow such a life. The first job she took after making up her mind to carve a career for herself in the world was with an airline. The position paid very well, required little mental effort, and provided exceptionally pleasant working conditions.

Much to her friends' amazement, however, she wasn't quite satisfied. Upon hearing of the Christopher plan to get large numbers of people with high purpose into the main fields that influence the thoughts and actions of millions, she decided to try for a job which would affect the many, rather than the few.

After several unsuccessful attempts, she finally landed an opening as secretary to the editor of a publishing house. Today, her sense of judgment has come to be valued so highly by her employer that she is frequently consulted for advice in the selection of book manuscripts for publication. She is, therefore, an important factor in determining the kind of material that hundreds of thousands of people will read. Partially at least, she is fulfilling the rôle of a lay apostle. And because she has realized the great need to have as many as possible go the *full* way and take up the religious life, she has encouraged a friend of hers to become a nun—the vocation she originally thought was to be her own.

INTO LABOR RELATIONS

In a nationally-listed merchandising concern whose headquarters are in the Mid-west, one of the officials in charge of labor relations is a middle-aged man who, as a youth, had his heart set on becoming a lay brother in a religious order. Back in Oregon where he was born he'd been attracted to a life where he could dedicate his entire service to God and to his fellowman. Though he was aware his health wasn't all it should be for such a demanding task, from his sophomore year in high school on through college he'd pursued his studies with this goal in mind.

When he finally made application to enter the order the authorities, after carefully examining his case, reluctantly informed him that while his health, with proper care, might stand up well enough in ordinary life, it might be too frail to bear the never-ending demands of the religious life on his time and energy. Disappointed—but not discouraged—he got on the staff of a West Coast newspaper and stayed there a few years, studying labor relations on the side. What attracted him to this phase of life were its opportunities to improve the lot of large numbers of working people while protecting, at the same time, the just rights of management. Today his influence is felt even outside the concern which employs him. At trade conventions, at labor gatherings, and in the normal conduct of his work in the labor relations field, he has been a tremendous force in bringing Christ into the market-place of every day affairs.

These are just five cases out of five hundred that could be mentioned. Yet there must be hundreds of thousands of other Americans like these who have thought at one time or another of dedicating their lives to religion (where there is still need for many more workers) but who for a variety of reasons have not done so. For some it may have been a lack of conviction that such was the right career for them. For others, a condition of health which would require more than usual attention, or insufficient schooling at an advanced stage in adult life, or other impediments, minor in themselves, but of sufficient consequence to warrant a decision that the religious life would not be suited to them, or they to it.

In the majority of these cases in which serious thought is given to a professionally religious life, there is, unfortunately, a tendency to lapse back into the crowd once that life, for any reason, proves unattainable. Such individuals often overlook the important service they can render to society if they are determined to do what they can—outside the religious life—to retain and develop the original noble impulse implanted by God; if they are determined to put it to use in some vital way in a profession which, though not in itself religious, abounds in apostolic opportunities.

Those who entertain even a passing inclination towards the religious life are motivated by high and unselfish ideals. There is a willingness to embrace a life requiring constant adaptation to the plans and demands of *others.* Because they are stimulated by such high purpose, these people have disposed themselves to devote the major part of their time and energies to working for *others,* with only a small portion of such time and energies set aside for their own convenience and entertainment. They are ready to accept a life of limited income, are ready to put aside the possibility of accumulating even moderate wealth.

For those who have already settled down in life it may be difficult, of course, to transfer to fields of activity where there is great need of apostolic lay action. However, there are tens of thousands of young men and women each year over the country who, though the professional religious life is not for them, would be heartened to know they can still have an important part to play, individually and personally, on a *full-time* basis.

Since they, above all others, harbor a particular sense of purpose for their lives, they might well be regarded as *first-line Christophers,* carrying into the important spheres of influence a vision and determination which are not always possessed by others.

SNATCH FAITH FROM DISASTER

Just before his death in 1936, the zealous lay apostle, G. K. Chesterton, made a significant statement that should have a special meaning for every first-line Christopher. He realized far better than most the need for haste in increasing the missioners of light to offset the promoters of darkness.

"The issue is now clear," he declared. *"It is between light and darkness, and everyone must choose his side."*

If this issue is faced squarely without any further delay, there is great hope for the future. It concerns all men of good will. Yet it should be expected that those who have felt the call of God at some time or another, would be more keenly aware of the peril. It should be expected that they would be more ready and anxious to do something about it and more quickly to be found leaping into the forefront of the ranks of those who are as determined to save the world as others are to wreck it.

In this time of world crisis brought on by advancing inroads of materialism and godlessness, these first-line Christophers have it in their power to snatch faith from disaster, if they can be found in sufficiently large numbers to carry Christ into the market-place. People like these possess the primary ingredient of purpose—to make God known, better understood, and more widely loved among all men. They recognize that man was born to work and, since God made the world and everyone in it, they further recognize that their first service belongs to Him. In a very real sense they can be God's assistants—Christ-bearers—their lives and their powers not dissipated but utilized in serving Him and all mankind.

If one by one they step forward into the ranks of those who are working for light and are not merely talking against darkness, they can do much to change the world itself for the better. The power of just one person such as they cannot be exaggerated, for they hold in their hands the Light of the world, the one Cure for all darkness.

ONE SMALL LIGHT

This point was brought home to me quite graphically some time ago at the Metropolitan Opera House in New York.

Final arrangements to hold a benefit concert were being discussed and, at the close of the talks, the assistant manager offered to show me the seating arrangement of the building.

The hour was late and all of the other employees had long since gone home. The interior of the auditorium was a blanket of darkness that clouded our view and, as we walked slowly forward, aroused our senses to vague imaginings at the sound of our own footsteps.

Asking me to wait where I was until he could switch on the main lights, the assistant manager left me and went on alone. His figure as he moved down the aisle, then across the stage, could scarcely be seen. Suddenly he stopped. There was the sound of a match scratching against wood. A tiny sliver of light appeared.

Small as it was, from where I stood at the back of the Opera House that speck of light was greater than all the darkness around it. A tiny piece of sulphur-tipped wood had made that possible. After that, to multiply that tiny glow thousands of times and dispel the shadows which still remained, was but the work of a minute. There was the click of a switch. From all corners of the auditorium clusters of electric lights flooded the Opera House and the darkness was gone.

That's how it is with all of us. The least person, no matter how insignificant, who is interested in bringing the light of Christ's truth to the whole world is likewise a pinpoint of light in the darkness and is, by God's grace, greater than all the encircling gloom.

All that is needed to remove the rest of the darkness is to multiply that speck of light a million times or more. Darkness disappears in the same proportion as light is added. It is as simple as that. In proportion as Christ-bearers dare to penetrate the darkness with the Light of Christ, so will it diminish and eventually disappear.

Some recognize this challenge. Others do not. One young woman entered the convent and prepared to embrace the religious life, only to realize at the last moment that such a life was not meant for her. Back in the world, she gave up all thought of continuing on as a *part-way* lay apostle. She took a job with the telephone company where the physical conditions are excellent so far as work was concerned, yet she has neglected to bring with her the spiritual impetus which had once sent her to embrace the religious life.

Another young woman, on the other hand, who also prepared to be a nun, did carry over her high sense of purpose into the world of everyday affairs when circumstances compelled her to give up a cloistered career. A leaflet which described the United Nations organization and the need for qualified men and women with sound values to work in furthering its aims, gave her the cue for which she was searching. In the beginning, however, time after time she was refused employment on the ground that she lacked the proper qualifications. Still she persevered. Finally, she was accepted for a position where she has innumerable opportunities to put Christopher action into practice in helping build a better world.

This woman, as well as a young man who once studied for the ministry in California and is now in charge of an important department of the state government there, together with an ex-seminarian who is the public relations head of a large manufacturing concern which has been free of both management and labor abuses during the entire twenty years he has held that office—each of these and countless others too numerous to mention have brought and still are bringing Christ into the market-place. All have the same things in common:

(1) High ideals and a supernatural purpose
(2) Readiness to embrace a life of self-sacrifice
(3) Recognition of the need for daily spiritual exercises
(4) Willingness to accept cheerfully a life of comparative poverty
(5) Apostolic desire to devote all one's time and effort to bringing God to men and men to God.

We are convinced beyond a shadow of a doubt that many others would plunge into the thick of things if they would just stop to realize the immeasurable good they could do. And there is a breath-taking hope for the future when the thousands of first-line Christophers begin to number in the *hundreds of thousands*!

IF YOU WON'T, WHO WILL?

To have such a lofty life objective—even if only in a passing way—is nothing short of a great gift from God. Even if it cannot be fulfilled completely, it should not therefore be rejected or completely ignored by those who have been so privileged. Perhaps God is calling them to a special apostolate in the world which could never be exercised by one set apart exclusively for the religious life. For as important and necessary as their work is, they cannot go into the many phases of the market-place. They can guide, direct and encourage, yes; but they depend on lay Christ-bearers to carry the torch into every segment of public life. Those in religious life *cannot* take a job, for instance, as clerk to a supreme court justice, teacher in a state college, official in a labor union, personnel director in a corporation, staff writer on a newspaper, secretary to a magazine editor, or one of a thousand other posts in vital spheres where so much is at stake.

Any, therefore, who have ever felt stirring within them

that divine urge to be another Christ in their own limited way—no matter who they are, where they are or what they are—should do everything in their power to nurture and strengthen it. If they are generous with God, He will be more than generous with them. If they are willing and determined in His name to go into the turmoil of the market-place, regardless of how pagan it may be, not to find fault with it but to make it even a tiny bit better because they have added their speck of light—then they will be embarking on a lifetime of thrilling, satisfying, even though hidden, venture that will continue on past death into eternity.

They will begin to experience, possibly for the first time in their lives, the sublime difference between the confining limitations of mere striving for self and the exhilarating privilege of the fixed purpose of serving all mankind. In a very real sense, there will never be a dull moment in their lives. The worse the problem is, the more they will relish tackling it. Misunderstandings, setbacks, ridicule, even an occasional "kick in the teeth" will be taken in stride. In fact they will count the day lost that doesn't bring to them some share, small or large, of the suffering that was Christ's and which he promised must be the lot of anyone who would be His co-worker.

Buoying them up every inch of the way will be the deeply satisfying and stimulating assurance that, inadequate as they may be, Christ works in, through and with them. The further they get into the apostolate, the more humble they will become, the more they will realize that they are nothing more than errand boys or messengers, but still, by God's grace, the connecting links between God and men. Oftentimes it may truthfully be said of them that "with you there, Christ is there"—and if they are not there, Christ is not there. Yes, make no mistake about it, they are His *personal representatives*. And the one thing He begs of people above all else is not merely to adore Him but, as a proof of their love, to bring Him into the midst of the darkness—even into the hate, the sordidness, the repulsiveness of every walk of life where paganism holds sway over weak, confused humanity.

SINK SPIRITUAL FOUNDATIONS DEEP

To do this on a life-time basis, it is only good sense for them to get into the routine of some sort of spiritual "daily dozen" in order to start sinking their spiritual foundation deep and to keep in good *spiritual* trim. Doing this will help them persevere over the long years in which they will be vitally needed. It will aid them to overcome paganism before paganism overcomes them. It will assist them to balance "action" with the Source of any good they may do. It will enable them to rise above the trials and temptations that the Devil, with all his subtlety and persistence, always employs to trip up any and all who make things uncomfortable for him. Faithfulness to daily spiritual exercises will serve to keep them ever conscious that they are in the presence of God and that they have a most important mission in life to perform. And they will soon find that their every action becomes a prayer.

It is an old axiom that "you can't give what you haven't got." They should not, however, mistake that to mean that if they are not spiritual experts they can't do anything. No, far from it. There's not a person in the world who cannot give something to the betterment of the world. No matter how far removed from God one may be, he still remains a child of God, and therefore he can still do something *for* God, thereby coming at least one degree closer to his Maker.

But it is likewise true that one who would play a special

rôle, such as that of a first-line Christopher, must make a special effort to develop his interior life and increase his spiritual power, not simply for his own self-sanctification, but above all else for the sanctification of the world.

The more one prays, the more one grows in the knowledge and love of God, the more hopeful one becomes, and therefore the more effectively brings Him into the world.

For Catholics, the following is offered as a suggested daily schedule:

(1) Morning prayers;
(2) Meditation or reflection—even 3 minutes a day would be of value;
(3) Whenever possible, attendance at Mass and reception of Holy Communion;
(4) Grace at meals, as well as recitation of the Rosary and the Angelus;
(5) Reading of a spiritual book (a minimum of 5 minutes a day) and a few verses of the New Testament;
(6) Special prayer to the Holy Spirit before more important tasks;
(7) Night prayers and examination of conscience.

This simple routine would take a very small portion of time out of the 24 hours a day, but would go a long way in making the entire day purposeful and fruitful. If it is not possible to follow any but a few of these exercises, each person should select what he or she likes. But whatever is decided on, it should be lived up to. The day should not be allowed to end without fulfilling whatever each has prescribed for himself or herself. The discipline of being faithful is valuable in itself, but the long-term worth of the daily "treatment" will be felt in an increasing way the longer a person perseveres in it.

Some time ago when talking with an outstanding magazine writer about this hope of guiding into vital fields as first-line Christophers the many thousands over the country who had contemplated entering the religious life, as well as all others interested in going "part way, full-time," this man made a quick reply that has stuck in my memory and has prodded me to do something about it. *"If you ever get enough people like that in the places that count and as much interested in saving everybody else as they are in saving themselves, you will certainly be throwing an awful lot of grace around in the world."* It was a rather blunt statement, but its truth was challenging.

WE MUST NOT FAIL THEM

Emphasis on a sturdy spiritual life is necessary above all else, but ranking next in importance is the broad vision of Christ. The Devil takes special delight in getting anyone with apostolic potentialities to become so preoccupied with nooks and corners that he misses the great issues that harass the world. After a while he can't see the forest for the trees. There is strong, gripping temptation to withdraw into one's little world, of getting the "God and myself" complex, instead of the fuller, truer and most essential "God, myself and everybody else" attitude.

It is so easy, strangely enough, for those who devote themselves most faithfully to spiritual exercises to become over-solicitous about saving self, body and soul, while ignoring the pitiful plight of the vast numbers over the earth who are starving—physically, mentally and spiritually. Yes, even those who at one time or other in their lives gave some thought of dedicating themselves one hundred percent to God and souls not infrequently show little hesitancy in taking back about eighty percent when they get into the narrow rut of their own limited spheres.

A special obligation rests on those of us who are Catholics. We are entrusted with the fulness of God's Truth. However, there is always the danger of our overlooking the fact that this Truth of God is meant for others as much as it is meant for us. We have a serious obligation to offer it to them at least by way of good example—but not to force it upon them.

As individuals, we often betray the Truth. Most frequently this betrayal is brought about by failing to have an all-embracing—that is to say, *Catholic*—desire to bring all men to that fulness of Truth which we are fortunate enough to possess. Yet these others who lack the fulness of the Truth of Christ are by no means all in utter darkness. They, too, possess in varying degrees the true Light Which enlightens every man that comes into the world. They, too, can be bearers of such Light as they possess.

The Gospels make it clear that Christ took men as they were and built on the raw material offered Him. To a chosen few He gave special training and instruction to equip them to be full-fledged, fully accredited apostles. Yet, at the same time, He wished every person who had even the smallest consciousness of His Truth to participate actively in spreading it.

He was willing to accept assistance from any well-meaning source and, in so doing, He occasionally ran counter to His disciples. They were obviously proud of themselves when one day they told Him that a certain man was *"casting out devils in Thy name, and we forbade him, because he followeth not with us."* But Christ corrected them: *"Forbid him not; for he that is not against you, is for you."* (*Luke* 9:49-50) He did not keep His first disciples waiting for years until their instruction would be so perfect that they would be certain not to misrepresent Him. On the contrary, He seems to have urged them to be His messengers from the start, sending them to hand on what Light they had and to publish the good news as they had taken it in.

And those possessed of the Light who carried it to others less fortunate, were rewarded by an ever-deepening insight into the Truth in all its fulness and beauty.

So it was then; so it is now. Any effort a man makes to grasp the Truth and live the Life is certain to bring him closer to Christ. *"Thou wouldst not have sought Me,"* He said to St. Augustine, *"had not I already been seeking thee."* God wants man, though He doesn't need him. His grace is penetrating, ever present and ever pressing upon us, and it will use any hold it has on a man to make its grasp more secure. Besides, it is a law of our nature that we can only take in new truth in terms of the old. No missioner begins his work by belittling even the crudest absurdities of the religion of the people to whom he has gone. The good missioner, like St. Paul on the Areopagus, looks for common ground.

Suppose the man with whom you go to work every day believes in some power he is willing to call God. And suppose that some lingering fragrance of the poetry of the Sermon on the Mount still encourages him to believe that God is a Father in heaven who cares for the birds of the air and the lilies of the field and even one hair on the head of a man. Suppose he has no affiliation with any church and is hardly able to grasp what the word "Christian" means, yet would resent being refused the name. Is he your ally or your enemy?

Perhaps he is a little of both. But you may still urge him to spread that portion of the Truth he already possesses to the many he can contact—and you cannot—who have never heard or imagined that the hairs on their heads meant anything to anyone. If you are thinking to yourself, "Who shall go?" and you feel your friend would answer, "Here I am; send me," why should you hesitate to send him into a darkness more complete than his? By his very going, he may come closer to Christ.

A doctor possessing the truth of medicine does not compromise with disease when he succeeds in getting a sick man to accept only a small fraction of that truth. Even getting his patient to follow *one* principle of good health—such as brushing his teeth—is a step in the right direction.

The acceptance of one simple principle, more often than not, arouses a voluntary desire for more, because the human mind has a natural love for truth which sometimes needs but the merest prompting to become more fully aroused. Yet even when the acceptance of a fragment of the truth does not lead to the gradual adoption of the whole, a one percent gain is not to be despised.

The Marxists today furnish one of the most graphic examples of unswerving allegiance to a creed without the slightest suggestion of compromise. Not for one moment do they water down their doctrine. Not in any way do they ever convey the idea that any other belief is the equivalent of theirs. Still, they have been unusually successful in getting millions to go along with them as well-wishers, sympathizers, fellow-travelers, and in dozens of other classifications ranging all the way from the "one percenters," on up.

All of these well-wishers, sympathizers and fellow-travellers serve a purpose for the cause of Marxism, little as they may realize it.

Quite apart from any deception they use in other matters, the Communists—to pay them the credit—have shrewdly seen that it is a sounder missionary approach to get people to move step by step towards Marxism over a period of years, than it is to expect them to advance too far, too quickly. During this transition process, one of the most effective means to ensure steady progress towards Marxism is to encourage novices to play a partial role in passing on, or otherwise promoting, some theory of atheistic materialism.

By the same token, if the 70,000,000 in our land who belong to no church could be encouraged to embrace and practice even one truth of Christ, they would be advancing, even if ever so slightly, in the right direction.

Not only did Christ, by word and example, make it clear that He welcomed any who would spread His Truth, in whatever measure. His greatest Apostle, Paul, was most explicit about it in his letter to the Philippians:

> "And many of the brethren in the Lord, growing confident by my bonds, are much more bold to speak the word of God without fear. Some indeed, even out of envy and contention, but some also for good will, preach Christ. Some preach Christ out of charity, knowing that I am set for the defence of the gospel. And some out of contention preach Christ not sincerely, supposing that they raise affliction to my bonds. But what then? So that by all means, whether as a pretext, or in truth, Christ be preached, in this also I rejoice, yea, and will rejoice." (*Phil.* 1:14-18) *

---

* Monsignor Ronald Knox, in his recent translation of the *New Testament* (made at the request of the Catholic Bishops of England) renders this passage as follows:

> "And most of the brethren, deriving fresh confidence in the Lord from my imprisonment, are making bold to preach God's word with more freedom than ever. Some of them, it is true, for no better reason than rivalry or jealousy; but there are others who really proclaim Christ out of good-will. Some, I mean, are moved by charity, because they recognize that I am here to defend the gospel, others by party spirit, proclaiming Christ from wrong motives, just because they hope to make my chains gall me worse. What matter, so long as either way, for private ends or in all honesty, Christ is proclaimed? Of that I am glad now; yes, and I shall be glad hereafter. . . ." (*Phil.* 1:14-18)

A MISSIONARY PROJECT

To be an effective apostolic instrument, therefore, a first-line Christopher must be anxious to "go" to all, especially those farthest from Christ, to "launch out" daringly—in short, to be a *missioner*. He should regard the job to be done as plainly a *missionary project*.

God has put that "little bit of the missionary" in every human being. The evil-minded have long recognized this and constantly keep reminding their followers "not to keep to yourselves what we give you, but spread it. Don't take any job. Take a job that counts—a job where you can spread ideas . . ."

If the missionary vision can spark the evil to action on a world-wide scale never witnessed before, it can be utilized with *far greater effect* for Christ-like work, since that spark was intended by the Creator, not for evil, but for *good*.

For those disposed to hit for the big world in the name of Christ—as He intended they should—the Christopher idea can be a help. It is nothing new; it is as old as the hills. It merely applies to the heart of America the same simple approach used by a missioner in bringing Christ into a pagan city in China.

Instead of sitting self-contained on the city's outskirts, complaining or criticizing, he goes in—again as Christ said to do. Even if he is alone, makes no apparent progress, perhaps is persecuted and even imprisoned, nevertheless he is *there*! He has fulfilled the first thing Our Saviour commanded in order for us to win the world, namely, to *"go."* And because he is there, Christ is working through him, bringing light into darkness, far more than even he realizes.

THE PROBLEM OF THE GOOD PAGAN

To first-line Christophers, more than to any others, there should be a ringing challenge in this missionary perspective and purpose. If enough show particular initiative in bringing the truth of Christ to the one hundred million of our people who, like sheep without a shepherd, are reached by practically no one in His Name, they can help save our country from a deadly paganism into which the majority of our citizens are retreating, step by step. And if enough make it their business to go into the mainstream of our life and restore to it the basic spiritual concepts upon which America was founded, there is high hope that they can do much to save from disaster not alone the United States but the world as well.

This paganism, which more and more deifies this life and rejects the hereafter, is well described by Rosalind Murray in her excellent book, *The Good Pagan's Failure.** She puts her finger on the roots of most of the confusion and tragedy that wracks our present-day world. It is not Communism, Nazism or Fascism. They are only symptoms, however terrible, of a more serious malady. They are like deficiency diseases that afflict the body when its normal vigor and resistance have fallen far below the danger point.

Miss Murray makes a strong point when she fixes most of the blame, not on the brigands who have and still are terrorizing the earth, but on the average "good pagan" who is one with Stalin and Hitler in his denial of God; is one with their complete rejection of the Divine Image in man. The only point of difference in the comparison is that the "good pagan" overlooks the devastating effects that must inevitably follow such malicious, short-sighted thinking.

---

* Longmans, Green and Co.

In one sense these neo-pagans are more dangerous than the Communists, for they reach in and effectively corrode large numbers whom the totalitarians can never reach. They are not vicious or cruel, *"but only those who build up the refinements of this world to the exclusion of the next."* They reject the laws of God and, as a result, they suffer the consequences of such rejection.

These consequences are inevitable. A man may play a poor game of golf when he knows the rules. When he rejects the rules, however, the plain fact is that he doesn't play at all! As poorly as men may act with the Ten Commandments, they certainly don't carry on any better when they toss those same Commandments aside.

Warnings of this trend toward paganism and materialism have been increasing on all sides. Archbishop Robert E. Lucey of San Antonio, Texas, pointed out this danger when he recently stated:

"It took us twenty centuries to build a none too strong Western civilization. We may see most of it destroyed in our own time. Communists take their religion seriously; many Christians do not. The missionaries of Communism work feverishly to teach their heresies; easy going Christians who are called to be apostles of truth, justice and love still indulge in the luxury of apathy, lethargy, complacence, stupid pride, race hatred and economic injustice. Meanwhile, millions of Christians are going into slavery worse than death."

Rabbi Samuel Thurman echoed the same thought not long ago when he told the Central Conference of American Rabbis in Kansas City:

"Man's all-consuming and all-embracing enterprise seems to be to impose man's design on the universe. . . . Fifty years from now a great-grandson will conclude that the rabbis of today had very little to say or do about God and altogether too much to say and do about the world.

"The ears of our own people are deaf to the voice of prophecy. They are much more attuned to the sirens of economic demands and material comforts. The spiritual has been supplanted by the secular."

Speaking on the modern church one Protestant called this same idea to his co-religionists' attention in the following words:

"It has forgotten its true business—the production of holiness. Holiness, not just consolation, moral uplift or social reform. . . . And the business of religion is . . . to give men eternity, and to give themselves to eternity—that so, by this resort to the center—they may integrate their whole existence. . . ."

In similar vein, Dr. Charles C. Morrison, editor of the *Christian Century,* a well known Protestant magazine, pointed out:

"The membership of Protestant churches has only a vague idea of what Christianity really is. . . . Protestantism, in our time . . . has not been generating a great faith of its own. We have been losing our religion to secularism. The result is that both the general community and the church membership are religiously illiterate."

EVIDENCE OF THIS NEW PAGANISM IN OUR YOUTH

This paganism is not confined to adults, either. Like the totalitarians, many parents have eliminated, or allowed to be eliminated from the training of youth, all thought of God and the supernatural, with the result that their children have had instilled in their minds the idea that this life is the beginning and end of everything. Two astounding sets of statistics confirm this fact. One concerns Germany; the other deals with the United States.

The first set of figures is contained in the Protestant

weekly, *Der Sonntag* of Dresden, which recently published the results of an inquiry it made among school children to determine the effects upon them of the de-Christianizing program that took place under the Nazis—effects which may well be felt for generations to come. 700 children, aged 9 to 12, were asked the simple question: *"Who was Jesus Christ?"* Only 7% of the children living in big cities and 1% of those living in suburbs were able to answer. *Of the 7% only 2% had been told about the Divine Saviour by their mothers.* Only 13 among 163 children knew the meaning of Easter. Of 179 city youngsters asked if they prayed daily, only 8 replied in the affirmative. Not more than 13 out of 480 children living in the suburbs said any prayers at all.

The second set of statistics emphasizes that what is taking place in America is much the same. Millions of our children are being deprived, just as effectively as the innocents under the Nazis, of the one most powerful force of self-control—the knowledge of Jesus Christ. The paganizing of our educational system has resulted in a changed outlook on the part of our youth and prepared the way for a wave of godlessness, juvenile delinquency and adult crime that increases by the hour. As Louis B. Nichols, Assistant Director of the F.B.I., stated before a recent conference of the Methodist Church:

"Criminals develop: they are not born. Somewhere in their development someone has fallen in the discharge of a duty . . . people for the most part commit crime because they do not possess a sufficient sense of moral responsibility . . . crime we will continue to have so long as man is dwarfed by a lack of moral and spiritual nurture."

The figures speak for themselves. A minimum of 6,000,000 persons in this country, or 1 out of every 23, have criminal records, an F.B.I. report shows. And, according to the *Methodist Voice* of Washington, D. C.:

"We have the highest rate of crime and delinquency in our history.

"We have three times as many criminals in our penal institutions as we have students in our colleges and universities.

"More prostitutes, under 18, were arrested last year than in any previous year.

"Eleven out of twelve of our young people do not attend any church.

"2,000,000 of our young men and women are infected, annually, with social diseases until it has become our Public Enemy No. One.

"During the war, 1,000,000 babies were born out of wedlock.

"60,000 of these babies were born to girls under 14 years of age.

"We have one murder every 40 minutes, 60 suicides every day, and one major crime committed every 22 seconds.

"In some places divorces equal marriages."

THE PRICE OF NEGLECT

To neglect this situation any longer is to invite disaster. It will leave the field wide open to those whose only "god" is the collectivist state and who see in man a mere beast of flesh and bone, devoid of an immortal soul. To neglect this task is to allow the "top-soil" of our free society to dry up and be blown away as so much dust.

Such a condition, while desperate, does *not* call for action marked by violence, nor by hysterical outbursts of emotion. Rather does it call for grim, apostolic determination on the part of all Christophers, of first-line Christophers in particular, to work as hard to integrate spiritual values into all phases of life as the enemies of civilization are striving to eliminate them. This positive note was stressed by the late Pope Pius XI when he said:

"We cherish the firm hope that the fanaticism with which the sons of darkness work day and night at their materialistic and atheistic propaganda will at least serve the holy purpose of stimulating the sons of light to a like and even greater zeal for the honor of the Divine Majesty."

If a person needs any further urging to play his or her part as a first-line Christopher and do something to relieve the present tragedy, he or she would do well to reflect for a moment on this possibility: more than a small portion of the world-wide confusion may be due to the fact that people like themselves, who have been given so much spiritually, still hesitate to share even a little of that treasure with those who have nothing at all. That "little," multiplied many times over by others who, like you, hold back, may make all the difference between spiritual life and death for countless millions.

The lack of a seemingly insignificant chemical, it was found not long ago, is the cause of the hitherto mysterious, widespread death of sheep. Dr. Leonard A. Maynard, director of the School of Nutrition of Cornell University, recently discovered that the absence of one small, vital nutrient in the soil, known as *cobalt,* has been the cause of widespread livestock loss. *"It has been found,"* Dr. Maynard states, *"that .1 mg* (an infinitesimal fraction of an ounce) *of cobalt daily makes the difference between life and death in a sheep; a lack of this minute amount was responsible for the death of tens of thousands of animals yearly before the discovery was made."*

To such a condition the sensible reaction should not be to blame the sheep for their fatalities. They have a right to expect "shepherds" to see to their care and help provide that which is missing.

That not enough "shepherds" have gone into the "highways" in the spiritual sense, has been due to the increasing tendency to put more value on the passing comforts of this life and less on eternal joys of the hereafter. Those who have scourged the earth have had one objective in common—the defiant rejection of a personal God and a future life. That rejection alone should be argument enough for any one, especially a person who once felt drawn to the complete service of God, to further with every bit of energy he or she can muster the one principle which is such a stumbling block to the godless.

A RARE OPPORTUNITY

For all Christophers, first-line lay apostles particularly, there is now an exceptionally rare opportunity to accomplish great things by showing devoted solicitude for the one hundred million in our country who are getting further and further away from the immutable principles of Christ. Communism and other evils may come and go, but this greater problem, involving a gradual loss of appreciation of the main foundations of our civilization, is far more serious than all of them put together. *It is the heart of America's sickness today.* In its wake will inevitably follow a returning paganism, a fading vision, a slow but sure degradation and slipping back to the revolting evils prevalent among mankind before the coming of Christ.

Not for one moment should we overestimate America's position in the world today. But we should not underestimate it, either. Whether we like it or not, we in this country have had thrust upon us a terrifying responsibility to show the way to a heartsick world. Only recently one magazine solemnly editorialized: "It is an open secret in the rest of the world that 20th century civilization would be guided in large part by the heart, the wisdom, and the power of the United

States. The secret has spread in every foreign newspaper, before every meeting of foreign ministers . . ."

It is much more than the dollars, food, medicine and material things of America that the world needs and really wants. What they crave above all else is the spirit that makes America the great nation it is. And that spirit above all else is God's truth proclaiming through the Declaration of Independence, the Constitution and the Bill of Rights that even the least individual as a child of God, has rights that no man or nation can take from him, the right to life, to liberty, and to the pursuit of happiness which begins here but will have its supreme fulfillment in eternity.

What an honor and a privilege, then, for anyone at this critical time to jump into the breech and help change the course of history. But who is better fitted, better equipped for this than a first-line Christopher? To them it can be said most emphatically and hopefully: *"You can change the face of the world!"*

THE TEST OF SINCERITY

It remains to be seen, however, whether they will gladly take up the challenge—or backtrack. There is little danger of exaggerating the important role that they can play, and it will be a terrible pity if they realize this only when it is too late—when they stand before the judgment seat of the Almighty. The test of their sincerity can be fairly accurately measured by how many go into the market-place, the apostolic vigor they show in seizing the initiative, and in the numbers in which they, as "committees of one" encourage other men and women to be other Christs.

If they have any doubt of the power they have in their hands (by God's grace) or of the immense and urgently needed contribution Christ expects them to make to the common good of all, they might consider for a moment the impelling resolve of Franz Werfel, expressed in his preface to the *Song of Bernadette.* *"I vowed,"* Werfel declared, *"that I would evermore and everywhere in all I wrote, magnify the divine mystery, the holiness of man, careless of a period which has turned away with scorn and rage and indifference from these ultimate values of our mortal lot."*

In one of his essays, "Can We Live Without Faith In God," he stresses the same spiritual concern, with explicit (even if qualified) tribute to Christ. "It is especially as a Jew," he stated, "by virtue of a primeval affinity of blood and character that I feel myself justified in the following view: this world that calls itself civilized can be spiritually healed if it finds its way back to Christianity . . . because the teaching of Christ . . . not only is not exhausted, but has scarcely been felt. Because in its metaphysical and ethical values it towers star-high above every trend of the present day. Because it places the gross, materialistic barbarian, the stockholder of nothingness, the possessed possessor of personal interests . . . before the sacred paradox, 'Live contrary to your interests for Truth and Life.'"

If one like Werfel felt so deeply, wrote so strongly, and fought so valiantly up to his very death, can those who possess Christ's Truth in its fulness do any less? If he and others like him, who have experienced no special calling by God, have dedicated themselves so completely to the furtherance of divine truth, will those who *have* experienced a personal invitation from on high, hesitate to be first-line Christophers? Will they hesitate to *"magnify the divine mystery, the holiness of man . . . evermore and everywhere"* in everything that they do?

If their hearts and souls are filled with faith in God, hope for the future, and love of humanity, they will seek out any post into which they can fit, in the fields of education, government, labor-management, writing, social service, library or any other sphere affecting the destiny of the many and not merely the few. They will not mind hardships, monotony, discouragements. They will deliberately take a low-paying job, if it is one of great missionary possibilities. They will find a certain joy in carrying a Cross. As they grow in love of people and the desire to help them all reach their eternal destiny, they will not count the cost of wear and tear on themselves. In fact, they will more and more see the wisdom of taking things a bit hard in this life and waiting for their rest in heaven.

"A WORLD TO WIN!"

Across the desk of a leading Communist in New York is stretched in large letters this challenging inscription: "A WORLD TO WIN!" It is a constant reminder to him and all who come to see him that there is nothing local or limited about the Communist goal. No matter how insignificantly placed they may be, their missionary aim is not two blocks or their own little environment. It is the *world*! Every move they make is a move to reach for *all* mankind. Because of their global vision, they become ten times as effective in whatever area they find themselves.

Where did the Communists get this broad-gauged vision? Why is it when they take a job it is seldom, if ever, a routine one? Why is it nearly always a creative post that touches the lives of the multitude, not merely the few? Why is it that every true Communist displays such driving purpose, enterprise and direction? Why is he willing to put up with endless delays, hard work, inconvenience, misunderstanding, boredom, setbacks, suffering, and even defeat, in his extraordinary allegiance to his cause?

In the answer to these questions, there are many factors. But outranking them all, believe it or not, is the broad-visioned daring of Christ in which they have been thoroughly indoctrinated—*while at the same time schooled to REJECT His Truth.*

Those who would recapture that daring of Christ and accept His Truth, those who would be other Christs—especially first-line Christophers—can yet take the play away from the godless.

Fired by the missionary spirit God has implanted in them, they can reach for the world as far as they are able. They can seek—whenever and wherever possible—jobs where they can bring into action, on a full time basis, their personal, individual power for the general good. They can influence the many, not merely the few.

They can show the way as lay apostles in bringing the world back to Christ!

XVI

INDIVIDUAL INITIATIVE IN AN ORGANIZATION

ANY GROUP or society or club is very much like a football team. Well organized, it is worth something more than the eleven players who happen to be on it. Yet unless these same players have a sense of personal responsibility and individual initiative, they will fall far short of their objective.

With regard to organizations, this is true whether the objective in question be good or evil. A small, well-organized group of subversives in Pittsburgh took over and dominated the policies of an important labor union because, individually, they never lost sight of their group's primary aim. And because they subordinated all other considerations to this end, they succeeded where otherwise they might have failed.

On a brighter note, from a Christopher point of view, not long ago a handful of alert unionists—Catholics, Protestants and Jews alike—finally were able to restore democratic leadership to another trade group which, for ten years, had been Communist-controlled. To do this meant persistent organizational work for over a year. Inactive fellow members were rounded up and encouraged to show personal interest, to attend meetings, to speak out on the issues which concerned them, to accept individual responsibility by working on committees and fulfilling a variety of other minor obligations, all of which eventually brought gratifying results.

The notable success of the Freedom Train in calling to the attention of the entire nation the great historical documents of America was due to a small organized group of businessmen. Theirs was a noble idea coupled with broad vision, simple planning, and efficient execution of the program agreed upon. What could easily have remained an empty dream, never to be fulfilled, became instead a vital reality and accomplished more than any other recent single effort in making the Declaration of Independence, the Constitution and Bill of Rights, and other documents of historic significance better known and more deeply cherished.

In one midwestern city a group of public-spirited citizens, realizing that many ideas in the minds of people have their origin in the printed word, banded together to force the public libraries of their community to include more books of better quality on their shelves.

In Washington, D. C., a few employees of a government office organized themselves to do something, in Christopher fashion, about the Russian menace to global peace. Distressed by continual talk on the subject with no accompanying action, twelve of them meet once a week during lunch hour to pray for the return of Russia to a Christian way of life. A local radio news commentator heard about the meetings and during one of his broadcasts referred to the need of prayer during these perilous times.

In each of the previous instances, sometimes one person, sometimes several individuals, were responsible for sparking group action. While the Christopher movement neither initiates nor sponsors groups of any kind, it is interesting to discover that organizations already established are including a Christopher purpose in their objectives. Others, recently started, are taking the Christopher idea as their guide and inspiration. One such group in Philadelphia has directed a large share of its energies to getting people into the main fields that influence the lives of millions—into education, government, labor-management, and communications.

In one large western university a few students, guided by a member of the faculty, combined to restore what they felt would be a healthier atmosphere to the student committee, the campus paper, student rallies, and other university youth activities. Recognizing that the chief reasons for the success of a small number of subversives within the student body who dominated these spheres was due, not so much to their strength, but to the apathy of the majority of sound-minded students, they resolved to play active roles in the various student projects. Under the leadership of one young man who had become familiar with the Christopher idea, they worked constantly to encourage more members of the student body to show an interest in their own affairs by taking responsible positions whenever and wherever possible. Moreover, they laid out a program through which *were* taught the details and important obligations of those holding such posts.

MANY JOIN BUT FEW WORK

This importance of positive, individual action in all kinds of organizations was pointed out quite clearly recently by E.

T. Leech, editor of *The Pittsburgh Press* of the Scripps-Howard newspaper chain. Answering the question as to what a God-fearing American can do in the face of the totalitarian menace to this country, Mr. Leech wrote:

". . . every citizen, young and old, is a part of some groups which have an influence in our social and public life. He belongs to a church or a union or a veterans' society or civic club or a school class or a nationality organization; most citizens belong to a number of groups. . . . Get a Communist into a club or a union or an office or a school or a fraternal society, and he'll go right to work. His first job is to convert some other member of the group to his viewpoint. Then there'll be two of them—and their next job is to try to convert two others—thus making four . . . they have done it over and over again. They are past masters as evangelists —as seekers of converts. They have been trained in that art.

"As for the average loyal American, he enjoys the greatest privilege—but also the most dangerous one—which democracy can offer . . . the privilege of complete indifference. And he enjoys it overtime . . . [Americans] are great joiners but poor participants in the affairs of the organizations which they join or the groups to which they belong by force of circumstances.

"Workingmen belong to unions—but most of them don't go to the union meetings. Businessmen belong to trade associations—but few go to the association conventions or take any part in the fixing of association policies. Farmers join agricultural bodies—but only a small number are active in what those bodies do. Veterans join special societies—but most never attend the meetings. Civic clubs enroll lots of members —but few active workers. In short, Americans belong to all sorts of things—but they just belong. They don't work; they don't speak; they don't meet; they don't vote."

Finally, after referring to the fact that subversives know

they have to control only a few people in order to control group policies, Mr. Leech concludes, "Here . . . is where the individual American citizen can answer the question: 'What can I do?' . . . He, too, can be a missionary, just as the Commies are—but on the American side. Go to meetings; don't be afraid to speak out; don't dodge a share of the responsibility; vote for good candidates . . . don't be indifferent. Be a working American, instead of merely a drifting one."

In groups people often assimilate each other's basic attitudes. Many of the ideas a person has and the thoughts he expresses have been absorbed, consciously or unconsciously, from friends and associates with whom he comes in contact. It is inevitable that a man or woman who goes to organization or club meetings regularly is bound to be affected by what his or her companions are doing and saying. It is the old story of *influence* or *be influenced*. Those with evil ideas can and are wreaking havoc in the lives of many good people whose main fault is that they are confused and uncertain as to their ultimate purpose as human beings, made in God's own image and likeness.

You people with good ideas, good motives, and an eternal goal—in short, you Christophers—will accomplish wonders in bringing Christ's Truth where there is ignorance and indifference the moment you realize the individual power for good which you can exert in any club or organization to which you may belong. Then will you more than match the daring pace set by the godless who are adept at the simple and indispensable art of knowing people, moving among them, understanding their problems, whims and fancies, sympathizing with them in their sorrows, rejoicing with them in their joys.

Yet remember this. People, whether in an organization or not, can tell in an instant whether you go among them to help them and guide them, or whether you go only when you want them to help *you*. The sincerity of your interest, the honesty with which you speak their language, the inoffensiveness with which you air your views—all these are necessary. But by the same token, however, you dare not compromise Truth. And it *is* vital that you do stay on the job.

WHERE YOU CAN BE A MISSIONER

You should use your efforts to see that your organization fulfills an objective which best serves the interests of the many, not merely the few. It should not be allowed to parallel the example of one group in Pennsylvania (organized for an apostolic purpose) whose members were exceptionally fine people, yet who did little more than meet regularly and complain about conditions in the world—and did nothing to improve them.

Fortunately, this sad state of affairs did not continue. During the course of one particular meeting a Christopher woke the members up to the fact that they were hoping to accomplish, by a once-a-month get-together of an hour or so, a program which never got beyond the talking stage. Anxious to strengthen the group by encouraging better individual participation in activities which would benefit large numbers of people, he inquired of the assembled men and women as to their varying occupations. To the surprise of all, it turned out that in almost every case they were holding jobs in which they did little more than earn a living.

Following up this information, the Christopher pointed out that in the one-hundred-and-forty-odd working hours in each month they might have been in jobs where not only could they earn a living, but could serve as missioners as well. Then he concluded with the suggestion that at least a few of them could easily shift to positions which influence the thoughts and actions of large sections of the population. That this

Christopher's words bore fruit is confirmed by the fact that, in the months which followed, several of the members went into government work and one returned to the teaching profession which she'd abandoned some years before.

Another group, which devotes itself to emphasizing the sacredness of marriage, was astonished to find out from one of their members that they were doing only half the job of which they were capable. This member, a newspaperman, was asked by a Christopher to explain the purpose of the organization. On being told, this Christopher commented, "What you're doing is fine. But aren't you keeping too much to yourselves? Why don't you get your friends to bring their ideas on the Christian principles of marriage out into the mainstream of everyday life to those who never hear of them and who need them far more than you do? And since you're in the newspaper business, why don't you use your organization to encourage more people like yourself to go into the writing field?"

The reply was brief, but to the point: "Say, you've got something there. Never thought of that before, but I can see now that we've been thinking of ourselves too much. You know what I'm going to do? I'm personally going to push those ideas for all they're worth!"

THEY MISSED THE POINT

A well-known author and foreign affairs expert who recently returned from Europe recounted the trouble one country is having with the Reds. He pointed out that one well-meaning group there makes a practice of reading and discussing the Papal encyclicals as the best means of stopping atheistic materialism. But while they keep talking about the importance of the encyclicals and how necessary they are, strangely enough they do little or nothing to put the Papal recommendations into practical application.

In contrast to this and on a more hopeful note, however, one very fine organization run along similar lines here in the United States, has put into everyday practice—with less stress on talk and more emphasis on action—these same encyclicals. Fired by a couple of tireless Christophers, whose every act bears striking testimony to the power of individual initiative in any group of people, this organization has been the means of affecting, for the better, the lives of hundreds of thousands of our citizens.

Unceasing, positive action for good is the best and surest guarantee of a free, God-fearing America of the future. Nothing less will do, for it was Christ Himself who said, "Not every one that saith to Me, Lord, Lord, shall enter into the kingdom of heaven: but he that doth the will of My Father Who is in heaven, he shall enter into the kingdom of heaven." (*Matt.* 7:21)

One important consideration of organizational activities is the opportunity and need for the zealous Christopher to assume group leadership. It is simply another case of influence or be influenced; lead or be led.

The active leaders of the various organizations in any given area are always few. These same leaders' names keep coming up as heads or officers of a number of various groups. For instance, in one Eastern city the commander of one of the local veterans' posts is also a member of the city's housing commission, is a campaign leader in the Red Cross drive, the Community Chest drive, the Infantile Paralysis and Cancer Fund programs, and is a member of several other civic and social clubs.

The net result of situations like this is that the bulk of

organizational work falls on the shoulders of a few zealous individuals who are overburdened and cannot do justice to a variety of tasks at one and the same time.

ORGANIZATIONS BY THE MILLION

When you consider the multiplicity of the varied types of clubs and organizations in the United States, you will begin to realize the tremendous field for *good* which is waiting to be reached. Wherever people gather, there ideas can be distributed more subtly than in most other spheres of endeavor. In this country alone there are approximately three million organizations of various kinds and functions. Included among them are the trade unions, some 15,000 women's clubs, 12,000 service clubs, countless national, student, labor, business, professional and other organizations, and a host of local religious, charitable, community and civic groups.

Also there are sports groups—teams of all kinds, gymnastic and outdoor clubs, hunting and fishing societies, bowling associations.

In addition, there are the mutual aid groups set up on a community or trade basis to care for the more unfortunate, dispensing all kinds of assistance to the indigent, the sick, the bereaved.

There are the fraternal organizations, the veterans' groups with national affiliations, the "hometowners"—the Iowans gathered in California, the men of Oslo living in Minneapolis. There are the young peoples' organizations, the hobbyists, the stamp and coin collectors, the clubs that fit every type of human interest imaginable.

Most of these groups include both men and women; but where, occasionally, an organization is composed exclusively of male members, almost invariably there will be an auxiliary for women. Through all of these channels it is possible to accomplish more than the original purpose for which such groups were formed. Individuals can be influenced on many subjects, the community guided, positions of leadership won. The godless find in organizations of all types a fertile field for their activities. We have much to learn from them.

THE "GRASS ROOTS"—AND THE ORGANIZATION

In recent years there has been much talk of "grass roots" movements, with the term being either used so loosely or misused altogether that people have come to suspect it as just another catch-phrase of the vote seeker or the political commentator. Actually there is such a thing as "grass roots" in our national life. The term denotes the average, down-to-earth men and women usually found in rural areas (yet not exclusively so) who are more concerned with everyday facts than tomorrow's fancies. They lead ordinary lives, enjoy simple if routine pleasures, play with their children, eat home-cooked dinners, listen to their favorite comedians on the radio . . . and consider the running of society out of their province.

The primary concern of each of these persons is his or her immediate family, supporting it, planning for it, holding it together. It *is* a big job and doesn't leave too much time for the problems of that bigger family called mankind. These are the grass-roots people whose horizons are too often limited by their most pressing needs and by their most immediate concerns. Now and then, of course, the narrow pattern of their living is disturbed by a war, by unemployment, by an election, by a newspaper headline, by a radio broadcast.

In all this picture, however, one thing has not been mentioned. That is the fact that at some point in his or her crowded schedule he or she goes to an organization or club meeting. Whether this is done to vary routine or to indulge in a less spectacular version of café society, is immaterial. The point is that each becomes, then, something more than an item in a family unit; he becomes, instead, a community individual. And that is exactly where each can come into contact with *ideas* outside the normal mold of family living.

In these community contacts at clubs and societies, ideas do take hold. You, the Christopher, interested in distributing Christ's Truth and the basic principles upon which our republic rests, will realize that to cultivate these grass roots you will have to spread the "seeds" of "grass." Merely to sit around and wait for things to happen is to waste your life in a barren existence; meanwhile watching other people with evil ideas plant and reap the harvest.

> ". . . But about the eleventh hour he went out and found others standing, and he saith to them: Why stand you here all the day idle?" (*Matt.* 20:6)

BE ONE OF GOD'S "SALESMEN"

To sell a product, salesmen are advised to make demonstrations. To win political campaigns, party workers ring doorbells. In both cases this means going from house to house, meeting people and telling them over and over again about a particular product.

Doing these things will involve repetition, and purposely so. For example, imagine you are in a subway, bus, or streetcar, and you see an ad for some sort of medication guaranteed to relieve coughs due to colds. The message leaves no conscious impression. You turn the pages of a newspaper, and you see the same advertisement. You hear its praises sung on the radio. Still this has no visible effect. One day, however, you come down with a cold. You begin to cough. You visit the drug-store on the way home from work and the man behind the counter shows you several brands of cough syrup. Which one will you buy? Chances are you'll purchase the medicine you've already seen advertised. You've looked at its name so often, heard about it over the air so frequently, that it begins to look and sound like an old friend.

That method can be carried over into an organization or club. A person at a meeting hears someone talking up the idea of preserving our God-given liberties. A day or so later he goes to his union and hears the same idea repeated, though perhaps with variations. Shortly afterwards while bowling with some friends, he hears the same idea repeated by a fellow bowling enthusiast. Now the idea becomes, in many ways, part of him. He has absorbed it, filed it away at the back of his mind. It is in his blood. Soon he is repeating that very idea in public as if it were his own, stating it with increasing conviction and increasing enthusiasm. In short, he has been sold on the idea of God-given liberties in a free democracy.

DANGERS TO BE AVOIDED

The godless are fully aware of the power of repetition. That is why they have developed the technique to its most effective point so as to undermine traditional institutions and fundamental concepts of freedom. And precisely because our freedom seems to be well founded, many good, if unthinking, citizens tend to laugh at the notion that totalitarian groups can wear away the hard rock of our God-given Constitutional guarantees of "life, liberty, and the pursuit of happiness."

It is this condition which poses one of the greatest threats to our free way of life. Our country faces a most sinister peril in this complacency, this failure to see the strength of godless erosion.

There are parts of these United States where once grew rich, abundant crops but which today are wastelands because not enough people made sufficient efforts in the direction of soil conservation. They did not protect the land either for themselves or for their children. "It's only a handful of earth lost here and there," many of them said. "No need to worry. There is a lot more left."

Today, those "handfuls of earth" represent a major agricultural disaster.

What erosion did to this soil of America, the constant inroads of godless elements can and are doing to the liberties which were purchased for us at such great cost by those who valued them even above life itself.

A second and equally important danger to be avoided can best be summed up in the phrase, "sins of omission." Many well-intentioned persons, even while joining various organizations to fight the life-sapping deterioration in our society, unwittingly encourage such deterioration.

One striking illustration of this occurred in a large city a few months ago. An investigation revealed that there was a growing trend on the part of better-qualified teachers of all religious convictions to withdraw from the educational field and go into pursuits where the work was easier and the financial return greater. With reference to one religious group alone, it was pointed out by a member of the board of education that of the teachers abandoning the profession at least forty percent were Catholic, while only seven percent of those entering public school classrooms as teachers were of the Catholic faith. About the same time, however, one Communist Party member boasted of the fact that eight hundred Marxists had enrolled as teachers in just one section of the city!

The paradox of the situation is this: several of those who had given up teaching for reasons that concerned themselves alone, not the general good, joined organizations dedicated to furthering Christian values and condemning the inroads of atheism and secularism. They made the serious mistake of thinking that joining an organization would be a suitable substitute for their individual responsibility and would dispense them of any personal effort beyond sitting on the side-lines and passing resolutions.

Little did they realize they were among the most effective promoters of the very disintegration they were condemning. Nothing pleases or helps those intent on destruction more than to have those with strong religious beliefs withdraw from the highways into the byways. While they were thus *subtracting* good from the schools, the enemies of our country were *adding* bad. While they were talking to themselves, the destructive elements were talking to thousands of students.

Strangely enough, it did not seem to occur to these teachers that they were like soldiers who desert during time of war. Even worse, they were more like soldiers who not only desert the service, but turn their uniforms and equipment and arms over to the enemy. Somehow they missed the one big thing: to get into a position where they can do good and to *work at it.*

What would you think if you heard, for example, that several farmers who had prided themselves upon raising crops of superior quality left their farms, then joined an organization to complain and pass resolutions against the farmers who had taken over their lands and who were ruining their soil? Farmers who want to produce good crops while preserving their healthy soil, actually go into farming. They plow, and plant, and work at it, individually. Very likely they will form associations for their mutual benefit and for the promoting of better farming methods. And they will find the associations valuable in aiding them in their efforts. But they know full well that all the farmers' associations in the world will not improve agriculture if nobody is plowing the earth, or if the only people who are doing the farming are deliberately destroying the value of the soil.

A third danger to be avoided is that of *cliques*—a major cause of a breakdown in any group. Everyone must be made to feel that he *belongs,* that he is part of all the organization's activities, and that he is missed when he is not present.

As a Christopher, motivated by the idea of being able to disagree without being disagreeable, one of our tasks will be to smooth out intragroup dissension and division. Frequently this can be done on a personal basis. Other times, of necessity, it must be accomplished in an official way.

A FINAL REMINDER

To spread the basic truths that make America as a free, God-fearing nation possible, you will constantly have to meet people. You can't do it in exactly the same way as the salesman or the political campaigner. *The Christophers* is not an organization, functioning as such. Rather is it a group of individuals motivated by an idea. If you were to ring a doorbell, put a foot inside the door, and say, "I'm here to sell you on the inalienable rights with which we were endowed by our Creator," that would be a strange approach, indeed. It would be fitting, however, for a Christopher to join some worth-while organization and strive to weave the Christopher idea into its activities, its conversation, into every opportunity offered of meeting and influencing people.

Really and truly to bear Christ when you are in a club, group, or organization, you will have to do your share in digging the "soil," in going among people, in planting the "seed" and cultivating it constantly so that one day, through the warmth of your love of mankind—because you love God so much—you will cover this nation with an eternal harvest for Christ. The work is hard . . . but the reward is great. And, in the words of the Scriptures: "*Now is the acceptable time . . . now is the day of salvation.*" (II Cor. 6:2)

XVII

PUBLIC SPEAKING

Presentation With a Purpose

THE BASIC RULE of public speaking is to know what you want to say and how to say it. A poor speech is usually the result of a failure to meet this fundamental requirement. Every talk must have a definite purpose, must stress some specific point: and the more this purpose is rooted in absolute truth, the greater will be its ring of sincerity. To you, the Christopher, this especially applies.

No matter what the subject, to begin to speak well in public you must be thoroughly imbued with a Christopher purpose. If you are, your very conviction will transmit itself to your listeners and overcome most of the technical speaking flaws you may possess. Secure in the knowledge that Christ works in and through you who would do His will, knowing what you want to say and believing in it, having an intense desire to reach as many as possible with the truth which you know, you *will* find a way of properly expressing yourself.

This is not to say, of course, that you will become a gifted orator overnight. The gift of public speech, like so many other gifts, is usually developed, not inherited. Many hours of hard work go into the making of an accomplished speaker. Even the orator from whose lips brilliant phrases just seem to pour has had his moments of open-mouthed silence, the early self-conscious days when he arose to speak and the words refused to come.

Moreover, many a man or woman, who is perfectly at ease in across-the-table conversation, often becomes very nervous when facing an audience. This happens even to the most seemingly self-assured individuals, yet such nervousness is not altogether a disadvantage.

One man who has been an active public speaker for some twenty-five years, who has taught classes, spoke in Madison Square Garden in New York, and engaged in debates before thousands of people, claims that in the course of a day he averages as many hours on a platform as he does in all his other activities combined. Yet he never goes before an audience without feeling somewhat tense.

"I'm rather grateful for that," he says. "Public speaking requires concentration, very much like hitting a baseball. The batter . . . has to be sharply alert, every muscle and nerve in tight coordination. Likewise, the effective public speaker must feel his body and brain move into high gear."

This moving into "high gear," then, is not something for you to fear. Rather should it be regarded as an advantage, when properly used. The only danger lies in becoming *so* tense that you will not adequately express yourself. If and when this happens, a moment or two of reflection on your rôle as a Christ-bearer should help to dispel any excessive nervousness. Coupled with this should be a determination to speak in public as often as you can find an opening. The more used you get to the audience and the limelight, the more quickly you will overcome the handicap of stage fright.

From a physical standpoint, nervousness develops from one of three sources:

(1) Failure to control your material,
(2) Failure to control yourself,
(3) Failure to control your audience.

CONTROL OF MATERIAL

To speak clearly is to think clearly—aloud. It is a mistake to trust to intuition. Who has not had the experience of realizing that there were many important things he should have said and didn't? Think out what you want to say *before* you attempt to say it.

Preparation of material is a prime requisite of successful public speaking. Even in extemporaneous addresses is this true. The best speeches of this kind are usually not as unprepared as they may appear on casual inspection. In most cases they consist of little parts of many speeches a speaker has made in the past. He carries them around in his mind like so many pieces of paper. His extemporaneous genius actually is a job of mental marshalling of data.

Since nearly all good talks are prepared, the method of preparation depends, in part, upon the nature of the speech. If you know, long in advance, that you are to make a speech of a certain length on a specified subject at a definite time, you can do a complete job of preparatory work. You can do research, consult files, gather advice, try out the entire talk on your family or your friends.

On the other hand, if you must speak on the spur of the moment, your problem is somewhat different. You must rely mainly on two things: your brain and your background.

Whenever you are called upon to speak, your brain will have to be alerted quickly to be ready for the task. You will have to decide immediately on the most important point you wish to convey and this decision should be made, if possible, before you get to your feet, *not* afterwards. Once the decision is arrived at, however, follow along that course. *Don't digress,* for not only will your listeners lose the theme of your talk, but you yourself will become increasingly confused. You will become so entangled in a maze of oratorical byways that you will find it ever more difficult to get on the highway again.

To broaden the scope of your knowledge, reading contributes a fund of information. It is suggested that you use such information in public speaking. The content of your talk should flow from within you, and this is where the Christopher has a particular advantage. He knows the ultimate goal he has to reach; he has a *purpose.* All his persuasion is geared to that end. His chart runs a steady course and is, therefore, that much more sure of success.

If you expect to speak often, you can do a great deal to increase the range of your material. Concentrated research is one method. It is the scholarly approach for those who have the time for intensive study. However, there are many other ways of widening one's background. You might, for instance, develop the habit of clipping out newspaper and magazine articles on a wide variety of subjects which concern you as a *missioner* for *good.* And you will be surprised at how much you can gather in a comparatively short time. As a result, you will accomplish a double purpose. You will increase the fund of knowledge held at your finger tips, and you will have a handy reference file in your home.

Occasionally you will hear or read of some incident that might be of value at some later date to illustrate some vital point. Clip out such an item or jot it down. In this connection it is suggested that you purchase from some stationery store both a letter file and a small 3″ x 5″ card file. Neither of these items need be expensive. The letter file can be used for those pieces of information which run to some detail. The card file can serve to list those references which tell their story in comparatively few words. From time to time, run through your little collection of incidents or anecdotes, discarding those references which are no longer useful. Keeping up to date in this manner is a constant preparation for public speaking that entertains yet conveys a message at the same time.

When you read a piece of good literature, a classic, a famous oration, an important document reprinted in the press, excerpts, perhaps, from the Declaration of Independence, don't hesitate to dwell on the more significant passages. Read them over, again and again—aloud. Soon they will become part of you without your consciously memorizing them. You will absorb thoughts, phrases, and a flow of speech. Both the content and manner of greatness will become part of you.

By no means, of course, is it suggested that you try to imitate anyone. You must be *yourself,* but in so doing you need not hesitate to improve yourself by exposing your eyes, ears, and brain to the works of great men and women.

Part of your preparation entails speaking aloud, though not necessarily to an audience. If there is some idea you want to convey, it might be advisable to try it out on your family or on a friend in the course of a casual conversation. This will give you a chance to organize your thoughts into concrete terms. And you will get some inkling of audience reaction.

MAKE AN OUTLINE

In preparing for a talk, an outline is a most suitable device. If the speech is long (fifteen minutes or more), an outline is almost a necessity. If the speech is brief (two to fifteen minutes), an outline is still desirable.

The outline should cover the main points of your address, yet it should not be too detailed or you may become more interested in following your outline than in paying attention to your audience. Your outline is your central line of argument, sketched very roughly. It is a reminder of what comes next. It should not be a completely written speech.

Occasionally, of necessity, your outline will go into some detail, as, for example, when you give exact quotations or list statistics and examples. Then it will be perfectly in order to write these items out and even read them to your audience. Your listeners will appreciate such brief interludes, and your speech will gain in authenticity. Christ Himself spoke in parables so as to make His divine truth understood by everyone.

A good talk, like a good story, has a beginning, a middle, and an end. This may sound basic, yet it is a phase of public speaking which requires a good deal of conscious attention. You undoubtedly can recall some speaker who, though he talked at length, just never seemed to get started. Then, again, there is the speaker who begins in the middle and ends there. He may talk well and may have a good point to convey, but, since he did not prepare the listener by an introduction and sum up his thoughts with a conclusion, more often than not much of what he said is lost. Finally, there is the speaker who starts with the end of his discourse. The audience may know his purpose, yet it will feel indifferent because he failed to develop his points effectively.

Repetition of main points is the hallmark of a well-presented talk. One successful orator offered this formula for a successful speech: "First I tell them what I'm going to tell them," he said. "Then I tell it to them. Then I tell them what I told them." The need to repeat, using different words and examples, is greater in speaking than in writing. A reader can always look back over a printed page; he cannot look back over your words without missing something else you are saying. The spoken word is fleeting. You should state an important idea several times so that your listeners can remember its meaning.

In using your outline, try to stay one step ahead of yourself. As you are finishing one point, take a quick glance at your outline so that your remarks will lead naturally to the next point. This makes for smoother transition and is especially necessary where one point is meant to complement another.

Your speech should be varied in style and illustration, but without real digression. Too much of a sameness, no matter how good in content, will eventually begin to disinterest your listeners.

Preparing a good talk is like preparing a good meal. For the eater, as for the listener, the enjoyment is almost unconscious. But the good cook, like the good orator, knows all about the vast quantity of conscious preparatory work that goes into a meal or a speech. The courses must be planned, the food bought, the tastes balanced, the service neat and attractive. A good talk, like a good meal, begins long in advance of the finished product.

KNOW YOURSELF

To know yourself is just as important as to know your material, and often much harder. You can be more objective about material than you can be critical about yourself. Yet knowing one's self is a gentle art, well worth the effort, for in public speaking the audience is constantly making a judgment of you as well as of your material.

The first tendency of a beginner in public speaking is to

imitate either real or imaginary characters and try to sound as they do. The effect on the audience is bad. They feel you are not being fair either with them or with yourself.

You are a personality with certain definite qualities of your own. You may be a cool, logical type, not prone to fiery speech, yet you still may be very effective. If you become imbued with the idea that you must increase the emotional content of your talk, you will finish by convincing your audience only of your poor taste. On the contrary, however, you may be essentially an emotional person whose whole tendency is to speak in forceful language. While it may be wise for you to learn some moderation, it would be a distinct mistake for you to force yourself into a pattern of speech unsuited to your temperament. In short, you should fit your style to yourself, gearing the pace of your words to your mental processes.

It is unnecessary to use artificial voice tricks. If you become excited you will shout. If that is your habit, fine. If it isn't, then it is inadvisable to use such an approach when speaking in public. The quality of public speech is not measured by the quantity of sound. A forceful statement, spoken quietly, sincerely, and slowly, can be more powerful than the loudest outburst of words.

Give your points a chance to impress themselves on your listeners. Even if you are a rapid talker, pause after a sentence or a significant passage.

Speak your own sentences, using words with which you are familiar. However, in your spare time you might do well to look up the meaning of new words so that they may become part of your vocabulary. An enlarged vocabulary is like an increased fund of knowledge. It equips you for all kinds of speaking.

Part of knowing yourself is being aware of your bodily movements. An old-fashioned form of public speaking prescribed certain physical gestures to accompany certain expressions. Today this form of speaking is considered out of date. Good gestures are *natural* gestures. The worst thing you can do is to give the audience the impression that you are more concerned with what you do with your hands or feet than with what you are trying to say. After a while your listeners will suspect that the important thing in your public appearance is not your thoughts but your physical extremities. On the other hand, if you forget about your gestures, so will your audience. If you concentrate on what you have to say—and talks with a Christopher purpose are needed urgently—your listeners will reflect your conviction.

Never assume that an audience will be angry with you if you give them a moment or two of silence to allow your words to impress themselves on their consciousness. More often than not, they will be grateful for the opportunity to digest your ideas.

It is a mistake for anyone to begin a talk with an apology. If you are unaccustomed to public speaking, there is no need to advertise the fact. Most audiences will accept you at face value, and, if your words reflect the sincerity of your conviction as a Christ-bearer, then your listeners will accept your message in the same spirit.

Your task, as a speaker, is to impress your motivation on those who hear you. As a Christopher, this should be especially easy since the truth of which you speak has stood the test of time and is rooted in eternity.

KNOW YOUR AUDIENCE

While all audiences have much in common, they still have their own individual characteristics. To know your audience is to speak more effectively to them. In doing this, there are several factors to be considered.

(1) *What is the interest of your listeners?* Not all people are equally interested in the same things. If you know the reason why they have gathered to hear you, you can proceed to use their interest to heighten their concern in your comments. Begin with those things that affect your audience and build on them. It is a sure guide to success.

(2) *What is the background of your audience?* In teaching, the instructor speaks in terms of the apperceptive background of his pupils, that is the quantity and quality of background which makes it possible for them to absorb what is being taught in the lesson. Every good speech is comparable to a new lesson. Its point of departure should be the knowledge already in possession of the listeners.

(3) *What is the occasion?* Speeches are not always made under the same circumstances. A speech should be adjusted to the mood of the moment. It should be part of the occasion.

(4) *What is the size of the audience?* You will not always find it effective to speak to six people as you would to six hundred. Smaller groups demand greater intimacy and informality. Larger groups require a more formal approach. If you know the size of your audience in advance, you will find it easier to prepare to speak to them.

When you have mastered the first three rules of good public speaking—mastery of content, of self, and of audience, there are a few additional suggestions it is well to bear in mind.

Use illustrations. The human mind can follow concrete examples more easily than abstractions. In public speaking it is advisable, as did Christ Himself on numerous occasions, to present illustrations. Explain what you mean by giving an example. Use stories. Retell real incidents. Cite newspaper reports. You will find that you can interest the most apathetic audience with the presentation of even one strong illustration, vividly told.

Look at your audience. This means that you should talk to more than one person among your listeners. Talk to all of your audience, but do not be afraid to pause frequently and look some one person directly in the eye. You will thus get some idea as to how your listeners are reacting to what you are saying. It also makes for audience-contact.

Never become angry with your audience. This is a variation of the Christopher theme of being able to disagree without being disagreeable. No matter how provoked you may be, don't show it. Don't shout; don't lose your temper. Your task as a speaker is to persuade your listeners, to win them over to the God-given truths which form the foundation of your philosophy. If you allow part of your audience, by its behavior, to turn you against the whole group, you have lost and your enemies have won. For a Christopher this point should be especially significant. Sometimes in the group which you are addressing there will be those in whom the idea of a Supreme Being arouses violent hatred. Guiding every action should be the words of Our Saviour Himself: "Love your enemies: do good them that hate you: and pray for them that persecute and calumniate you."

In the spirit of Christ's love, then, you can go far in reaching the world if you will have the patience and courage to persist in your work of carrying Christ to all men.

XVIII

REMINDERS FOR A CHRISTOPHER

TWO BUSINESSMEN IN a Chicago restaurant recently were discussing a topic of grave concern to most thinking people everywhere—the threat of atheistic materialism to world peace. During the concluding conversation over coffee and cigarettes, one of the pair made an enlightening observation. As his companion finished a lengthy outburst on the danger of totalitarianism to our whole industrial and financial structure, he put in:

"You're right—one hundred percent. But if you'll pardon my saying so, many of us seem to have quite a lot in common with the Commies. Now wait a minute," he held up a restraining hand as the other businessman half arose out of his chair in angered surprise: "Let me finish. Sure, we're against Communism, but isn't it merely for one reason—economic? Everything we've said so far seems to prove it. What bothers us is that it will hit us where it hurts the most—in our pocketbooks. If we were honest with ourselves many of us would admit we're almost as much against religion as the totalitarians are."

This incident is told for one purpose: to spotlight a similar tendency among many basically good people, businessmen and botanists, tradesmen and teachers, journalists and juveniles, alike. They are opposed to Nazism, Fascism and Communism, but primarily for *material* reasons. The spiritual reason, upon which their whole civilization rests, these people disregard almost entirely. They are almost as much opposed to any moral force—to the very force that makes their way of life possible—as are the totalitarians.

They are concerned about the threat to their freedom, but they ignore the cure which they hold in their own hands. They are like sick people who are against disease, yet they don't want the doctor.

Fundamentally, these men and women are solid citizens. But they leave out of their lives and out of their thinking the one essential point, the "divine spark," whose source is none other than the Creator of the universe, of everyone and everything in it. They forget that America's greatness lies in her possession of the heritage handed down from the Founding Fathers. As John Foster Dulles has said: "There is no doubt whatever in my mind but that moral force is the only force that can accomplish great things in the world. If you look back to the history of our own country, you will find that our finest institutions were primarily molded by the Christian belief of our Founders. They believed that there was such a thing as moral law, and that there was a Creator who endowed men with inalienable rights. They believed, too, that this nation had a great mission in the world to carry those concepts of righteousness to other people."

The suggestions offered last July by the National Conference on the Education of Teachers, at Bowling Green, Ohio, serves to emphasize the fact that this concept has been allowed to slip into the background. Totaling ten in number, some of these suggestions recommended that a teacher should strive to possess all the human qualities—love of children, sympathetic understanding, fairness, patience, humor and a sense of justice. They recommended that a teacher should be intellectually alert and curious, have a pleasing personality and appearance, enthusiasm, vigor, vitality, poise and charm, and should have a healthy physical and mental outlook on life, with well rounded interests.

The Conference stated further that a teacher should develop a love for the democratic way of life and should understand the importance of developing world citizenship and better human relationships.

Few would disagree with these suggestions. As far as they go, they deserve the emphasis they received. Yet they are suggestions that aim for effects without first recognizing a Cause. They lack one thing which Miss Sara A. Bair, after thirty-nine years of teaching, put into words so well.

Answering the questions of a newspaperman, Miss Bair revealed a strong sense of dedication, an impelling determination to serve others, to leave the world better than she found it, to put into life as much as possible and to take out as little.

"I've always said a good teacher has the divine spark. It's difficult to put into words, but I should say it is a real love for and interest in people."

That love for people (for the love of God) is invariably the driving force, the "divine spark," of those who do most for God and for country—as well as for themselves.

This same recognition of fundamentals is to be found in the statement of another teacher, a public school instructor in Mississippi, who was awarded the title, "Best Teacher of 1947." Her salary is only $1,900 a year, but rather than give up the privilege of her chosen profession she has taken extra work after school to meet living expenses. That this teacher has a Christopher purpose and sense of dedication to her work is evident from her remark:

> "There is no more exalting profession in the world, except that followed by those who preach the word of Jesus. I quake in my boots when I think of my responsibilities. I feel I am rendering a service to humanity—and Lord knows they need it."

What Miss Bair saw, what the Mississippi teacher saw, what one of those two businessmen saw so clearly is that good qualities in any line of endeavor are but effects of which faith, hope and charity are the cause.

The purpose of this book is to encourage people to restore spiritual values in every sphere, every nook and cranny of American life. The more attention given to these values, the less need will there be for combatting erroneous ideas.

But, since it is so easy for all of us, human as we are, to forget the primacy of the spiritual, it is well to be reminded, over and over again, of certain elementary guides and sign-posts which will help us on the way. In this chapter, then, are set down a few reminders which may be worth a glance from time to time. They are but variations on the triple theme—faith, hope and charity—which it has been the purpose of this whole book to emphasize.

(1.) *Depend more on God, less on self.* All of us should pray as if all depended on God and should work as if everything depended on ourselves. Yet we should *not* forget for one moment that, as St. Paul said, we are not *"Sufficient to think anything of ourselves, as of ourselves, but our sufficiency is from God."* (II *Cor.* 3:5) The more we realize our strength is rooted in God, the more we will acquire, and be inspired by, an exhilarating assurance that nothing can daunt us . . . *"For though I should walk in the midst of the shadows of death, I will fear no evils, for Thou art with me."* (Ps. 22:4)

(2.) *Share the Truth, don't hoard it.* One of the easiest ways to keep your faith is to "give it away." On the other hand, one of the surest ways to lose your faith or to weaken it, is to keep it to yourself. One thing that stifles peoples' lives and makes their work meaningless, is *possessiveness.* It entangles not only the evil and the miserly, but even those who, by their daily actions, seem closest to God. The miser refuses to think of anything but his money and himself. A person can be equally miserly in spiritual things, thinking only of self and God while failing to complete the triangle: (1) God, (2) self, (3) others.

(3.) *Be world-minded, not local-minded.* We have a personal responsibility to save the world, not merely to save ourselves and our immediate surroundings. Christ expects us to think and work in terms of helping to bring God to the world, and the world to God. As Americans, we have a special opportunity. Barbara Ward, foreign editor of the *London Economist,* and a zealous Christ-bearer in her own right, stated recently: "I believe that the American people—the only people in the world who thought of an ideal first and then built a state around it—will prove in the long run happier, freer, and more creative when they carry that ideal of a free society out into the world, than if they sit at home and hug it to themselves."

(4.) *Go among people, don't avoid them.* The Gospels reveal how our Lord was ever on the move, not merely to enjoy Himself but always with the hope and prayer that as He moved among the people, He would reach some who could be reached in no other way. His was the loving purpose of bringing God to men and men to God. He went to dinners, to weddings, to all sorts of gatherings. He engaged in conversation with all types of persons and in all sorts of places—on the roadside, on busy city streets, in village squares, in wheat-fields, at the seashore, at the side of a well, in the desert, on the mountainside—anywhere and everywhere. And the people flocked to Him because He first went to them. (". . . *My delights were to be with the children of men." Prov.* 8:31)

Whenever He prayed, He invariably and immediately followed through with some concrete act of love for man. Only as we go among people, however distasteful this may be at times, and though avoiding them might be much the easier course to take, will we truly be Christophers, bearers of Christ. We shall bring Christ's peace and truth to the world in the measure that we imitate His everlasting quest for souls.

(5.) *Push on, don't stand still.* "The dogs bark, but the caravan moves on," runs an ancient proverb. We should not feel unduly concerned, therefore, about unfair criticism. We should learn, in fact, to expect it as part of the price of being a follower of One Who pushed on in the face of falsehood, misunderstanding, and ingratitude.

(6.) *Aim to serve, not to be served.* The noted critic, John Mason Brown, gave vivid testimony to the joy of service, in these words: ". . . no one, I am convinced, can be happy who lives only for himself. The joy of living comes from immersion in something that we know to be bigger, better, more enduring and worthier than we are. People, ideas, causes—these offer the one possible escape not merely from selfishness but from the hungers of solitude and the sorrows of aimlessness. *No person is as uninteresting as a person without interests.* The pitiful people are those who in their living elect to be spectators rather than participants; the tragic ones are those sight-seers who turn their backs deliberately on the procession. The only true happiness comes from squandering ourselves for a purpose."

(7.) *Be gentle, don't hurt.* It's the old, old story which one remarkably keen student of human nature put into words so well: *"You can catch more flies with honey than with vinegar."* It often takes a few more moments and a little added effort to be gentle and considerate, but it pays rich dividends. A hasty, sarcastic word, however, can quickly undo or offset many advances towards good. Seldom is anybody won by being nagged, irritated or belittled. Hurting those most hostile to religion is one sure way of driving them even farther away.

(8.) *Submit ideas, don't impose them.* Most people resent intrusion, especially in the name of religion. Beware of the attitude of proving you are right and others wrong. On the other hand, however, they are frequently more receptive when truths are *offered* to them, not *forced* down their throats. Christ Himself never intrudes. *"Behold I stand at the gate and knock,"* (*Apoc.* 3:20), He declared. He is right at the threshold, ever ready, even knocking on the door as a reminder that He is anxiously waiting to help. But He carefully avoids pushing in. He leaves it entirely to each individual to extend the invitation. He builds the fire but He does not strike the match. If Christ Himself is so insistent that cooperation with Him must be entirely voluntary, even at the risk of rejection and denial of Him, a Christopher can be no less considerate.

(9.) *Better to be optimistic than pessimistic.* A bottle of wine lying in the grass by the side of a hot, dusty road and apparently left behind through oversight by picnickers, was spied by two thirsty tramps. One of the tramps rushed forward with glee and picked it up. As he held it aloft, however, his smile turned quickly to a scowl. *"It's half empty,"* he complained. The other tramp, taking the bottle from his companion's hands, exclaimed cheerfully, "Yes, but it's half full, too!" . . . A Christopher, above all others, should stress the hopeful side of things, while still remaining realistic. That people are as good as they are, with so many unsound ideas being spread over the world, is surprising and encouraging. Yet even if things were twice as bad as they are now, there would still be great hope, thanks to God. *"An optimist sees an opportunity in every calamity; a pessimist sees a calamity in every opportunity."*

(10.) *Cheer, don't depress.* "No good deed goes unpunished" runs the favorite quip of one zealous Christopher who has had her share of "knocks," but who realizes that a sense of humor is one of the best helps in maintaining a sense of proportion. It is a good sign when people are not inclined to laugh at others, but are able to laugh at themselves. To be able to come up smiling in the midst of discouraging obstacles is a great asset for any Christopher. It shows strong faith in God and in others. Those who lack faith in anyone outside themselves tend to be depressed. The forbidding chill of those who are self-centered, rather than God-centered, once caused G. K. Chesterton to remark: *"They do not have the faith and they do not have the fun!"* The only ones who are truly gay of heart and ever hopeful are those who are fundamentally spiritual. They know the hidden meaning of St. Paul's words: *"Rejoice in the Lord always; again, I say, rejoice."* (*Phil.* 4, 4)

(11.) *Be more of a "go-giver" than a "go-getter."* All of us must have the necessities of life, but we have to be careful lest we favor ourselves too much. We have to be on guard against becoming so preoccupied in securing conveniences and luxuries that we miss the real joy of living—*which is living for others!* Repeatedly Christ said to *"go"* and *"give."* Seldom did He say to *"go"* and *"get."* The example He Himself set and which all men can understand, can be summed up in these five words: *"He went about doing good . . ."* (*Acts.* 10:38) The same should be said of all Christophers.

(12.) *Be daring, not timid.* Being bold does not mean being reckless, any more than being timid is a synonym for prudence. Timidity, in fact, is frequently a vice which poses as a virtue. No one in the world should be more daring than a follower of Christ. No one should be willing to risk more, to venture farther. Before them always should be Our Lord's daring challenge to Peter: *"Launch out into the deep!"* Peter's first reaction was certainly not one of boldness, but rather one of timid protest: "Master, we have labored all the night, and have taken nothing." He did not mention his being in the warm, shallow water close to shore where there are few fish to be caught. But then, suddenly stirred by Christ's daring, he quickly added: *"But at Thy word, I will let down the net."* (*Luke* 5:4-5) Taking Christ literally, he did "launch out into the deep," into the dangerous waters far from shore. And the result? The nets were so filled with fish that they were breaking, their ships so full that they were almost sinking. Our Lord, immediately after Peter reached shore, added one significant remark to the episode: *"Fear not: from henceforth, thou shalt catch men."* And Peter carried that daring into everything he did for the rest of his life. Those who would be true Christophers will have to be equally daring, avoiding all timidity. If we followers of Christ ever take seriously our Lord's command to "launch out into the deep," into the midst of the one hundred million in our land and the billion over the world who are not being reached by anyone in His name, our nets, too, will be breaking. For us, this is a tremendous responsibility!

(13.) *Admit your mistakes, don't deny them.* A few years ago, Albert Einstein made a most startling about-face. He publicly acknowledged that the universities and the newspapers that boasted of their everlasting loyalty to truth were failures when the acid test of Nazism came. The only ones who didn't whimper, but who consistently and continually championed the sacred rights of every man, woman and child, were those who were definitely for God, not against Him.

"Being a lover of freedom," said Einstein, "when the revolution came to Germany, I looked to the universities to defend it, knowing that they always boasted of their devotion to the cause of truth; but no, the universities immediately were silenced. Then I looked to the great editors of the newspapers whose flaming editorials in days gone by had proclaimed their love of freedom; but they, like the universities, were silenced in a few short weeks. . . .

"Only the Church stood squarely across the path of Hitler's campaign for suppressing truth. I never had any special interest in the Church before, but now I feel a great affection and admiration because the Church alone had had the courage and persistence to stand for intellectual truth and moral freedom. I am forced thus to confess that what I once despised I now praise unreservedly."

By admitting his mistake, Einstein accomplished a great deal of good. He brought to the attention of millions a truth which they might otherwise never have known. To acknowledge one's errors is humiliating, but it is often through humiliations, willingly endured, that we deepen and strengthen our spiritual roots.

(14.) *Be humble, not proud.* Most of us get into one sort of trouble or another because we try to fool ourselves. There is the everlasting temptation to pretend to be something we are not. A photographer who aimed to please everybody, once advertised: *"As you look to me, $1.00; as you think you look, $1.50; as you would like to look, $2.00."* So many headaches can be avoided by following the simple advice: *"Be yourself!"* If God gives us only one talent, He wants us to use it efficiently, but He certainly does not wish us to try to fool the public, to give the impression that we have five or ten talents. Of a young businessman who had unusual success, despite certain limitations, someone wisely said, *"He is smart enough to know what he doesn't know."* Pride can trip up any of us. It is the most insidious of sins. It reaches into the most protected and sacred spheres. It is the Devil's Number One Specialty. *"I will not serve!"* said Lucifer. And *"by that sin fell the angels."* Pride will react on us in proportion as we exaggerate self and overlook the fact that anything and everything we have, little or much, comes from God.

(15.) *Inspire confidence, don't dishearten.* "There is no surprise more magical than the surprise of being loved," Charles Morgan once said. "It is God's finger on a man's shoulder." There's a bit of nobility in the worst of human beings because all are made in God's image and that image can never be completely effaced or lost. Never write anybody off! There's always hope! Even the man who has decided to have nothing whatever to do with God isn't frozen in that state of mind. Deep in the very roots of his being, and just because he is created in the Divine Image, there is an ever-present tug toward God. It is the privilege of Christophers to help him become aware of this tremendous tug. For this very reason, that in the very being of every man there is a pull toward God, Christophers can honestly say to anyone, with little danger of hurting his or her feelings: "There's a lot of good in you!" They can inspire confidence by a word or by a friendly glance. After all, this is a part of that great virtue of charity. And for a definition of charity, someone once offered:

It's silence when your words would hurt
It's patience when your neighbor's curt
It's deafness when a scandal flows
It's thoughtfulness for other's woes
It's promptness when stern duty calls
It's courage when misfortune falls.

(16.) *Disagree without being disagreeable.* A child who had spent quite a bit of extra time at her prayers one particular evening and had been questioned by her mother as to the reason, replied: "I was praying that all bad people would be good, and all good people nice!" One of the greatest injuries to religion comes from a few of its most loyal adherents who are correct in all matters, *save one.* They persist in being disagreeable when it would be just as easy to remain agreeable, even while differing. If they realized how that slightly sour note has a big effect in keeping large numbers away from religion, many would undoubtedly change to a more pleasant attitude without delay. It is most important for a Christopher to be *pleasantly* firm when it is necessary to be firm. But being disagreeable is a sign of weakness.

(17.) *See both points of view, not merely your own.* An anonymous author sums up this point as follows:

"When the other fellow acts that way, he's *ugly;*
When you do it, it's *nerves.*
When he's set in his ways, he's *obstinate;*
When you are, it's just *firmness.*

When he doesn't like your friends, he's *prejudiced;*
When you don't like his, you are simply *showing good judgment of human nature.*
When he tries to be accommodating, he's *polishing the apple;*
When you do it, you're using *tact.*
When he takes time to do things, he is *dead slow;*
When you take ages, you are *deliberate.*
When he picks flaws, he's *cranky;*
When you do, you're *discriminating.*"

(18.) *Be patient, not impetuous.* There is little danger of making a mistake by proceeding gently, patiently, though persistently. But much harm can result from being unpleasantly brusque.

"Why were the saints, saints? Because they were cheerful when it was difficult to be cheerful, patient when it was difficult to be patient; and because they pushed on when they wanted to stand still, and kept silent when they wanted to talk, and they were agreeable when they wanted to be disagreeable. That was all. It was quite simple and always will be."

(19.) *Be a doer, not just a talker.* A frequent inmate of the county jail in a small midwest community has for his motto, "Death before dishonor." Writing it down on a piece of paper wasn't enough for him. He had it *tattooed on his arm!* To him can be applied the question frequently on the lips of a skeptic: "Do you talk and *do,* or do you only *talk?*" This skeptic would always explain that he had heard many enthusiasts talk about the great things they planned to do. But, he complained, they never got past the talking stage.

This danger has been eloquently expressed by C. S. Lewis'

devil in *The Screwtape Letters* as he refers to his effort to tempt the good man: "The great thing is to prevent his doing anything. As long as he does not convert it into action, it does not matter how much he thinks about this new repentance. Let the brute wallow in it. . . . The more often he feels without acting, the less he will ever be able to act, and, in the long run, the less he will be able to feel."

Talk without performance is evidence of lack of sincerity. (*"Even as the body without the spirit is dead, so also faith without works is dead." James* 2:26)

One of the easiest ways to *be* good is to *do* good.

(20.) *Don't flee suffering; use it.* At the recent *Life* Round Table on the *Pursuit of Happiness,* a panel of eighteen men and women spent fifteen hours discussing the third right enumerated in the Declaration of Independence. Of the distinguished group selected for this panel, no one did more to emphasize spiritual values than a girl, Betsy Barton, who lost the use of both legs fourteen years ago in an automobile crash. In closing Miss Barton said: "It is my experience that suffering and pain are, unfortunately, the great character builders—not that suffering is good in itself, but because it often helps to shift our expectation of happiness from without to a search for it from within . . . Mystics have shown us that when they set out to achieve spiritual understanding, they cleared the way by depriving themselves of *things,* by their own will. But we are so suffocated with things and with distractions that the real pursuit of happiness is almost impossible. . . . I feel that we should learn how not to be afraid of being alone. Then we would not seek to run from alone-ness into distractions. If self-understanding is a component of happiness (as we agreed) this is best achieved in silence, in stillness and in solitude . . . Happiness is primarily an inner state, an inner achievement. In other words,

I would like to close by saying that the Kingdom of Heaven is within us." . . . As Betsy Barton pointed out, suffering may be the means whereby we achieve self-understanding. And it is in the measure that we achieve self-understanding that we are able to reach out with understanding to others. Happiness is not to be found in the pursuit of *things,* nor in the possession of *things.* It comes as a by-product of *living* and *giving,* of suffering and participation in the sufferings of others. ". . . *Through many tribulations we must enter into the kingdom of God.*" (*Acts* 14:21)

(21.) *Keep first things first.* Our Lord over and over again stressed we should do *first* what most of us by nature are inclined to do *last.* He didn't say, for instance: "Love thyself and then if it isn't too much bother, take an interest in the welfare of others." He put it just the other way—and He put it crystal-clear: *"Love thy neighbor."* How much? *"As thyself!"* He could have urged us to be "simple as doves and wise as serpents." But here again He specified first the quality that presumes being on one's toes: *"Be ye wise as serpents and simple as doves."* (*Matt.* 10, 16) As things now stand, most good people are "simple as doves," which requires little effort, whereas most of those who are bent on evil are "wise as serpents." Once there are found enough followers of Christ who strive to combine both qualities, then great things are bound to happen. And, again, Christ did *not* say: "Go ye into the byways and the highways." He purposely put the more important and the least likely first: *"Go ye into the highways and the byways."* Christians at present are largely confining themselves to the "byways." Those who are striving relentlessly to destroy the world and enslave mankind, concentrate almost entirely on the "highways." They know that once they control the main spheres of influence (education, government, labor-management, the writing field) they automatically control the "byways" as well. It isn't hard to understand, therefore, why the Christopher objective lays special stress on (a) *"Love thy neighbor;"* (b) *"Be ye wise as serpents;"* and (c) *"Go ye into the highways."*

XIX

CHRIST SPEAKS TO YOU

NOTHING could be more fitting than that Our Lord should have the last word. So, in this final chapter, Christ Himself speaks to you, His Christ-bearer, in His own words.

HIS CLAIM TO BE HEARD

(1.) *"I and the Father are one."* (*John* 10, 30)

(2.) "Amen, amen I say to you, before Abraham was made, I am." (*John* 8, 58)

(3.) *"I am the way, and the truth, and the life. No man cometh to the Father, but by me."* (*John* 14, 6)

(4.) "Heaven and earth shall pass, but my words shall not pass." (*Matt.* 24, 35)

(5.) *"For this was I born, and for this came I into the world, that I should give testimony to the truth. Every one that is of the truth, heareth my voice."* (*John* 18, 37)

(6.) "I am the light of the world; he that followeth me, walketh not in darkness, but shall have the light of life." (*John* 8, 12)

(7.) *"Now this is eternal life; that they may know thee, the only true God, and Jesus Christ, whom thou hast sent."* (*John* 17, 3)

(8.) "I am the resurrection and the life; he that believeth in me, although he be dead, shall live." (*John* 11, 25)

(9.) *"I am the vine; you the branches: he that abideth in me, and I in him, the same beareth much fruit: for without me you can do nothing."* (*John* 15, 5)

(10.) "Every plant which my heavenly Father hath not planted, shall be rooted up." (*Matt.* 15, 13)

(11.) *"Blessed art thou, Simon Bar-Jona: because flesh and blood hath not revealed it to thee, but my Father who is in heaven. And I say to thee: That thou art Peter; and upon this rock I will build my church, and the gates of hell shall not prevail against it. And I will give to thee the keys of the kingdom of heaven. And whatsoever thou shalt bind upon earth, it shall be bound also in heaven: and whatsoever thou shalt loose on earth, it shall be loosed also in heaven."* (*Matt.* 16, 17-19)

(12.) "And whosoever shall fall on this stone, shall be broken; but on whomsoever it shall fall, it shall grind him to powder." (*Matt.* 21, 44)

(13.) *"I am the door. By me, if any man enter in, he shall be saved."* (*John* 10, 9)

(14.) "I am the bread of life; he that cometh to me shall not hunger: and he that believeth in me shall never thirst." (*John* 6, 35)

(15.) *"Amen, amen I say unto you, Except you eat the flesh of the son of man, and drink his blood, you shall not have life in you. He that eateth my flesh, and drinketh my blood, hath everlasting life; and I will raise him up in the last day. For my flesh is meat indeed: and my blood is drink indeed. He that eateth my flesh, and drinketh my blood, abideth in me, and I in him. As the living Father hath sent me, and I live by the Father; so he that eateth me, the same also shall live by me."* (*John* 6, 54-58)

THE COMMISSION TO GO

(16.) "All power is given to me in heaven and earth. Going therefore teach ye all nations: baptizing them in the name of the Father, and of the Son, and of the Holy Ghost. Teaching them to observe all things whatsoever I have commanded you: and behold I am with you all days even to the consummation of the world. (*Matt.* 28, 18-20)

(17.) *"Go ye into the whole world, and preach the gospel to every creature. He that believeth and is baptized, shall be saved: but he that believeth not shall be condemned."* (*Mark* 16, 15-16)

(18.) "As the Father hath sent me, I also send you." (*John* 20, 21)

(19.) *"You have not chosen me: but I have chosen you; and have appointed you, that you should go and should bring forth fruit, and your fruit should remain."* (*John* 15, 16)

(20.) "The harvest indeed is great, but the laborers are few. Pray ye therefore the Lord of the harvest, that he send forth laborers into his harvest." (*Matt.* 9, 37-38)

(21.) *"And other sheep I have, that are not of this fold: them also I must bring, and they shall hear my voice, and there shall be one fold and one shepherd."* (*John* 10, 16)

(22.) "Come ye after me, and I will make you to be fishers of men." (*Matt.* 4, 19)

(23.) *"Launch out into the deep, and let down your nets for a draught."* (*Luke* 5, 4)

(24.) "Fear not: from henceforth thou shalt catch men." (*Luke* 5, 10)

(25.) *"Behold I send you as sheep in the midst of wolves. Be ye therefore wise as serpents and simple as doves."* (*Matt.* 10, 16)

(26.) "Let us go into the neighboring towns and cities, that I may preach there also: for to this purpose am I come." (*Mark* 1, 38)

(27.) *"In this is my Father glorified: that you bring forth very much fruit, and become my disciples."* (*John* 15, 8)

(28.) "You are the light of the world. A city seated on a mountain cannot be hid. Neither do men light a candle and put it under a bushel, but upon a candlestick, that it may shine to all that are in the house. So let your light shine before men, that they may see your good works and glorify your Father who is in heaven." (*Matt.* 5, 14-16)

(29.) *"And every one that hath left house, or brethren, or sisters, or father, or mother, or wife, or children, or lands for my name's sake, shall receive a hundred fold, and shall possess life everlasting."* (Matt. 19, 29)

BY MEANS OF LOVE

(30.) "Thou shalt love the Lord thy God with thy whole heart, and with thy whole soul, and with thy whole mind. This is the greatest and the first commandment. And the second is like to this: Thou shalt love thy neighbor as thyself. On these two commandments dependeth the whole law and the prophets." (*Matt.* 22, 37-40)

(31.) *"A new commandment I give unto you: that you love one another, as I have loved you."* (John 13, 34)

(32.) "This is my commandment, that you love one another, as I have loved you." (*John* 15, 12)

(33.) *"By this shall all men know that you are my disciples, if you have love one for another."* (John 13, 35)

(34.) "Greater love than this no man hath, that a man lay down his life for his friends." (*John* 15, 13)

(35.) *"You are my friends, if you do the things that I command you."* (John 15, 14)

(36.) "For the Son of man also is not come to be ministered unto, but to minister, and to give his life a redemption for many." (*Mark* 10, 45)

(37.) *"You have heard that it hath been said: Thou shalt love thy neighbor, and hate thy enemy. But I say to you: Love your enemies: do good to them that hate you: and pray for them that persecute you and calumniate you. That you may be the children of your Father who is in heaven, who maketh his sun to rise upon the good and bad, and raineth upon the just and the unjust."* (*Matt.* 5, 43-45)

(38.) "If you love them that love you, what reward shall you have? Do not even the publicans this? And if you salute your brethren only, what do you more? Do not also the heathens this?" (*Matt.* 5, 46-47)

(39.) *"As long as you did it to one of these my least brethren, you did it to me."* (*Matt.* 25, 40)

(40.) "Dost thou see this woman? I entered into thy house, thou gavest me no water for my feet; but she with tears hath washed my feet, and with her hairs hath wiped them. Thou gavest me no kiss; but she, since she came in, hath not ceased to kiss my feet. My head with oil thou didst not anoint; but she with ointment hath anointed my feet. Wherefore I say to thee: Many sins are forgiven her, because she hath loved much. But to whom less is forgiven, he loveth less." (*Luke* 7, 44-47)

(41.) *"Amen, I say to you, this poor widow hath cast in more than all they who have cast into the treasury: For all they did cast in of their abundance; but she of her want cast in all she had, even her whole living."* (*Mark* 12, 43-44)

(42.) "Father forgive them, for they know not what they do." (*Luke* 23, 34)

(43.) *"They that are in health need not a physician, but they that are ill. Go then and learn what this meaneth: I will have mercy and not sacrifice. For I am not come to call the just, but sinners."* (*Matt.* 9, 12-13)

(44.) "The son of man is come to save that which was lost." (*Matt.* 18, 11)

(45.) *"The son of man came not to destroy souls, but to save."* (*Luke* 9, 56)

(46.) "So I say to you, there shall be joy before the angels of God upon one sinner doing penance." (*Luke* 15, 10)

(47.) *"Even so it is not the will of your Father, who is in heaven, that one of these little ones should perish."* (*Matt.* 18, 14)

(48.) "The bruised reed he shall not break; and smoking flax he shall not extinguish: till he send forth judgment unto victory." (*Matt.* 12, 20)

(49.) *"John the Baptist came neither eating bread nor drinking wine; and you say: He hath a devil. The Son of man is come eating and drinking; and you say: Behold a man that is a glutton and a drinker for wine, a friend of publicans and sinners."* (*Luke* 7, 33-34)

(50.) "Woman, where are they that accused thee? Hath no man condemned thee?" Who said: "No man, Lord." And Jesus said: "Neither will I condemn thee. Go, and sin no more." (*John* 8, 10-11)

(51.) *"Bring forth quickly the first robe, and put it on him, and put a ring on his hand, and shoes on his feet; And bring hither the fatted calf, and kill it, and let us eat and make merry: Because this my son was dead, and is come to life again: was lost, and is found. And they began to be merry."* (*Luke* 15, 22-24)

THE GAIN OF SUFFERING

(52.) "Remember my word that I said to you: The servant is not greater than his master. If they have persecuted me, they will also persecute you: if they have kept my word, they will keep yours also." (*John* 15, 20)

(53.) *"If the world hate you, know ye that it hath hated me before you."* (*John* 15, 18)

(54.) "I have given them thy word, and the world hath hated them, because they are not of the world; as I also am not of the world. I pray not that thou shouldst take them out of the world, but that thou shouldst keep them from evil." (*John* 17, 14-15)

(55.) *"Amen, amen I say to you, that you shall lament and weep, but the world shall rejoice; and you shall be made sorrowful, but your sorrow shall be turned into joy. A woman, when she is in labor, hath sorrow, because her hour is come; but when she hath brought forth the child, she remembereth no more the anguish, for joy that a man is born into the world. So also you now indeed have sorrow; but I will see you again, and your heart shall rejoice; and your joy no man shall take from you."* (*John* 16, 20-22)

(56.) "Then shall they deliver you up to be afflicted, and shall put you to death: and you shall be hated by all nations for my name's sake. And then shall many be scandalized: and shall betray one another: and shall hate one another." (*Matt.* 24, 9-10)

(57.) *"These things I have spoken to you, that in me you may have peace. In the world you shall have distress: but have confidence, I have overcome the world."* (*John* 16, 33)

(58.) "He that loveth his life shall lose it; and he that hateth his life in this world, keepeth it unto life eternal." (*John* 12, 25)

(59.) *"If any man will come after me, let him deny himself, and take up his cross daily, and follow me."* (*Luke* 9, 23)

(60.) "He that findeth his life, shall lose it: and he that shall lose his life for me, shall find it." (*Matt.* 10, 39)

(61.) *"Amen, amen I say to you, unless the grain of wheat falling into the ground die, itself remaineth alone; but if it die, it bringeth forth much fruit."* (*John* 12, 24-25)

(62.) "And if thy right eye scandalize thee, pluck it out and cast it from thee. For it is expedient for thee that one of thy members should perish, rather than thy whole body be cast into hell." (*Matt.* 5, 29)

(63.) *"The kingdom of heaven suffereth violence and the violent bear it away.* (*Matt.* 11, 12)

(64.) "You have heard that it was said to them of old: Thou shalt not commit adultery. But I say to you, that whosoever shall look on a woman to lust after her, hath already committed adultery with her in his heart." (*Matt.* 5, 27-28)

(65.) *"Blessed are the clean of heart: for they shall see God."* (*Matt.* 5, 8)

(66.) "Blessed are the poor in spirit: for theirs is the kingdom of heaven." (*Matt.* 5, 3)

(67.) *"Blessed are they that hunger and thirst after justice: for they shall have their fill."* (*Matt.* 5, 6)

(68.) "Blessed are they that suffer persecution for justice' sake: for theirs is the kingdom of heaven." (*Matt.* 5, 10)

(69.) *"Blessed are ye when they shall revile you, and persecute you, and speak all that is evil against you, untruly, for my sake: Be glad and rejoice, for your reward is very great in heaven. For so they persecuted the prophets that were before you."* (*Matt.* 5, 11-12)

(70.) "And fear ye not them that kill the body, and are not able to kill the soul: but rather fear him that can destroy both soul and body in hell." (*Matt.* 10, 28)

(71.) *"But he that shall persevere to the end, he shall be saved."* (*Matt.* 24, 13)

(72.) "Come to me, all you that labour and are burdened, and I will refresh you. Take up my yoke upon you, and learn of me because I am meek and humble of heart; and you shall find rest to your souls. For my yoke is sweet and my burden light." (*Matt.* 11, 28-30)

(73.) *"Do penance, for the kingdom of heaven is at hand."* (*Matt.* 4, 17)

(74.) "This kind can go out by nothing but by prayer and fasting." (*Mark* 9, 28)

(75.) "*Go behind me, Satan, thou art a scandal unto me: because thou savourest not the things that are of God, but the things that are of men.*" (*Matt.* 16, 23)

(76.) "No man can serve two masters. For either he will hate the one, and love the other: or he will sustain the one and despise the other. You cannot serve God and mammon." (*Matt.* 6, 24)

THE FINAL ACCOUNTING

(77.) "*Let not your heart be troubled. You believe in God, believe also in me. In my Father's house there are many mansions. If not, I would have told you because I go to prepare a place for you.*" (*John* 14, 1-2)

(78.) "For God so loved the world, as to give his only begotten Son; that whosoever believeth in him, may not perish, but may have life everlasting." (*John* 3, 16)

(79.) "*For the Son of man shall come in the glory of his Father with his Angels: and then will he render to every man according to his works.*" (*Matt.* 16, 27)

(80.) "Everyone therefore that shall confess me before men, I will also confess him before my Father who is in heaven. But he that shall deny me before men, I will also deny him before my Father who is in heaven." (*Matt.* 10, 32-33)

(81.) "*Lay not up to yourselves treasures on earth: where the rust and moth consume, and where thieves break through, and steal. But lay up to yourselves treasures in heaven: where neither the rust nor moth doth consume, and where thieves do not break through, nor steal."* (*Matt.* 6, 19-20)

(82.) "For what doth it profit a man, if he gain the whole world, and suffer the loss of his own soul? Or what shall a man give in exchange for his soul? (*Matt.* 16, 26)

(83.) *"When thou makest a dinner or a supper, call not thy friends, nor thy brethren, nor thy kinsmen, nor thy neighbours, who are rich; lest perhaps they also invite thee again, and a recompense be made to thee. But when thou makest a feast call the poor, the maimed, the lame, and the blind; And thou shalt be blessed, because they have not wherewith to make thee recompense: for recompense shall be made thee at the resurrection of the just."* (*Luke* 14, 12-14)

(84.) "The land of a certain rich man brought forth plenty of fruits. And he thought within himself, saying: 'What shall I do, because I have no room where to bestow my fruits?' And he said: 'This will I do: I will pull down my barns, and will build greater: and into them I will gather all things that are grown to me, and my goods. And I will say to my soul: Soul, thou hast much goods laid up for many years, take thy rest; eat, drink, make good cheer.' But God said to him: 'Thou fool, this night do they require thy soul of thee: and whose shall those things be which thou hast provided?' So is he that layeth up treasure for himself, and is not rich towards God." (*Luke* 12, 16-21)

(85.) *"Give an account of thy stewardship: for now thou canst be steward no longer!"* (*Luke* 16, 2)

(86.) "Depart from me, you cursed, into everlasting fire which was prepared for the devil and his angels." (*Matt.* 25, 41)

(87.) *"Come, ye blessed of my Father, possess you the kingdom prepared for you from the foundation of the world."* (*Matt.* 25, 34)